1989

Interpreting Mozart
on the Keyboard

Da Capo Press Music Reprint Series

EVA AND PAUL
BADURA-SKODA

Interpreting Mozart
on the Keyboard

TRANSLATED BY
LEO BLACK

NEW PREFACE BY
EVA BADURA-SKODA

DA CAPO PRESS • NEW YORK • 1986

Library of Congress Cataloging in Publication Data

Badura-Skoda, Eva.
  Interpreting Mozart on the keyboard.

  (Da Capo Press music reprint series)
  Translation of: Mozart-Interpretation.
  Reprint. Originally published: New York: St. Martin's, 1962.
  Bibliography: p.
  Includes index.
  1. Mozart, Wolfgang Amadeus, 1756-1791. Works. 2. Piano music — Interpretation
(Phrasing, dynamics, etc.) I. Badura-Skoda, Paul. II. Title.
ML410.M9B1413   1986   786.1'092'4   85-24566
ISBN 0-306-76265-X

English translation by Leo Black
© 1962 Barrie and Rockliff (Barrie Books Ltd)
2 Clement's Inn, Strand, London WC2
First published in German under the title *Mozart-Interpretation*
© 1957 by Eduard Wancura Verlag, Wien

Published by Da Capo Press, Inc.
A Subsidiary of Plenum Publishing Corporation
233 Spring Street, New York, N.Y. 10013

PREFACE

Interpreting Mozart on the Keyboard first appeared in England in 1961, and in the United States in 1962. During the past years, as copies of the original publication and its several editions became scarce and the book finally went out of print, my husband and I made earnest plans to prepare a new, enlarged edition much broader in scope than the earlier version. It was our intention to expand the subject matter to contain additional research and observations on the interpretation of not only the instrumental works of Mozart but also his vocal compositions.

Unfortunately, neither of us has been able thus far to find time for this task. Paul Badura-Skoda is a performing artist who continues to give nearly one hundred concerts a year and has yet to finish several demanding recording projects. Withal, he has managed to write a book on Bach interpretation that will soon be published. My own schedule has been crowded with musicological activity encompassing work on Mozart piano editions and Dittersdorf symphonies, as well as a history of the fortepiano and iconographical and biographical studies of Schubert.

As it may be several years, therefore, before the co-authors of the present volume will be in a position to collaborate again to produce those additional chapters on the interpretation of Mozart's compositions, we gladly agree to the reissuing of our original work, unaltered, for library collections and for the use of music students, scholars, and performers — not to mention the growing community of Mozart lovers.

— EVA BADURA-SKODA
Vienna, Austria
September 1985

INTERPRETING MOZART
ON THE KEYBOARD

Unfinished oil painting of Mozart by his brother-in-law, Joseph Lange, *c.* 1782–83 (?) (*Mozart Museum, Salzburg.*)

EVA AND PAUL
BADURA-SKODA

Interpreting Mozart
on the Keyboard

TRANSLATED BY
LEO BLACK

ST. MARTIN'S PRESS

NEW YORK

Printed in the United States of America

Contents

List of Plates

THIS book has been written after long, affectionate study of Mozart. The discoveries and insights granted us during this study daily increased not only our love for his music, but also our admiration for this unique man and artist. We now find it hard to realize that some people, not only music-lovers, but professional musicians, see nothing in Mozart's music. Simple and uncomplicated as it seems to the layman, every musician realizes its underlying complexity, its balance of content and form, so hard to recreate; truly, to play Mozart is the acid test of musical taste.

As everybody realizes, good Bach-playing needs stylistic awareness—acquaintance with the style of the time and of the composer—and this is just as true of Mozart. Without a knowledge of Mozart's style, such as the present book aims at providing, one cannot fill out the sketchy passages in many of his compositions in roughly the way he might have done himself; nor can one produce stylistically accurate cadenzas for his concertos, amplify his sparing dynamic markings, play his ornaments correctly, and so on. (Incidentally, if our musical examples differ from the texts of the best-known printed editions, this is because wherever possible we have quoted from Mozart's manuscripts or from the next most reliable source.)

Naturally, there are certain limits to any knowledge of Mozart's style. So in treating various problems some purely personal views are bound to be expressed. Nor have we even tried to make all our conclusions wholly acceptable—our main aim has been rather to bring to light problems of Mozart-interpretation, and to help solve them.

Although we have often chosen the piano works as a starting-point, this book is by no means directed merely to pianists. We have also examined many compositions for other instruments, and violinists, singers and conductors will find here much that concerns them.

We are glad of this opportunity to thank most sincerely our revered teachers, the late pianist, Dr. Edwin Fischer, Professor Wilhelm Fischer and Professor Viola Thern, for everything they taught us. It is also our pleasant duty to thank very warmly all those who helped us in our work on the German edition, above all Professor Alfred Orel, the conductor George Szell, Professor Hellmut Federhofer, and Dr. Oswald Jonas. We are also very grateful to the directors and staff of various libraries: New York Public Library, Music Department (Dr. J. Braunstein); German National Library, Berlin (Dr. Virneisl); the West German Library, Marburg/L. (Director Cremer); the University Library of Tübingen (Dr. von Reibnitz); the Library of the Gesellschaft der Musikfreunde, Vienna (Dr. Hedwig Kraus); and the Music Department of the Austrian National Library in Vienna (Prof. Dr. L. Nowak). As for the translation into English, we should like to express our thanks to publisher and translator for their kind co-operation, to Mr. H. C. Robbins Landon, Mr. Paul Hamburger and Mr. Fritz Spiegel for their help and good advice, and to Miss Emily Anderson for the kind permission to use her translation of Mozart's letters. We also wish to thank those publishers referred to in the translator's note. We are much obliged to Mrs. Christa Landon, Mr. Maurits Sillem and Mr. Albi Rosenthal for helping us with reading and correcting the proofs.

We would like to thank the following publishers for the use of quotations from books published by them:

Cassell & Co. for C. P. E. Bach: *Essay on the True Art of Playing Keyboard Instruments*, trs. W. J. Mitchell, 1949.

Oxford University Press for Leopold Mozart: *Treatise on the Fundamental Principles of Violin Playing*, trs. Editha Knocker, 1948.

T. Schirmer & Co. for Busoni: *Sketch of a New Aesthetic of Music*, trs. T. Baker, 1911.

Vienna   THE AUTHORS

THE following standard translations of contemporary documents have been used in the text:

C. P. E. Bach: *Essay on the True Art of Playing Keyboard Instruments*, trs. W. J. Mitchell, 1949, London.

Busoni: *Sketch of a New Aesthetic of Music*, trs. Thomas Baker, 1911, New York.

Karl von Dittersdorf: *Autobiography*, trs. A. D. Coleridge, 1896, London.

Leopold Mozart: *Treatise on the Fundamental Principles of Violin Playing*, trs. Editha Knocker, 1948, London and New York.

W. A. Mozart: *Letters of Mozart and his Family*, trs. Emily Anderson, 1938, London.

A small number of passages from C. P. E. Bach appeared to require rather more literal translation for the special purposes of this volume, and these I have translated myself, clearly indicating the material which is not taken from the excellent version mentioned above. In the brief passages from Quantz, Türk, Schumann, Liszt, Busoni, etc. the translations are my own.

L.B

INTRODUCTION

THE problem of musical interpretation must be as old as music itself. Put at its simplest, it is the problem of leaving the listener with the most powerful, direct, deep and lasting impression possible. This is expressed in the classical legend of Orpheus, whose songs have a miraculous effect, whose playing is so moving and enchanting that it overcomes the gods and even death itself. The ultimate goal of all musical activity is to make an impression on the soul of the listener. That is the goal, but the way to it is a long and uncertain one. There are indeed a few favourites of Fortune for whom at first everything seems automatically to go right; but in the long run they, too, find that art is the result of hard work and often of suffering—or even, quite often, of a process of destruction (illness, sin) that blights the soul and lays it bare. The essence of artistry lies in the power to create, to love, and the desperate need to communicate—the path is 'infinite pains'. The chequered careers of these 'favoured' artists are no reflection on their degree of vocation. Nor can the essence of greatness, of creativity, be wholly communicated or passed on, and ultimate perfection in playing remains a secret reserved for the moment of performance.

But one thing is common to artists of all ages; they were not born as finished artists—their path was that of effort and endurance. Disappointment lies in store for anyone who thinks that all he has to do is to wait passively for the moment of enlightenment. Favoured or not, he who wishes to achieve anything must seek to exploit his talents to the full and to increase his knowledge. This means that the musician, the interpreter, must come to grips with the essential problems of musical interpretation.

Of course, musicians have always been concerned with the basic questions of interpretation, and much has already been said and written on the subject. However, great interpreters have held contradictory views, and it often seems hard to reconcile various principles. Take, for instance, those laid down by two such authorities as C. P. E. Bach and Busoni. Bach said:

> A musician cannot move others unless he, too, is moved: He must of necessity feel all of the effects that he hopes to arouse in his audience . . .[1]

whereas Busoni wrote:

> If an artist is to move others, he must not be moved himself—otherwise he will lose control of his technique at the vital moment.[2]

I

It may sound a paradox, but the ideal interpretation should fulfil both these conditions. One plays with absolute conviction, yet somewhere inside there is a controlling function that must remain unmoved, otherwise one's feelings overflow the banks laid down by the intellect and the result is amateurish. The following sentences from Busoni's *New Aesthetic of Music* show incidentally that he was by no means hostile to 'feeling'; his words were originally written in reply to the criticism that he played without feeling:

> Feeling, like honesty, is a moral necessity, a quality nobody may renounce . . . even though in everyday life one can forgive lack of feeling if it is compensated by some more brilliant quality of character . . . in art it [feeling] is the ultimate moral quality.[3]

Every musical phrase can be regarded as the symbol of a certain expressive content. The true artist is privileged not merely to recognize this content, but to fix it so firmly in his consciousness that his intellectual and spiritual qualities are set free for other tasks. Thus even when the artist knows that a phrase expresses sorrow, he cannot afford to feel miserable every time he plays the passage, particularly when practising or rehearsing. The vital thing is that he knows what the phrase means—and what sorrow means; and that he is able to portray it without losing control of himself. Unless he can objectivize the waves of feeling conjured up by the music, i.e. subordinate them to a higher level of consciousness, he will be incapable of the intellectual effort needed to mould a large-scale musical form as an organism; he will be too concerned with the succeeding emotions and will lose sight of the horizon. He must view the work as a whole if he is to fill every part of it with the appropriate expression of feeling, and to give the listener the impression of a coherent, harmonious whole.

The relationship between composer and interpreter is another problem that has been much discussed. Should the interpreter use a composer's work to express himself and his 'emotions', or should he stand out of the way, hide behind the work, force his own personality into the background? The answer must depend not only on the temperament of particular interpreters but on the taste of the time. The Romantics demanded that the interpreter, too, should be allowed free scope for his imagination and for interpretation. Franz Liszt wrote in one of his letters:[4]

> The virtuoso is not a mason, chiselling his stone conscientiously according to the sketches of the architect. He is not a passive tool for reproducing feelings and thoughts, without adding anything of his own. He is not a more or less experienced 'interpreter' of works which leave him no scope for his own comments. . . . For the virtuoso, musical works are in fact nothing but tragic and moving materializations of his emotions; he is called upon to make them speak, weep, sing and sigh, to recreate them in accordance with his own consciousness. In this way he, like the composer, is a creator, for he must have within himself those passions that he wishes to bring so intensely to life. . . .

Many modern composers go to the opposite extreme in their views; they demand that the interpreter shall simply play the notes put before him, with no comments of his own, as impersonally as a soldier carries out the orders of his superior officer. Ravel is believed to have said, 'I will not be interpreted!' and Stravinsky has made similar remarks.

Ravel's words are obviously a protest against too subjective, romantic interpretation of his works, against the fact that many performers take too little trouble to find out what the composer really wants, and to express it. His deliberately wrong use of the word 'interpretation' does not affect the basic idea.

Liszt's words are no surprise, coming from a romantic and, moreover, from an improviser of genius; his ideas reflect the interpretative style of an age that has finally passed away. But it must not be forgotten that now, as always, romantic works demand a freer, more personal interpretation than do the works of other periods. The interpreter of romantic music will always stand especially in need of improvisation, 'the magic of the moment', if he is to express the moods intended by the composer.

It is, however, harder to understand the views of the various modern composers who tend toward the opposite extreme. It is quite impossible to perform a piece of music 'impersonally', for even the coldest, most matter-of-fact musician interprets, i.e. he expounds, communicates, translates, whether or not he realizes that he is doing so. If a composer wished to ensure a slavishly impersonal performance of his work, he could never be content with merely writing his music down, but would always have simultaneously to make a gramophone record of the work, which the performer (for one could hardly go on calling him the interpreter) would simply have to imitate as best he could. But there is no need to emphasize that such soulless imitation would be the death of all musical performance. On the other hand, once the performer is recognized as an interpreter, not an imitator, then a record of the composer's performance can naturally assist him very much, particularly as he is glad of any help in understanding what the composer is trying to say. Incidentally, composers' recorded performances of their works are the best proof that even those among them who stand out for objective performance can rarely remain at all objective or impersonal when they themselves perform. Above all, they can rarely play a work the same way even twice running. Quite the opposite; composers tend to play their own works not merely with more life, less constraint and more naturally, but also often with more imagination than do the fanatical advocates of literal exactness.

All the same, most composers nowadays tend to undervalue the function of the interpreter, and to allow him less freedom than is in fact his due. Since their own psychological world and processes of thought are naturally clear and obvious, they are often under the illusion that they have expressed their thoughts quite clearly in musical notation. But there is a great difference between a musical text's relation to actual music and the way the plan of a house is related to the finished building. Given a good plan, even an untalented but conscientious builder can erect a building that answers its purpose, whereas in performing a work even the most gifted interpreter can at times go so appallingly wrong that the composer's intentions are completely distorted. This is often the case in our concert halls, and not only in performances of modern music! Even if two interpreters adhere as strictly as possible to the 'given markings', they will never reproduce the work in the same way, whereas it is a fact of daily experience that machines, council flats, etc., are as alike as two peas. Although musical notation is becoming constantly subtler, our way of notating acoustic processes with optical symbols must remain an imprecise transcription. The sequence of tension and relaxation and the wide scale of sensory values can never be exactly pinned down by graphic means. Printed music replaces a continuum by points, and only the intuition and skill of the interpreter can link these up and bring them to life.

There have been many attempts to demonstrate the great changes that take place, during the course of generations, in the current picture of some great composer of the past. It almost looks as if any period's idea of Bach, Beethoven or Mozart told us more about the period than about the composer. If we now imagine we appreciate Mozart's greatness more completely and deeply than our grandfathers did, there is only one thing that may entitle us to do so: the ever more prevalent conviction that we must respect composers' intentions, and that it is impossible to study too fully the text of their music and the customs of their time. In other words, we must do everything possible to ensure that our playing is faithful to the work and to its style.

What does this involve? First, it must be made clear that faithfulness to a work is not to be confused with what we may call literal exactness.* In the history of interpretation there is a contrast between a period about the turn of the century, which tended to allow great freedom—indeed, arbitrariness—in interpretation, and one since about 1920 in which the tendency has been to remain 'faithful to the text', to adhere rigidly to the printed score. Unfortunately, this often resulted in academic adherence to the printed text. The demand for adherence to the text was a welcome and most important development, but nowadays we have learnt, from our efforts to understand genius and the historical situation in which it flourished, that literal exactness alone cannot ensure faithful and stylish interpretation—that classical composers' works not merely permit, but demand of the performer a degree of freedom; the one thing we can be absolutely sure they did not want is inexpressive, dry performance.

Let us return to our basic demand in interpretation—to achieve the deepest and most lasting effect possible†—and proceed from there. From

---

*It has nothing to do with the above-mentioned refusal to reproduce a composer's performance by mere imitation; imitation can lack style just as creative interpretation can be stylish.

†Incidentally, one must beware the fallacy that composers are not interested in effectiveness, or even in superficial 'effects'! Many composers have delighted in 'effects', and Mozart was no exception. He justifies many an idea in his works with the words, 'It makes a good effect'.

this standpoint, the question, 'Exact or free interpretation?' at first seems a subsidiary one. For if we insist on exact interpretation, we do so not for its own sake, but in the conviction that Mozart's works are most effective when reproduced in a Mozartian style (so far as this is possible; by 'style' we mean the totality of the psychological phenomena to which a creative artist is subject, by which he is formed and which, for his part, he influences). If some particular performer were able to play Mozart so as to make a stronger and deeper effect than anyone else, we should willingly be converted to playing Mozart in 'his style' from then on.* But this is not very likely to happen. Mozart's works, of all music, possess such incomparable organic unity, so complete a balance between content and form, that any interpolation of foreign elements, even on the part of a genius, would ruin their harmony— that harmony which seems to lift his music above mere human frailty.

Although faithfulness to a particular work and to the style as a whole is very necessary, it carries with it a danger of attaching too much importance to the intellect. An excessively intellectual approach blocks the paths to the unconscious, to the earth, where all musical performance has its roots. For when all is said and done, art can only be grasped intuitively. No amount of historical research, on its own, can make a performance truly stylish; the work must sound 'as if it had never been played before'. Historical discoveries can often increase the liveliness of a performance; one has only to think of our rediscovery of baroque music's rhythmic subtleties, which the nineteenth century completely failed to appreciate. The intellect must support intuition, and often guide it, too; it organizes, divides, analyses. But these particles, separated by the intellect, can only be moulded into a living entity through a long experience of feeling and intuition. Throughout history, the living breath of music has been great men's instinct for grasping melody, tension and relaxation, extension and contraction. This is why there must be a little of the gipsy in every musician. Theoretical study is only the preparation—a necessary preparation, like practice at an instrument. But the artistic experience depends solely on the life that imbues one's playing. Edwin Fischer always used to impress on his pupils:[5]

> Do not destroy this world of artistic visions that come up from your unconscious—make room for it; dream dreams, see visions, don't listen to records till you in turn become a record, forever repeating yourself: suffer, rejoice, love and live a life that constantly renews itself.

*Composers' minds, too, can work this way: 'I wish you could have been at Liszt's this morning. He is quite extraordinary. I was absolutely spellbound by the way he played some of the Novelettes, the Fantasia and the Sonata. Often not at all as I had intended, but with genius, so tenderly and boldly as even he can not always play. Only Becker was there—with tears in his eyes. . . .' (Letter from Robert to Clara Schumann, Leipzig, 20th March 1840, from Clara Schumann, *Jugendbriefe Robert Schumanns*, Breitkopf and Härtel, Leipzig, 1886.)

Chapter One

MOZART'S SOUND

ONLY in rare and exceptional cases can one reconstruct with any exactness the actual sound of a Mozart work at the time of its first performance. But even if one were to produce the same acoustical conditions—perhaps using old instruments in a rococo hall—this would be nothing like enough to achieve a historically faithful presentation. Other things, too, would have to be the same as in Mozart's day: aesthetic standards and social conditions. But since the eighteenth century, as we well know, the aesthetic and general outlook of musicians and public has altered greatly, even if we ignore the complete change in the structure of society since Mozart's time.

Still, we usually play music not because we are interested in history, but, firstly, from a delight in playing and in sound itself, and, secondly, because we like a particular work. On the other hand, we cannot do full justice to music from other periods unless we hear it as its creator did, and attempt to reproduce it, as far as possible, in the style and with the resources of the period when it was written.

But even the use of historical instruments poses a number of difficult problems. To begin with, really good historical instruments are very rarely available. Imitations may be more mechanically reliable, but it is very rare for them to sound as distinctive and satisfying as do originals. Although a few historically genuine instruments have been preserved so that one can indeed play them (we refer here to pianos), even these show their age. Usually the case, being wooden, has dried so much that the instruments constantly go out of tune. If a modern pianist gives a recital on a Mozart piano, he has to choose whether to retune the instrument after each item or to afflict the ears of the public with impurities of tuning.

The question of using old instruments reminds us of a remark by the late Curt Sachs, the famous expert on old instruments, to the effect that the longer and more intensively he had to do with old instruments, the less desire he had to hear them. According to Sachs, it is a proven fact that the organs in the various Leipzig churches during Bach's time varied greatly in pitch. But the wind instruments that Bach employed were incapable of adapting themselves to the varied pitch of the organs, so that they must

1. Forte-piano with pedal-board built in, dating from about 1812. It resembles Mozart's pedal-piano which he had built during the 1780s, while living in Vienna. (*Collection of Musical Instruments, Kunsthistorisches Museum, Vienna.*)

inevitably have been out of tune when Bach had to transfer a performance from one church to another, as often happened; there were not enough wind instruments for each church to have a set with the appropriate tuning. On the other hand, the contention that *all* eighteenth-century performances must have suffered from faulty intonation cannot be proved. Wind instruments survive from this period which are wonderfully well tuned and, despite their age, can be played scrupulously in tune. Eighteenth-century recorders and flutes, in particular, were often constructed with remarkable care. Moreover, it is known that even in Mozart's time singers and string players were expected to be able to alternate between pure and tempered intonation, to match the accompanying instrument; this can only be done by a highly trained ear.

There is a further problem in using historic instruments; we are no longer able to play them as they used to be played. Not only has our performing technique altered, but our perception of sound is attuned to modern conditions, and complete re-education would be necessary in order to learn how to play old instruments approximately as they used to be played in Mozart's time. If some particular musician, after years of contact with old instruments, succeeds in reconditioning himself in this way, a public accustomed to the sound of modern instruments will probably find his reconstruction of an older ideal of beauty peculiar or downright unpleasant. The practical musician cannot propose to do away with the acoustical and technical alterations of the last 150 years, even though these alterations often meant sacrificing some particular effect of tonal beauty, for he will find his approach condemns him to isolation. The revival of old ideas of sound, and the use of old instruments, is extraordinarily interesting for the historian; but for the musician, because of the general alterations in our aesthetic attitude, it is for the most part impracticable.

This is why there are limits to the extent to which nowadays one can carry the demand for a re-creation of the 'original sound'. Although we must avoid the last generation's mistake of regarding their technical and instrumental achievements as the *ne plus ultra*, we must all the same be healthily critical of the instruments and acoustical conditions of past ages. To regard everything old as beautiful, simply because it is old, would surely be as much of a mistake as to apply present-day aesthetic standards uncritically to the art of past ages. In re-creating a work in performance we are always faced with the task of finding a compromise between historical knowledge and the world of present-day perception.

There are good reasons why on this question of sound one should think rather less strictly than on other stylistic questions. Tone colour (in physical terms, the total of harmonics above a fundamental) is unlike the basic elements of music (melody, harmony, rhythm, tempo, dynamics, etc.) in that it is usually not a decisive factor in the musical substance of a work. For this reason, Bach and Handel could frequently arrange their own and other people's compositions, and Mozart, for example, arranged a wind octet for strings, an oboe concerto for flute, etc. Sound, as such, only becomes important when a musical idea owes its birth to an auditory image of some specific sound. Indeed, many musical ideas have been produced with a quite definite instrumental sound in mind—one thinks, for example, of horn motives, or of an oboe cantilena that suggests a shepherd's pipe. In these cases there is some psychic relationship between the original sound and the composer's ideas for his composition. For example, if in the development of instruments the sound of the horn were to alter so much that it sounded like a factory siren, this would finally put an end to the association of 'open spaces, woods, hunting, nature' which at the moment it can still evoke, even though nowadays the horn is very rarely used in hunting. If any musician is now interested in gaining a clear idea of the sound of instruments in Mozart's time, he should examine the changes that have taken place in this direction during the past 200 years.

The tonal picture has altered in many respects; the developments of recent centuries have aimed at a greater volume of tone, greater compass, better intonation and, very often, greater ease of performance. It is easy to see the reasons for this alteration. For example, one reason for the increased volume of sound in present-day performances is that concerts in private rooms are becoming rarer and rarer, while it is now quite common for an audience of 2,000 or 3,000 to hear solo and chamber music recitals. One principal reason for the greater volume of tone produced by modern instruments, and the greater loudness of present-day performances, lies, of course, in the development of music itself; even Beethoven's ideal of sound differs clearly from Mozart's, and it is largely because of his influence that piano-makers have ever since his time aimed at a fuller, rounder tone, with less contrast of registers and, above all, more power.

But in achieving greater volume, the character of piano tone has been steadily altered. It seems that the human ear only reacts favourably to very bright sounds, rich in overtones, when they are not very loud. Forte, these sounds tend to make a sharp, shrill effect, and fortissimo they are almost unbearably strident.* So it is not at all surprising that, in comparison with Mozart's piano, even Beethoven's, and *a fortiori* the pianos of the nineteenth and twentieth centuries have not only a fuller, louder tone, but also one that is darker and usually also duller. This was an inevitable development in the manufacture of pianos. Compared with the modern piano, Mozart's piano, with its many overtones, produces an extraordinarily thin, translucent, effect, sharply defined, and 'silvery'. The instrument was more delicately built, the strings were thinner, and this made its tone relatively weak. The levels of volume to which we are accustomed were impossible until the introduction of the steel frame by A. Balcock in 1825,[6] and the associated increase in string-tension.† Moreover, the eighteenth-century piano has leather-covered

---

*Those who own records of old instruments (clavichord, eighteenth-century fortepiano) will be able to confirm this statement. These delicate instruments sound attractive only if the loudspeaker is not allowed to exceed the original level of volume as recorded. Reproduced too loudly, the bright tone of these instruments becomes displeasing.

†To make clear the difference between a fortepiano of Mozart's time and a modern

hammers, not the felt ones now customary, slimmer in shape, so that these pianos have a very bright tone, rich in overtones, something between that of a harpsichord and a modern piano.

Hardly any instrument of the modern orchestra is still the same as in Mozart's time. Often technical imperfections stimulated mechanical improvements, which in turn altered the tone. But no other instrument was so strongly affected, so fundamentally rebuilt, as was the piano. When Mozart was young, the pianoforte was a very recent invention,[7] an instrument rarely to be found. Even in the seventies Mozart seems to have had no piano at his disposal in Salzburg, as one can gather indirectly from a letter from his mother to Leopold Mozart:[8]

> Indeed he plays quite differently from what he used to in Salzburg—for there are pianofortes here, on which he plays so extraordinarily well that people say they have never heard the like.

But by the end of the eighteenth century the pianoforte was usurping the cembalo's leading role. We know that Mozart, who has often been justly called the first important virtuoso pianist, was very fond of the pianos of his day and preferred them to the harpsichord.[9] Doubtless the piano was his favourite instrument; so much can be gathered simply from the fact that he wrote such a great number of works for the piano. His piano works—particularly the concertos—reflect his most personal thoughts, and it was in these works that he attained the highest peaks of instrumental art. His piano style shows clearly that he was a born pianist, who had an amazing way of exploiting his instrument's technical and acoustical possibilities, reaching their utmost limits, but not letting these hinder him. His well-known letter from Augsburg to his father (17th October 1777), contains an enthusiastic description of the Stein piano. In Augsburg, as everywhere that he played, his piano playing won golden opinions.

> Everything was extraordinary, tasteful and remarkable. His compositions were thorough, fiery, varied and simple; the harmony so full, so powerful, so unexpected, so elevating; the melody so agreeable, so playful and all so original; his performance on the fortepiano so pleasing, so pure, so full of expression, yet at the same time so extraordinarily fluent that one hardly knew what to listen to first, and the whole audience was moved to ecstasy ...*

as a contemporary wrote. The *Musikalische Real-Zeitung*, Dresden, 1789 (p. 191), wrote:[10]

---

piano, one need only compare their weights: a Walter piano weighs about 140 lb., a Steinway concert-grand more than 1,000. Transportation of instruments must have been a good deal easier then! 'Since my arrival, your brother's fortepiano has been taken at least a dozen times to the theatre or to some other house', Mozart's father wrote to Nannerl (12th March 1785). One wonders whether Mozart would nowadays have had his piano moved twelve times in three weeks.

*From Mueller von Asow, *Briefe W. A. Mozarts*, I, p. 271.

On the 14th April the famous composer W. A. Mozart from Vienna played on the fortepiano before His Eminence, and he has also performed here in Dresden in many aristocratic and private houses, with limitless success. His abilities at the clavichord and fortepiano are quite indescribable: one should add also his extraordinary ability to read at sight, which is truly incredible— for even he is hardly able to play a piece better after practice than he does at a first reading.

Unlike the cembalo, the fortepiano is known to have made possible dynamic gradations from *pp* to *ff*, and many varied modes of touch, even though its technique is in many ways different from that of the modern instrument. It should not be supposed that our piano is capable of subtler nuances; the Mozart pianos of Stein and Walter, for instance, were clear and very bright in the upper register, and this made it easier to play cantabile and with full colour. The lower notes had a peculiar round fullness, but none of the dull, stodgy sound of the low notes of a modern piano. Whereas the tone becomes steadily thinner toward the top, the highest register sounding almost as if pizzicato, the full sound of the bass is by far the most satisfying register of the Mozart piano. The strings are so thin that chords in the bass can be played with perfect clarity even when they are very closely spaced. On a modern piano such chords usually sound sodden and earthy—so stodgy that one can hardly pick out the individual notes. This is why such chords as the following one:

(which often occur in Mozart) are enough to challenge a modern pianist's taste and feeling for style. We shall show later on how to overcome this technical problem.[11]

Thus it is not so easy to re-create on a modern piano the full differentiation of tone of a Mozart piano, and perhaps this is the main reason why many pianists recommend the avoidance of the pedal in playing his music. But all eighteenth-century fortepianos had a knee-lever, which had exactly the same function as the present-day sustaining pedal, and which Mozart very much appreciated. We know of his letter from Augsburg to his father (17th October 1777), in which he praises the efficiency of this mechanism in Stein's pianos:

> The last [Sonata], in D,[12] sounds exquisite on Stein's pianoforte. The device too which you work with your knee is better on his than on other instruments. I have only to touch it and it works; and when you shift your knee the slightest bit, you do not hear the least reverberation.

The use of the knee-lever, i.e. the lifting of the dampers, gave a richer and more satisfying tone even to the Mozart piano. When it is said that the pedal should not be used in playing Mozart

> because Mozart never reckoned on this pedal as a regular adjunct, and regarded its use, at most, as a rare exception, a quite special effect[13]

this must be contradicted. It is very improbable that Mozart was sparing in his use of the tonal possibilities of the right knee-lever.[14] There are passages in his piano works which in fact rely on a pedal effect—for example, the very beginning of the D minor Fantasia (K.397), or bar 46 of the Fantasia from the C major Fantasia and Fugue (K.394):

There are many cantabile passages which can be played much more expressively and effectively with the aid of the pedal (Piano Sonata in A major (K.331), first movement, variation IV, bar 3):

The piano solo at bar 40 of the Romanze from the D minor Piano Concerto, too, would sound very meagre if the pedal were completely avoided.

Why should Mozart, the unchallenged master at exploiting all the timbres and tonal possibilities of his instruments (think of the wonderful soft trumpet solo in the first Finale of *Don Giovanni*, the treatment of the clarinet in the Trio K.498 or the Clarinet Concerto, or the Wind Serenade K.361)—why should he not have used a mechanism about which he wrote so enthusiastically? Unfortunately, this opinion is very widespread, though the only possible argument in its favour is that—if we had to choose between two extremes— a performance of Mozart's music would be more tolerable when played without pedal than when overpedalled. Naturally, the use of the pedal must in no way be allowed to mar the clarity of performance, and one should expressly warn against excessive pedalling. Even with the dampers raised, the pianos of Mozart's time sounded much more translucent than those of the present day.

The fortepiano of Mozart's time had a compass of only five octaves (from F, fourth ledger line below the bass clef, to F above the treble clef). The apparent ease with which Mozart observed the upper limits of this compass is almost unbelievable. If it should in fact happen that in the recapitulation of a second subject the theme threatened to go above top F because of its transposition into the tonic, the motive would be altered, and in so subtle a

way that necessity became a virtue; often this is done in the simplest possible
way (B flat Concerto (K.595), third movement, bars 112–13):

Here, at the recapitulation (bars 251–2), the original diatonicism is altered
into chromaticism:

In Beethoven's works one not infrequently comes across passages in which the
compass of the contemporary piano seems to have imposed unwelcome
limitations on the composer's fantasy (e.g. G major Piano Concerto, first
movement, bar 318, or E flat Concerto, first movement, bar 332). In Mozart,
on the other hand, it is hardly ever necessary, nor in most cases possible, to
make alterations such as many present day pianists make in these passages
from Beethoven. One can point to two possible exceptions to this rule in
Mozart: in the G major Piano Concerto (K.453), third movement, bar 56, to
retain the original upward motion (as in bars 40 and 48) would mean reaching top G:

and in the Three-piano Concerto (K.242), third movement, bar 155 onwards, a literal transposition of the figuration from bar 34 makes it necessary
to play a top A:

In this concerto one could also perhaps extend the compass in bars 50–1 of the second movement, to correspond with bars 22–3. But these alterations are by no means absolutely necessary.

The lower limits of the compass are another matter. Here one is more often aware that Mozart did not regard his piano's bottom F as a natural lower limit, but would occasionally have used the low E, E flat or even C, had his instrument permitted. In fact, he did! He was so fond of the bass register that he had a pedal board made for his own use, as Leopold wrote to Nannerl in St. Gilgen:

> He has had a large fortepiano pedal made, which is under the instrument and is about two feet longer and extremely heavy.[15]

The Danish actor and musician, Joachim Daniel Preisler, also mentions this pedal piano in his diary (he came to Vienna in the course of his studies in 1788):

> Sunday the 24th August. In the afternoon, Jünger, Lange and Werner came for us, to go to Kapellmeister Mozart's. The hour of music I heard there was the happiest ever granted me. This little man and great master improvised twice on a pedal piano, so wonderfully! so wonderfully! that I did not know where I was. Weaving together the most difficult passages and the most ingratiating themes.*

Michael Rosing, who went with Preisler (together with Peter Rasmus Sabye) confirms Preisler's reports in his own diary:

> 24th August, 1788: about 4 in the afternoon, Jünger, Lange and Dr. Werner came to take us to Kapellmeister Mozart's—he played free fantasias for us in such a way that I longed to be able to do the same myself; particularly his pedal in the second fantasia made the greatest impression. Happy and overwhelmed at having heard Mozart, we returned to the city.†

*From Joachim Daniel Preisler's *Journal over en Rejse igiennen Frankerige og Tydskland i Aaret 1788*, Copenhagen, 1789, quoted and translated into German by O. E. Deutsch in *Dänische Schauspieler zu Besuch bei Mozart* ('Visit of Danish Actors to Mozart'), *Oesterreichische Musikzeitschrift*, 1956, pp. 406 et seq.

†O. E. Deutsch, ibid., p. 410.

Frank, a doctor, also reported about this pedal:

> I played him a fantasia he had composed. 'Not bad', he said to my great
> astonishment. 'Now listen to me play it.' Wonder of wonders! Under his
> fingers the piano became quite another instrument. He had reinforced it with
> a second keyboard that served as a pedal.[16]

Thus what was used was a pedal board, such as nowadays one only finds on
an organ. An additional instrument such as Mozart possessed can only very
rarely be found in museums and collections of instruments. The illustrations
of pedal pianos opposite pp. 6 and 22 will perhaps give an idea of how such an
instrument looked. Its lowest note was the bottom C of the modern piano,
and its compass was about two octaves. The instrument shown opposite p. 22
has a so-called 'broken' octave as its lower octave, i.e. omission of the chromatic notes C sharp, D sharp, F sharp and G sharp saves four keys. Thus the
bottom note is not E as it might appear, but C. E and G are the first two
'black' keys.

Mozart could write the autograph of the D minor Concerto as he did (cf.
p. 204) only because he had a pedal piano (a fact that has hitherto been overlooked, strangely enough). Today, unfortunately, this passage can no longer
be performed as it stands.

Mozart would scarcely have had a pedal piano built without some special
reason. He certainly used it quite often to extend the compass in the bass, or
to double important bass notes and motives. Thus it is not out of style to
remember the pedal piano in certain cases where this is particularly justifiable, and, for example, to play the bass augmentation of the fugue subject
from the Fantasia and Fugue (K.394) doubled an octave lower:

or the chromatic bass in the development of the first movement of the E flat
Concerto (K.482), descending to bottom E flat:

(*Sustained notes on the analogy of the orchestral basses*)

Mozart may also have used the low pedal notes in the original cadenza for the A major Concerto (K.488):

But all these are probably exceptional cases. In general one will be better advised to adhere to the traditional Mozart text, particularly as there is a great danger of making the tone of the modern piano thick and unclear by using its deep bass notes.

It was once objected that the notes of a Mozart piano die away too quickly, i.e. that it is almost as short-breathed as the harpsichord. This is a doubtful assertion, and should not be regarded as supported by the passage in Mozart's famous letter of 17th October 1777 about the Stein piano, where he says:

> But now I much prefer Stein's, for they damp ever so much better than the Regensburg instruments. When I strike hard, I can keep my finger on the note or raise it, but the sound ceases the moment I have produced it.

Surely Mozart was referring, not to the tone of the piano, but to the efficiency of the dampers and release mechanism, whether one played legato or staccato.

It can happen even nowadays that with a bad piano the hammer does not fall back into place when one plays legato (i.e. keeping the finger on the key), but stays pressed against the string. Since modern hammers are felt-covered, this merely results in an undesired damping of the string. But the narrow leather hammers of the time would have given a disagreeable 'buzzing' tone, like the noise produced by touching a vibrating string on a present-day piano with some metallic object, such as a screwdriver.

Incidentally, we had a chance to inspect a Stein piano in private possession in New York, and this convinced us that the tone of such pianos was by
no means short-breathed and wooden. In the middle register of the piano
the note is perceptible for several seconds after the attack, as with every good
eighteenth-century instrument.

Throughout the first paragraph of this letter Mozart is referring, not to the
Stein piano's quality of tone, but only to its mechanism. For the letter continues:

> In whatever way I touch the keys, the tone is always even. It never jars, it is
> never stronger or weaker or entirely absent; in a word, it is always even. . . .
> His instruments have this special advantage over others that they are made
> with this escape action. Only one maker in a hundred bothers about this.
> But without an escapement it is impossible to avoid jangling and vibration
> after the note is struck.

Moreover, eighteenth-century pianos often had other devices for altering
the tone, beside the obligatory knee-lever to lift the dampers and the sordino
knee-lever found in some instruments (corresponding to our una corda pedal
shift mechanism)—for instance, a lute-stop, or the so-called bassoon-stop—a
fillet of parchment which was pressed against the string and produced a bur-
ring noise. Some pianos even had a percussion mechanism, which could be
brought into action with the foot. These mechanisms akin to harpsichord
stops were hardly more than playthings. Did Mozart perhaps employ the
bassoon-stop or the percussion mechanism in the ritornellos of the Turkish
March from his A major Sonata? Nowadays we must use different means to
conjure up the typically Turkish quality of the piece—by subtleties of touch,
by 'pointing' the rhythm, etc. In fact, the piano is particularly well suited to
a play of tone-colour, since the tone of the present-day piano, as against that
of other instruments, e.g. the oboe or 'cello, is intrinsically indifferent,
'characterless', and needs to be given form. It is wrong to say that on the
piano one can merely play loud, soft, legato, staccato, etc., and that it is
impossible to achieve a true play of tone-colour, to imitate a woodwind
instrument or a 'cello pizzicato. From the standpoint of physics, the piano's
tone can, of course, not be altered. But it is one of the inexplicable secrets of
interpretation that the player can communicate to the listener not only
moods, but particular acoustical images. How else could one understand the
artistry with which pianists such as Cortot, Wilhelm Kempff or Edwin
Fischer handle piano tone? Unfortunately, it is impossible to demonstrate
the wonderful wealth of tone-colour possibilities without audible examples.
Amazing effects can be achieved by changes of register, or, equally, frequent opposition of high and low, crossing the hands, alternation of legato and
staccato, full textures and two-part writing, rolling trills in the bass, etc.
Mozart's piano writing contains trumpet flourishes, the gently melting tones of
the flute, the veiled sound of the basset horn, noisy orchestral tutti, just as it
contains utterly magical sounds that could belong only to the piano. But the
most intimate and inward expression of all can be achieved by using the

piano's *una corda*-tone—as if the player were breathing the music into the listener's ear. . . . To play Mozart without the magic of a richly varied tonal palette is not only inartistic, it is out of style.

For eighteenth-century pianos were wholly suited to a play of varied tone-colour. Everyone who plays Mozart nowadays could profit from occasionally playing an instrument of that period. Practice at an old fortepiano is the most direct way to gain an idea of the sound which must have been in Mozart's mind. This kind of personal study cannot be replaced by even the most exhaustive description of the Mozart piano, and certainly not by merely listening to records of the instrument.* It would be a most welcome thing if for many present-day Mozart performances pianos were available whose sound resembled that of genuine historic pianos, without the latter's faults which result from their age (rapid deterioration in tuning, unreliable mechanism). But, unfortunately, such pianos are only very occasionally made, and are for the most part not available, so we must reconcile ourselves to the prevailing conditions.

Not only have pianos altered a great deal in sound since the eighteenth century; the sound of the strings, above all of the violin, has changed. The higher bridge, alterations to the bass-bar, higher tuning (it is well known that the tuning A has constantly risen, in terms of cycles per second, and now lies roughly a semitone above that of Mozart's day), but especially the use of steel strings—all these have so altered the character of the tone that present-day violins have a tone that is more piercing, brighter and richer in overtones. Use of the Tourte bow, developed in the nineteenth century, and the technique of bowing customary since then, make it possible for modern violinists to produce a tone that is much more powerful, but which sounds much less warm and tender than the typical violin tone of the eighteenth century could be. There have been only isolated attempts to approach the violin tone of Mozart's day by using gut strings and historical bows. Our ear has become used to the sharper tone of the steel E-string, and, since the latter is much more reliable in such things as firmness and security of intonation, it is unlikely that large numbers of violinists will decide to re-introduce gut strings. Perhaps it is just possible to use plastic or some other artificial material to make strings which would give a more noble sound than that of steel strings, without losing any of the latter's powerful tone. But such an invention is only likely if musicians give voice to a stronger demand for the specifically warm sound of gut strings. Until then it appears that we must reconcile ourselves to this alteration in tone, as to the fact that although the development of the horn has made the instrument easier to play, and capable of producing a chromatic scale, the individual quality of the natural horn's tone seems to have been lost for ever. The 'Viennese' horn comes nearer to the

---

*There are two astonishingly well-preserved Walter pianos, for example, in the Kunsthistorisches Museum Collection of Instruments, Vienna; another, belonging to the Mozarteum in Salzburg is exhibited at the moment in the Mozart Museum there. There is a good Stein piano in the Fia-la-Ahlgrimm collection, Vienna, and another in the Neupert Collection, Nuremberg, a third one in our own collection.

sound of old natural horns than do those made in the French style.

About the development of other wind instruments it should be said that, as a result of changes in technique and improved mechanism, the tone of all of them has undergone great changes—flute and oboe perhaps least, the trumpet perhaps most. Incidentally, the eighteenth-century bassoon must certainly have sounded louder; here, for once, there has been a development in the opposite direction.

The nineteenth-century developments that variously affected the loudness of instruments altered the natural factors on which the classical instrumental ensemble founded its acoustical balance. Naturally, we must take this into account today. There are fewest difficulties in this direction when the ensemble concerned is homogeneous (as in the string quartets and wind serenades). But even the combination of violin and piano brings to light tricky problems, not only as regards loudness, but also because overtone relationships have been changed by alterations in the tone of both violin and piano. The violin has become not only louder, but brighter, more piercing and rich in overtones; on the other hand, the piano has lost much of its overtone richness as it has gained in loudness—it has become duller. Pianists have to exercise great flexibility in playing with a violinist (and, of course, this also applies to all the chamber music with piano, and to the piano concertos); now they must produce the merest breath of sound, to imitate the delicate tone of the Mozart piano, and the next moment they need much greater intensity, in order to do justice to a piano cantilena. It is a well-known acoustical fact that it is difficult to make a loud but dull instrument 'penetrate' in ensemble playing. In the violin sonatas the danger is indeed more that the piano will play too loud and drown the violin. But one should also take note of the passages where a melody is first given out by the violin and then taken over by the piano. Here, if the pianist plays too softly, the musical line can be destroyed instead of being enhanced as the course of the music demands. There is particular danger in passages where the violin is given the lower line of a melody played in thirds. Here, for once, it is the violinist who must accommodate to the pianist, otherwise the acoustical balance may be disturbed because the lower line is inappropriately emphasized. In the classical period there were no violin sonatas 'with piano accompaniment' (though nowadays we are forced to hear Mozart's violin sonatas performed in this way). On the contrary, Mozart called them 'Sonatas for Piano, accompanied by a Violin'; but it will be best to speak of two equal instruments, each of which must in turn stand out or allow its partner to dominate.

The sound of the orchestra has also altered in the last two centuries. As compared with that of Mozart's day, the present-day orchestra hardly ever allows the wind instruments (including the horns) to sound loud enough, while the strings are relatively too loud. The sound of wind instruments was much loved in the eighteenth century, especially by Mozart, and at the time great importance was attached to a clear overall sound. It is therefore certain that most of Mozart's works gain from performance by a small body of strings rather than by the forty or fifty customary nowadays. But, of course, in deciding the size of the orchestra, one must be guided not only by the character of the work concerned, but also by the acoustics of the hall; it is simply that as a rule one should beware of using forces that are too large. We advance this opinion, although we know that Mozart did come across very large orchestras, as is seen from his letter of 24th March 1781, in which he writes about the orchestra of the Vienna Tonkünstlersozietät: 'The orchestra consists of 180 players.' And on 11th April 1781 he reports:

> I forgot to tell you the other day that at the concert the Symphony[17] went magnificently and had the greatest success. There were 40 violins, the wind-instruments were all doubled, there were 10 violas, 10 double-basses, 8 violoncellos and 6 bassoons.

Such enormous forces seem, however, to have been very much the exception at the time. Usually Mozart could only count on, say 6 + 6 violins, 4 violas, 3 'celli and 3 basses.[18] His ideal seems to have corresponded to the composition of the Mannheim orchestra:

> Now I must tell you about the music here. . . . The orchestra is excellent and very strong. On either side 10 or 11 violins, 4 violas, 2 oboes, 2 flutes and 2 clarinets, 2 horns, 4 violoncellos, 4 bassoons and 4 double basses, also trumpets and drums. They can produce fine music. . . .[19]

The astonishing shortage of violas is typical of practically all eighteenth-century orchestras. Haydn often complained about this, and Mozart, who frequently divides his viola parts, must also have wished for a larger number of violas for performances of his works.

Thus for most of Mozart's works large resources are inappropriate. There is a widespread prejudice among conductors and orchestral musicians that only large forces 'sound well', and that they are indispensable for large halls. One of the most welcome developments in the last few years has been the formation, in various countries, of numerous chamber orchestras with very small forces (four first, four second violins); these have proved that even a few instrumentalists can produce enough sound to fill the largest hall. (A very thorough discipline is necessary, of course; there is no room here for the last-desk player who always marks time for three bars after the leader has entered!) These chamber orchestras have greatly enriched our musical life, not only because they have given new life to a valuable, forgotten corpus of music, but, above all, because they have got us back into the way of listening to sounds that are slender and translucent.

When piano and orchestra play together it is a definite advantage that the modern piano has a much greater volume of sound at its disposal. The forte of a Mozart piano was just loud enough to emerge audibly against an orchestra playing piano. In former times the orchestra had for this reason always to make allowances for the weakness of fortepiano tone.*

*cf. pp. 211 et seq. as regards the question of t? bination of piano and orchestra.

It is certainly true that nowadays we are accustomed to a much greater degree of noise than in earlier times—street noises, the thunder of railways and the roaring of aeroplanes, the stentorian tones of larger-than-life loud-speakers in cinemas and at public gatherings, and enormous orchestras in the concert hall. If we were to recreate the absolute intensity levels of the eighteenth century, it is certain that the resulting sound would at first seem much too thin and lacking in penetration. We must reconcile ourselves to the fact that a forte, if it is to sound like one to us, must in acoustical terms be louder than in Mozart's time. For all that, even today a Mozart forte should still not have the volume of tone of a Wagner forte.

A forte, however, is not only an acoustical but a psychological effect. And here it is quite the other way round; in Mozart a forte, though in fact having a smaller degree of loudness, will usually require more psychological intensity than a forte in Wagner, since for Mozart, *forte* may already mean 'full out', whereas in Wagner *f* is only rarely a dynamic climax, in view of his use of dynamics as loud as *fff*.

Mozart was familiar with all the dynamic gradations between *pp* and *ff* (*pp*, *p*, *mp**, *mf*, *f*, *ff*). Unfortunately, he was often content, in accordance with tradition, to give mere hints about dynamics. To complete these in the way required by the music is a difficult problem in interpretation. Nineteenth-century editors of Mozart's works almost always went too far in this direction—too many dynamic nuances destroy the line, *il filo*, as Leopold Mozart called it. But the other extreme—renunciation of all additions to the often hasty dynamic indications—can lead to results that are at least equally misguided. Here Quantz's demands, in his famous textbook, still apply:

> From all that has so far been said, one can now see that it is by no means enough merely to observe piano and forte at those points where they are written; but that an accompanist must also know how to introduce them judiciously in many places where they are not indicated. To achieve this, good teaching and great experience are necessary.[20]

The older and more mature Mozart became, and the greater the independence with which he went his way as man and artist, the more obviously did he try to avoid any ambiguity in his notation. Thus, among the works of his maturity we find a few in which the dynamic indications are worked out in full. The wonderful A minor Rondo (K.511) is a good example of the wealth of nuance which Mozart desired in performances of his works. Here, for once, the manuscript contains exact and frequent performing indications, so that in matters of dynamics and phrasing this piece serves as an excellent starting-point for a study of Mozart's style.

It is quite clear that in Mozart's works, *p* and *f* are merely basic types. Thus a *p* in Mozart can mean *p* or *pp*, but also *mp* in present-day notation, while *f* takes in all the gradations from *mf* to *ff*. Naturally, one can only decide in each individual case which degree of loudness is to be chosen, and one often

*The modern *mp* corresponds to the eighteenth-century *pf*.

needs to know a work very well indeed if one is to decide correctly in some particular case. As an obvious example, not every forte requires maximum dynamic intensity. In his *Violinschule* (XII, §17), Leopold Mozart writes:

> . . . wherever a forte is written down, the tone is to be used with moderation, without foolish scrapings, especially in the accompaniment of a solo part. Many either omit to do a thing altogether, or if they do it, are certain to exaggerate. The affect must be considered. Often a note demands a strong accent, at other times only a moderate one, and then again one which is hardly audible.

It is difficult to draw up general rules for this, but it may be said that *ff* is indicated by the marking *f* in a final tutti with trumpets, timpani and string tremolo, also in the emotional outbursts that occur in the development sections of many of his mature sonata movements.

It is in the instrumental concertos, above all, that we see the full importance of the division of *p* and *f* into several degrees of loudness. During the soli, Mozart mostly prescribed a uniform *p* for the orchestra, whether they are given important motivic material or mere accompanying figures (sustained or reiterated chords). In purely accompanying harmonies, the powerful modern orchestra should be particularly careful to keep down to *pp*, whereas it is not merely permissible but necessary to enhance the melodic climaxes by also allowing the orchestra a higher dynamic level.

As we have said, Mozart was often extraordinarily sparing with his dynamic indications. In particular, the solo parts of the piano concertos only rarely contain any markings at all. For all that, it is usually not difficult to recognize the right dynamics by examining the musical structure. One could give the following rules here, as an aid.

In pianoforte writing a forte is appropriate in the following cases:

1. Octave passages and full chords (cf. Sonata in F (K.533), second movement, development; Piano Concerto in C (K.503), first movement, bars 298 et seq.).

2. Passages in broken chords over several octaves (cf. C minor Concerto, first movement, bars 332 et seq.).

3. Cadential trills in allegro movements, and virtuoso scales in development sections (e.g. almost always before a cadenza).

4. Tremolo and quasi-tremolo figures such as broken octaves (cf. C minor Fantasia (K.475), first Allegro, bar 3; Piano Concerto in E flat (K.482), first movement, bars 345 et seq.).

5. Also often in runs for the left hand (C minor Concerto, third movement, bars 41 et seq.; A minor Sonata, first movement, bars 70 et seq.; D major Sonata (K.576), third movement, bars 9 et seq.).

Naturally, there are exceptions to these rules. In the finale of the A minor Sonata (K.310), the principal theme occurs in octaves in the left hand, bars

64 and also 203. Both times Mozart expressly demands *p* for these legato octaves.

The theme of the Variations on Sarti's *Come un' Agnello*, which in many editions is marked 'piano dolce', should certainly not be quoted as an exception to the rule that octaves indicate *f*. The marking mentioned is not authentic. Mozart also quoted this theme in the second finale of *Don Giovanni* and added a forte marking. It is very unlikely that he wanted this theme to be regarded as having a different character in the Variations.

In the coda of the C minor Concerto, third movement, the piano's octaves suggest a *f*. But in Mozart the sombre character of chains of chromatically rising first inversions always has sinister associations. This is a problematic passage; one could compare the introduction to the *Don Giovanni* Overture (bars 23 et seq.).

It need hardly be emphasized that the very rare *pp* and *ff* markings actually prescribed by Mozart deserve quite particular attention (e.g. A minor Sonata, first movement, bars 62 and 66).

Of course, Mozart's way of limiting himself to the markings *f* and *p* is no mere sign of economy or haste. His dynamics (and in many ways those of his period) are even more a matter of design than of colour. Piano and forte are juxtaposed like light and shade, as the aesthetics of the time had it. This very play of contrasts is typical of Mozart and must not be blurred. There are far fewer dynamic transitions than one hears nowadays, and in Mozart they are almost always explicitly marked 'crescendo' or 'decrescendo'. The long crescendo practised by the eighteenth-century Mannheim school is an effect which Mozart used only rarely, but when he did so he indicated it with pedantic exactness, e.g. in the Posthorn Serenata (K.320), first movement.

The word 'calando' is frequently found in Mozart's autographs. For him it simply means 'becoming softer', and not, as at a later date, also 'becoming slower'. This is shown, for instance, by the following passage from the A minor Sonata, first movement, bar 14, in which a slowing-up of the tempo would be unmusical and out of place:

If 'calando' also meant 'becoming slower', here there would have to be a subsequent 'a tempo', such as Mozart was accustomed to write after, for instance, a 'rallentando'.

Nowadays there are certain misunderstandings about the accentuation signs in Mozart. He often used the sforzato sign, *sf*, simply as a substitute for the markings > ∧ < >, which at the time were not yet customary. It makes a great difference whether the *sf* marking comes in a context of forte or piano, whether it is a deliberate accent on a weak part of the bar or merely

2. Eighteenth century forte-piano (by A. Stein) with small upright pedal-piano built on. (*Metropolitan Museum, New York.*)

marks and underlines the melodic climax of a phrase, as in the second bar of the B minor Adagio for piano:

In a *p* the *sf* marking often merely means a relatively weak accent. Many otherwise good performances are marred because sforzati are strewn undiscerningly about a piano passage.

Mozart's 'forte-piano' marking, '*fp*', means much the same as *sf*. The note should be attacked abruptly, then suddenly decrease in loudness, so that there is no gradual slow decrescendo, such as one so often hears nowadays. There is a passage of this kind, for example, in the D minor Concerto (K.466), third movement, bars 341 et seq.:

In the next example (E flat Concerto (K.449), first movement, bars 219–20), *p* should already have been reached by the second crotchet:

If Mozart wanted a sustained chord to die away gradually, he wrote *sf>p*, as, for example, in the second movement of the C major Piano Concerto (K.503), bar 2.

Naturally, the *fp* accent should not be exaggerated. For instance, the countless *fp* markings in the middle movements of the sonatas K.309 in C and K.310 in A minor are never to be taken as more than indications of a slight accent for expressive purposes. One can find an explanation of the *fp* marking in Quantz (XVII/VII, pp. 252 et seq. of the original edition). And Leopold Mozart, too, explained it in his *Violinschule* (XII, §8):

> It is customary always to accent minims strongly when mixed with short notes, and to relax the tone again. . . . And this is in reality the expression which the composer desires when he sets *f* and *p*, namely forte and piano, against a note. But when accenting a note strongly the bow must not be lifted from the string as some very clumsy people do, but must be continued in the stroke so that the tone may still be heard continuously, although it gradually dies away.

And elsewhere (footnote to I, iii, §19):

> just as the sound of a bell, when struck sharply, by degrees dies away.

Mozart also often used the marking *mfp*. It has almost the same significance as *fp*, only the initial accent is naturally to be played rather less strongly. With dissonances (or suspensions) it often seems to be simply an indication that the dissonant (or suspended) note is to be played a little louder than the ensuing resolution. One should certainly make a distinction between this *fp* and Mozart's very frequent dynamic marking *for : pia*, which he uses when, for example, in an adagio the first crotchet is to be sustained *f* and the second played *p* (subito) (e.g. Adagio in B minor (K.540), bar 9, or the C minor Fantasia (K.475), bars 11 et seq. Here the Alte Mozart-Ausgabe (*A.M.A*). wrongly alters Mozart's *for : pia* into *fp*. With *fp*, the piano marking would begin with the second semiquaver of each bar, whereas Mozart wanted it to begin only at the fifth semiquaver.)

There is some dispute as to the interpretation of chords written in the following way:

which constantly occur in the piano works where *f* chords are to be especially well marked and full in sound (e.g. K.503, first movement, bars 298 et seq.). We believe that this notation is to be regarded as, in the main, a marking for accentuation. It will only rarely be right to play the shorter middle or lower parts with literal exactness. In many cases a sharply broken-off arpeggio may also be intended (K.310, second movement, bar 82), but there is no proof of this (Mozart's customary arpeggiando marking is a transverse stroke through the chord: cf. p. 98). According to Türk (*Clavierschule*, second edition, 1802, p. 329), such chords are to be played exactly as written.

The rococo music of the eighteenth century delighted in echo effects; Mozart must also occasionally have used them, but relatively less often than his contemporaries. For there is no lack of such effects, not only in works by the musicians of the 'age of sensibility', but also in those by composers of

2. The Mozart Family. From a painting by della Croce. (Mozart Museum, Salzburg.)

the succeeding generation. In his textbook Quantz gave the following instruction:

> When there are repeated or similar ideas, consisting of half or whole bars, either at the same pitch or transposed, the repetition of such a passage can be played rather softer than its first statement.[21]

and Türk, in his piano methods of 1789, 1792 and 1804, again advocates a frequent use of echo dynamics, also without any mention of particular composers.

In the music of a classicist such as Mozart, one should, however, be careful in introducing this effect. There is nothing more wearisome than the constant stereotyped recurrence of echo effects, which can often hopelessly break up the overall line. They are only in place in markedly *galant*, playful turns of phrase (e.g. in the E flat Concerto (K.482), third movement, bars 120–1, 173–4, 180–1), but certainly not in codettas, in which one of the hall-marks of Mozart's style is the strengthening effect of repetition. From the few works for which Mozart did provide scrupulously exact dynamic markings, one can easily see that he only wanted the echo effect to be used very rarely. Thus in the entire A minor Sonata there is only one passage of this kind, in the first movement, bar 18 (and in the recapitulation, bar 99). In the 'Haffner' Symphony, for example, Mozart again expressly denies himself any echo effect when motives are repeated (Presto, bars 11–12, 17–19, etc.), although here the effect could well be used; he uses it only once (bars 102–3).[22]

On the other hand, there are countless examples of passages in which Mozart wished a repetition to be louder. If, for example, a two- or four-bar idea is first given out by the piano on its own, and is repeated with orchestral accompaniment, this scoring naturally precludes any echo effect. Such passages occur, for example, in the E flat Concerto (K.482), first movement, bars 312–15, in the Two-piano Concerto (K.365), first movement, bars 96–99, etc. In bar 155 of the first movement of K.482, the repeat of the motive from bar 153 is given added rhythmic life, and this also precludes any echo effect. However, there is a charming 'double echo' in the E flat Concerto (K.271), third movement, bars 196–200 (and the corresponding passages).

It is certain that Mozart set great store by strict observance of his dynamic markings. In his letters, which are always a mine of information for the Mozart scholar, he says:

> I began to teach . . . Mlle. Rosa [the Sonata] three days ago. We finished the opening Allegro today. The Andante will give us most trouble, for it is full of expression and must be played accurately and with the exact shades of forte and piano, precisely as they are marked.[23]

This brings us back to the demand for 'faithfulness'—in the favourable sense. . . .

Mozart was a born enemy of all exaggeration. In a letter to his father in 1781, he summed up his artistic credo:

. . . as passions, whether violent or not, must never be expressed in such a way as to excite disgust, and as music, even in the most terrible situations, must never offend the ear, but must please the hearer, or in other words must never cease to be *music* . . .[24]

and this could well be applied to his sound-picture. In Mozart, the sound should always have something noble and aristocratic about it. Mozart was indeed no stranger to sweet and voluptuous sounds, to the darker levels of sensibility; there is a measureless variety of moods in his music: but even in his most expressive moments, the sound-picture remains translucent and beautiful.

Chapter Two

PROBLEMS OF TEMPO AND RHYTHM

I. TEMPI

. . . One must also be able to divine from the piece itself whether it requires a slow or a somewhat quicker speed. It is true that at the beginning of every piece special words are written which are designed to characterize it, such as 'Allegro' (merry), 'Adagio' (slow) and so on. But both slow and quick have their degrees. . . . So one has to deduce it (the tempo) from the piece itself, and it is this by which the true worth of a musician can be recognized without fail. Every melodious piece has at least one phrase from which one can recognize quite surely what sort of speed the piece demands. Often, if other points be carefully observed, the phrase is forced into its natural speed. Remember this, but know also that for such perception long experience and good judgment are required. Who will contradict me if I count this among the chiefest perfections in the art of music?

I

THESE words come from Leopold Mozart's *Violinschule* (I, iii, §7).[25] 'Long experience and good judgment' help us to judge the right tempo, but a feeling for style is also very necessary. No one tempo is right to the exclusion of all others. The individual musician retains a certain freedom which should not be undervalued—within a certain range, any tempo *can* be artistically valid. Here we will try to show the limits of this freedom.

It is constantly said that 'The old masters would have been horrified at the tempo of present-day performances. Surely they can't have played so fast in the old days!' Now, it is a tempting assumption that in an age of speed we have increased the tempo of musical performance; but this seems doubtful. To say 'the older, the slower' is certainly wrong. If we go back through history, we find that in the mid-eighteenth century J. J. Quantz, Frederick the Great's famous flute teacher, worked out mathematically exact tempi with the aid of the human pulse, which he took as beating at eighty to the minute. For an 'allegro assai' in $\frac{4}{4}$ he prescribes 'a minim to one pulse beat', i.e. MM. $\downarrow = 80$, but for an 'allegro assai' in alla-breve time he demanded a tempo twice as fast, and this gives astonishingly fast tempi for the works of his generation. It seems that in the second half of the eighteenth century basic tempi were, if anything, quicker than ours, not slower. Quantz did indeed expressly say that his tempo indications should not be taken too literally, and that in choosing a tempo one should bear in mind various other factors, particularly 'the quickest notes that occur in a passage'.

Apart from the pulse, there are other inborn 'pacemakers' in the human constitution (for example, normal walking speed), and these seem so deeply ingrained that they would hardly be influenced by time or a changing world.

Mozart left neither metronome markings nor tempo-calculations based on the pulse. As regards his tempi we have to rely on the few imprecise indications found, for example, in his letters, where he will complain about the excessively fast tempi of some performers, or will warn against playing certain movements too slowly. These remarks about tempo in his letters are refreshingly direct; they were part of his every-day musical activities, and were certainly not written with an eye to posterity. Although it would be hard to base any general principles on these remarks, we should mention the most important of them, if only because one has to be thankful for any remarks of Mozart's that cast light on this 'most difficult and chief requisite in music'.

Mozart wrote about the 'Haffner' Symphony (7th August 1782):

> The first Allegro must be played with great fire, the last—as fast as possible.

And about the *Entführung aus dem Serail*, in the famous letter of 26 September 1781:

> The passage 'Drum beym Barte des Propheten' is indeed in the same tempo, but with quick notes; but as Osmin's rage gradually increases, there comes (just when the aria seems to be at an end) the allegro assai, which is in a totally different measure and in a different key; this is bound to be very effective. For just as a man in such a towering rage oversteps all the bounds of order, moderation and propriety, and completely forgets himself, so must the music too forget itself.

He says of the end of the first act:

> Then the major key begins at once pianissimo—it must go very quickly—and wind up with a great deal of noise.

When in the same letter he says, about the Overture to the *Entführung*:

> and I doubt whether anyone, even if his previous night has been a sleepless one, could go to sleep over it.

it seems that here again he meant the tempo to be anything but boring.

On the other hand there is no lack of remarks showing clearly how much he opposed excessively quick performance of his works:

. . . before dinner he [the Abbé Vogler] scrambled through my concerto at sight (the one which the daughter of the house plays—written for Countess Lützow). He took the first movement prestissimo, the Andante allegro and the Rondo even more prestissimo. He generally played the bass differently from the way it was written, inventing now and then quite another harmony and melody. Nothing else is possible at that pace, for the eyes cannot see the music nor the hands perform it. Well, what good is it?—that kind of sight-reading and shilting are all one to me. The listeners (I mean those who deserve the name) can only say that they have seen music and piano-playing. Well, you may easily imagine that it was unendurable. At the same time I could not bring myself to say to him, Far too quick! Besides, it is much easier to play a thing quickly than slowly: in difficult passages you can leave out a few notes without anyone noticing it. But is that beautiful? In rapid playing the right and left hands can be changed without anyone seeing or hearing it; but is that beautiful? And wherein consists the art of playing prima vista? In this; in playing the piece in the time in which it ought to be played and in playing all the notes, appoggiaturas and so forth, exactly as they were written and with the appropriate expression and taste, so that you might suppose that the performer has composed it himself.[26]

And a little later Mozart preferred the playing of the 16-year-old beginner Aloysia Weber to that of the celebrated Abbé Vogler:

Mlle Weber . . . played the clavier* twice, for she does not play at all badly. What surprises me most is her excellent sight-reading. Would you believe it, she played my difficult sonatas at sight, *slowly* but without missing a single note! On my honour, I would rather hear my sonatas played by her than by Vogler![27]

We do not think that Mozart's assessment of Aloysia's musical abilities was affected by the fact that he was in love with her. Mozart's judgment in musical matters was at all times incorruptible—one should compare the letter he wrote to his father about this time, on the subject of Aloysia's singing. It is by no means purely laudatory!

The Mannheim composer F. X. Sterkel also aroused his disapproval. He played five duets,

so fast that it was hard to follow them, and not at all clearly, and not in time.[28]

Mozart is constantly raising objections when clarity and rhythmic exactness suffer through over-fast tempi. Here he was at one with his father; Leopold also often found tempi too fast:

Indeed, I am no lover of excessively rapid passages, where you have to produce the notes with the half tone of the violin and, so to speak, only touch the fiddle with the bow and almost play in the air.[29]

In the letters from Mozart's later years, after the death of his father, he does not discuss tempi, but his contemporaries' remarks are some guide. Rochlitz's

* *Translator's Note*: Originally 'clavir', so probably the clavichord.

recollections of Mozart in the Leipzig *Allgemeine Musikalische Zeitung* of December, 1798, seem very authentic, even though he has often been mentioned as a rather over-imaginative writer:

> Nothing roused Mozart to livelier protest than did 'botching' of his compositions when performed in public, mainly through excessively fast tempi. 'They think that will add fire to it', he would say, 'The fire has got to be in the piece itself—it won't come from galloping away with it'. . . .

Hardly twenty years after Mozart's death there were clear differences of opinion about the tempi in his works:

> One need only remark, for example, the widely differing tempi adopted in differing places for some pieces, even very famous and characteristic ones. To mention only one, I heard Mozart's Overture to *Don Giovanni* played under the great man himself, by the Guardasonic Society [as it then was] of Prague, and I also heard it in various other places, including Paris, Vienna and Berlin. The Adagio was taken a shade slower in Paris, in Vienna quite noticeably faster and in Berlin almost as fast again as under Mozart, and in all three places the Allegro was played either faster or slower than he played it.[30]

It is interesting that many reports suggest that Mozart tended to take his allegro movements at a moderate speed. Nowadays movements simply marked 'allegro' are often played too fast. If Mozart wanted a movement played really 'fast', then he marked it 'presto' or 'allegro assai'. An unadorned 'allegro' carries the original meaning of the word—gay, cheerful. The well-known D major Rondo (K.485), for example, is wonderfully effective when played 'gaily', graciously, even if in a flowing tempo—and how uninteresting it is when played merely 'fast'!

As regards andante and adagio movements, Mozart's remarks and those of his contemporaries rather suggest that he preferred a flowing tempo. Of course, one does sometimes hear a grave, stately adagio played at a very ungrave, overfast tempo; but the opposite, the andante movement played with excessive slow pathos, is much commoner. In a letter to his father he gives advice to his sister about the piano concertos K. 413-15:

> Please tell my sister that there is no adagio in any of these concertos—only andantes.[31]

In Mozart's time 'andante' was not really a slow tempo—that was a nineteenth-century development. For Mozart it was a fairly flowing tempo, still in accordance with the original meaning of the word, 'moving', and it lay roughly half way between slow and fast. He marked the MS. of the F major Rondo (K.494) 'Andante', but two years later he used it as the Finale of the F major Sonata (K.533), marking it 'Allegretto'. So there can have been no very great distinction between the tempi 'andante' and 'allegretto'. Naturally, not all Mozart's andante movements require the same tempo, and there are a number where one should take care not to play too fast. There must always be a clear distinction between the light, 'grazioso' andante movements* and those which are intimate and deeply felt (e.g. those in the C major Concerto (K.503) or in the A minor Piano Sonata (K.310)). Mozart made the following remarks about the Fugues which he sent to his sister in Salzburg in 1782:

> I have purposely written above it *Andante Maestoso*, as it must not be played too fast. For if a fugue is not played slowly, the ear cannot clearly distinguish the theme when it comes in and consequently the effect is entirely missed.[32]

The andante of the B flat Violin Sonata (K.454) is another one which should certainly not be taken too quickly; Mozart originally marked this movement 'Adagio', then crossed this through and replaced it by 'Andante'. The reason will be clear to those who know the sonata. The unusual extent of this movement is itself enough to necessitate a more 'flowing' tempo that will hold the form together. On the other hand, bars 30–3 show that this 'andante', which resembles an adagio, must be played relatively calmly, since if the initial tempo is too quick these bars can hardly be played with the appropriate expressiveness. (We would propose a tempo of $\quad = c.$ 52.) The Andante of the C major Concerto (K.503) should be taken even more easily. This movement is certainly very akin to an adagio in character.[33]

Similarly, Mozart marked the second movement of the Sonata K.309 'Andante un poco Adagio'. On 6th December 1777, he wrote to his father about this movement:

> the Andante (which must not be taken too quickly) she plays with the utmost expression.

In a $\frac{3}{4}$ adagio the tempo should flow so that one can still feel the rhythm in whole bars. In this way figurations in small note-values can be played melodically and evenly, without superfluous accents, yet lose none of their expressiveness.

One interesting tempo indication is that given by Nissen for Pamina's famous G minor aria from *The Magic Flute*, 'Ach, ich fühl's': this is also marked 'Andante'. In his biography of Mozart, Nissen, who came to Vienna in 1793, reports that at the time the tempo of this aria was '6 to 7 Rhein. Zoll', according to the tradition inherited from Mozart. ('Rhein. Zoll' was a pendulum measure that can be regarded as a primitive forerunner of the metronome.) Although the time-gap of over a year means that we cannot be sure of the correctness of the tradition, this single concrete tempo indication still deserves close attention. Whether one takes it literally or only roughly, it means an andante which to our way of thinking is unbelievably fast: converted into a metronome marking it is $\quad = 138$–48.[34]

---

*A fine example of the light, floating andante is the 'andante grazioso' middle movement of the E flat Trio (K.542), proposed tempo $\quad = c.$ 58. Nor should the andante grazioso of the A major Sonata (K.331) be taken too slowly, $\quad = c.$ 138–44, but 'grazioso', i.e. with charm and an undulating rhythm; e.g. a very slight ritardando in bars 12 and 18. For Variations I–IV we recommend $\quad = 144$–52, for the Adagio variation $\quad = c.$ 72–76, for the final variation $\quad = c.$ 132–38).

At first sight this seems such a fast tempo that one would dismiss it as impossible.* But it is very important to know that almost all the later composers who left exact metronome markings for their Andante movements held the same view. Chopin's Andante in the D flat Nocturne, op. 27, no. 2 (♩ = 50) is just as fast! Beethoven's original marking for the second movement of the second Symphony, ♪ = 92, also shows that he regarded this tempo as a flowing one, as did Schumann, if we look for instance at the Andante ♩ = 100 in *Träumerei*. One can trace this view down to Hindemith, who has marked the third movement of his Third Sonata (a typical andante), 'Mässig schnell'—'moderately fast', ♩ = c. 84.

In considering this vital problem of tempi, one should bear in mind that a full tone produces a kind of 'inertia'; the more slender the tone, the more mobile it is. This is a decisive factor in Mozart's music. If one takes the trouble to secure a tone that is free from thickness, it is astonishing how much room there is for expression, even in a flowing andante. The individual notes may perhaps lose a little, but the coherence of complete phrases more than makes up for this.

In general composers imagine their slow movements as going faster than interpreters in fact play them. Recordings and live performances by present-day composers have shown us, on the other hand, that in performing their own works they often choose slower tempi than those they have indicated by their metronome markings. This is mainly explained by the fact that all sound has to be realized, and is bound to move more easily in the composer's mind than when played or sung, with all the various factors of inertia (mechanical and acoustical) that are involved. All the same, the tempo should not be allowed to slow down too much in performance, as, unfortunately, is often the case.

It is not surprising that Mozart's music has given rise to more differences of opinion about tempi than has that of later composers, who often provided metronome markings as a basis for interpretation. There are many musicians who hold that Mozart's music must be played as 'weightlessly' as possible, lightly and quickly; the justification for this is sought in Mozart's childlike temperament, his effortless way of overcoming even the greatest technical difficulties when composing, or in the inherent grace of his idiom, which is indeed far less 'weighty' than that of Beethoven or Brahms. Other musicians hold the opposite view, seeing the tragic, demonic elements in Mozart as the most striking. In their determination to reject the idea of Mozart as an euphoric Olympian who poured out melody throughout his life, they often run the risk of reading tragic qualities into works which really are playful and relaxed, and whose charm is easily destroyed by an over-serious, too weighty approach.

Naturally, both views contain an element of truth: Mozart's music con-

*This is just the sort of piece where the tempo often drags, in the interests of 'expression'. Bach's aria from the *St. Matthew Passion*, 'Erbarme Dich mein Gott', which conveys the deepest emotion, should not be performed too slowly; nor should the E flat minor Prelude from *The Well-tempered Clavier*, Book I, be allowed to drag.

tains both euphoria and tragedy: this is one of the things that mark his unique place in the history of music. In even his most *galant* works there is a trace of deep seriousness, and the reverse is also true. The predominant character of any particular work is very important in choosing its tempi. For example, the first movement of the tragic C minor Concerto (K.491) would lose much of its expressive depth if taken too quickly, as would the second movement of the E flat Concerto (K.271). (For the latter we would suggest a tempo of ♪ = *c.* 80–84. Here it is best not to try to be too exact, since the movement has something of the character of a recitative, and a certain freedom is thus in order.) Brilliant movements, with less spiritual depth, demand quick tempi if they are to make the maximum effect—for example, the first movement of the Coronation Concerto, the first movements of the Piano Sonatas K. 284, 309 and 311, the first and third movements of the piano-duet Sonata K.381 and the first movement of the Sonata for two pianos K.448 (♩ = *c.* 152). (It is interesting that nearly all these movements are in D major.)

Mozart's articulation marks* often hint at the appropriate tempo. In the outer movements of the Concerto in B flat (K.595), there are subtleties of articulation which are impossible to convey if the tempo is too quick.

First movement, bar 99 (suggested tempo ♩ = *c.* 129–32):

In the third movement, too, the articulation provides a pointer to the correct tempo (bars 1–8):

bars 102 et seq.:

*See the Chapter on 'Articulation'.

bars 150 et seq.:

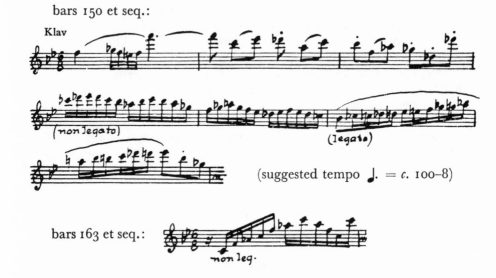

(suggested tempo ♩. = c. 100–8)

bars 163 et seq.:

non leg.

Another movement in which a fairly moderate tempo matches best the character of the music is the Finale of the Piano Concerto in E flat (K.449); this is why Mozart marked it 'Allegro ma non troppo'. At an excessive tempo it loses its incomparable magic. (Suggested tempo ♩ = c. 108–16.)

In his tempo markings Mozart was a good deal more exact than is often assumed. Since even nowadays there is still a good deal of confusion about the meaning of Mozart's tempo markings, we shall try to arrange them in a scale:

Largo is the slowest tempo, since, as far as we know, Mozart does not use the marking 'lento' in the piano works. An example of the marking 'largo' is the introduction of the first movement of the Violin Sonata in B flat (K.454); we would suggest a tempo of ♪ = c. 69–72.

Adagio. Although this is definitely a marking for a slow tempo, it should be realized that an eighteenth-century adagio has to flow rather more than a nineteenth-century one. In Mozart one should as a rule adopt a rather more flowing tempo for the adagio movements of the *galant* works (e.g. Concerto for Three Pianos, second movement, suggested tempo, ♪ = c. 80–4) than for the markedly lyrical adagio movements in his late works (Sonata K.457, second movement, ♪ = c. 76, or ♪ = 76–80 in the A flat section in the middle; Fantasia in C minor (K.475), opening, ♪ = c. 72–80; bars 11 onward, ♪ = c. 80–4; the D major section, c. 80–8; Adagio in B minor (K.540), ♪ = c. 76, etc.). The festal Adagio at the beginning of the C major Fantasia is a special case, and should be taken at ♪ = c. 92; we also feel the Adagio of the D major Sonata (K.576) at a rather more flowing tempo, ♪ = c. 92–6.

Larghetto. It is unfortunate that larghetto should widely and wrongly be regarded as slower than adagio. See discussion of K.491, p. 266.

Andante. As already remarked, andante is the most problematic tempo marking in Mozart's music. Often he qualifies it to show whether he intends a slower or more flowing tempo. He indicates a steady tempo by 'Andante un poco adagio' (second movement of the Piano Sonata K.309, second movement of the Piano Concerto K.238: ♩ = *c.* 56), 'Andante con espressione' (Piano Sonata K.311, second movement), 'Andante cantabile con espressione' (Piano Sonata K.310, ♪ = *c.* 80–8, with some agogic freedom, the middle section rather quicker, to *c.* 96), 'Andante sostenuto' (second movement of the Violin Sonata K.296). A flowing andante is most often marked 'Andante grazioso' (Piano Sonata K.331).

Andantino should also indicate a rather flowing andante (second movement of the Concerto K.449, ♩ = *c.* 50–2). But more often the marking *Andante* is not qualified, and a great deal of trouble is often necessary to find the right tempo. We find the choice of a tempo particularly difficult for the Andante movement of the F major Sonata (K.533), which has to be played with solemnity and yet must flow (♩ = *c.* 58–63), with a slight quickening in the more excitable development section. A definitely stormy *Andante* occurs in the C major Fantasia (K.394) (♩ = *c.* 66).

Allegretto is very like andante and only moderately fast. In outer movements it can be more like an allegro, whereas as a marking for a 'slow movement' it should be taken as a very flowing andante. (An example is the second movement of the F major Concerto (K.459)). In the third movement (*Allegretto*) of the D major Sonata (K.576), which is often unfortunately taken too fast, we recommend ♩ = *c.* 92.

Allegretto grazioso. Whereas the suffix 'grazioso' in an andante movement indicates a more flowing tempo, in allegretto movements the opposite holds good. Grace goes with leisure. Typical of this kind of movement are the Finale of the G major Trio (K.496), and, above all, the Concert Rondo in D (K.382) (♩ = 56–60).

Tempo di menuetto. This is a frequent marking, which, like the marking 'menuetto', should be defined more exactly. Mozart's minuet, unlike that of the baroque period, was a placid dance in $\frac{3}{4}$ time, and his minuets are often played too fast. One should not take the 'tempo di menuetto' Finale of the Three-piano Concerto (K.242), or the Minuet from the A major Sonata (K.331), faster than ♩ = 126–32. No one definite basic tempo can be laid down for Mozart's minuets. The famous one from *Don Giovanni* must indeed be taken very steadily (♩ = *c.* 84–92), whereas such minuets as those in the last three symphonies require a tempo almost twice as fast (♩ = between 152 and 168). Mozart marked most of these quicker minuets 'Allegretto',

---

*Chopin was very exact about his tempo markings, and in the Nocturne, op. 27, no. 1 ('Larghetto') he writes a final long ritardando, which *ends* 'adagio'; this shows clearly that larghetto is to be played quicker than adagio.

as against the true 'tempo di menuetto'. An important point is that the minuet must have three clear beats in a bar, not one (as in Beethoven's scherzos, for example).

However, the Viennese minuet was obviously taken a good deal quicker than the Italian type. On 24th March 1770, Mozart wrote from Bologna to his sister about a ball in Milan:

> The minuet itself is very beautiful. It comes, of course, from Vienna and was most certainly composed by Deller or Starzer. . . . The minuets in Milan, in fact the Italian minuets generally, have plenty of notes, are played slowly and have several bars. . . .*

Allegro. This, Mozart's commonest marking, takes in everything that comes under the heading 'quick'. Suffixes for a steady allegro are 'allegro ma non troppo' or 'allegro maestoso'. But even among the allegro movements where there is no more exact marking one must make a clear distinction between lyrical cantabile movements (Piano Concerto in A (K.488), first movement) and the 'fiery', virtuoso ones (e.g. the first movement of the 'Haffner' Symphony). In the autograph of the C minor Sonata (K.457), the first movement is marked 'Allegro', whereas in the first edition it is headed 'Allegro Molto'; naturally one will choose a fairly brisk allegro here ($\bignote = c$. 80–8).

Allegro vivace (Concerto K.449, first movement) means that the allegro is to be lively, but not necessarily quicker, whereas

Allegro molto and *Allegro assai* are more akin to Mozart's quickest tempo, presto. The correct marking for the 'allegro assai' in the Finale of the C minor Sonata is around $\bignote. = 72$–6.

Presto should be played as fast as possible, i.e. while still allowing every note and every articulation mark to come through clearly, and without obscuring the translucency of the texture.

Prestissimo does not occur in Mozart's piano works, so far as we know.

Mozart was very exact about tempo markings—this we can gather indirectly from a well-known passage in a letter (7th June 1783) about Clementi:

> Clementi is a *ciarlatano*, like all Italians. He writes 'Presto' over a sonata or even 'Prestissimo' and 'Alla-breve', and plays it himself allegro in $\frac{4}{4}$ time. I know this is the case, for I have heard him do so.

One sees that Mozart felt there were clear differences between allegro ₵, allegro $\frac{4}{4}$, presto ₵ and presto $\frac{4}{4}$, etc.; that when he wrote 'Allegro $\frac{4}{4}$', he did not mean 'allegro alla breve', and vice versa. How seldom this fact is taken into account in performance!

---

* *Translator's Note*: Literally, 'have many bars'.

Mozart also deliberately uses the alla-breve sign in slow movements. Here it indicates that there are to be only two accented beats in the bar, and not four. Even at a slow tempo this is not merely possible but indispensable, musically speaking, and it is a pity that in the old Breitkopf complete edition (*A.M.A.*) there are countless places where the alla-breve sign is omitted from andante and larghetto movements. In the larghetto of the Piano Concerto in B flat (K.595) it is of decisive importance. There is no question of Mozart's having added it by an oversight: this can be seen from the single fact that except in the closing bars there are none of the customary demisemiquaver passages customary in a larghetto movement. (Suggested tempo: ♩ = *c*. 76.)

Alla-breve time is again a characteristic feature in the slow movement of the D minor Concerto (K.466), which combines the raptness of a nocturne with wonderful serenade-like grace (as in the staccato accompaniment of bars 11–12!). Here the test of the right tempo is whether one can make the transition to the stormy middle section without any noticeable acceleration. The larghetto of the C minor Concerto is discussed in a later chapter.

Although a $\frac{6}{8}$ time-signature rules out any exact indication of the accentual scheme applicable to the movement, there are subtle musical ways of showing the distinction between a $\frac{6}{8}$ bar with only two beats and one where there are more notes of rhythmic importance (cf. the effect of the alla-breve sign in $\frac{4}{4}$). The themes in the Finale of the Piano Concerto K.482 show a clear duple division of the bar, whereas, for example, those in the third movement of the Piano Concerto K.595 contain from four to six melodic accents in each bar. The latter movement should therefore be played somewhat slower (♩. = 100–8) than the more virtuosic Finales of the Piano Concertos K.450, 456 and 482 (♩. = 108–16); not the least compelling reason is that the first subject of K.595's Finale is almost identical with the tune of the song 'Komm, lieber Mai', whose word-setting shows four syllables to a bar. The first movement of the D major Sonata (K.576) also has more than two melodically important notes to a bar, and should therefore not be taken too quickly (♩. = *c*. 92–6).

As we mentioned at the beginning, every interpreter is left a certain freedom in choosing the right tempo, within the bounds of the artistically valid. It would be pointless to try to tie all artists down to particular metronome markings, for there are too many purely personal variations involved. Over a number of years the radio station R.I.A.S. in Berlin constantly found that all conductors adopted slower tempi in morning concerts than in the evening, so that the same programme would be several minutes shorter in the evening than when broadcast before lunch. Even more than the time of day, the personal condition of the artist plays a part—whether he is tired or exuberant, placid or excited; and obviously much depends on his temperament or on the race he belongs to. Age, too, has a great effect on the way one feels tempi. As the ninth of his ten 'golden rules', Richard Strauss wrote in a young conductor's album:

> When you think you have reached the ultimate prestissimo, then double the tempo![35]

Twenty-three years later, in 1948, Strauss added the remark:

> Nowadays I would alter it to 'then halve the tempo'. (To conductors of Mozart!)

Furtwängler, too, is famous for the relatively slow tempi he preferred toward the end of his life. More than anyone else he demonstrated that a feeling of absolute rightness depends less on the tempo itself than on the maintenance of tension and psychological interest.

Perhaps it is as well that Mozart could not leave behind any metronome markings; the current passion for 'faithfulness to the text' might lead musicians to follow such markings against their own inner conviction, and nothing leads to such lifeless rigidity as this kind of violation of one's instincts. A wrong tempo played with utter conviction is the lesser evil. Metronome markings should show neither more nor less than the correct mean tempo within a particular range, and where we have suggested figures, this is how they should be regarded.

II. 'Playing in Time'

> Time makes melody, therefore time is the soul of music. It does not only animate the same, but retains all the component parts in their proper order. Time decides the moment when the various notes must be played, and is often what is lacking in many who have otherwise advanced fairly far in music and have a good opinion of themselves. This defect is the result of their having neglected time in the first instance.[36]

Musical performance that fails to keep in time will always sound amateurish, apart from the fact that it makes the tempo unrecognizable. Unfortunately, there have always been musicians who played every bar at a different tempo, and usually they were proud of it. Schumann, in his *Musikalische Haus- und Lebensregeln*, compared their playing with the singing of drunkards, and Mozart expressed himself still more strongly on the subject of what is possibly the most serious of all musical defects:

> Further, she will never acquire the most essential, the most difficult and the chief requisite in music, which is, time, because from her earliest years she has done her utmost not to play in time. Herr Stein and I discussed this point for two hours at least and I have almost converted him, for he now asks my advice on everything. He used to be quite crazy about Beecke; but now he sees and hears that I am the better player, that I do not make grimaces, and yet play with such expression that, as he himself confesses, no one up to the present has been able to get such good results out of his pianofortes. Everyone is amazed that I can always keep strict time.[37]

Rhythmically exact playing, the alpha and omega of all good interpretation, costs much labour; even pianists with a natural feeling for rhythm must work very hard at the outset if they are to achieve absolute rhythmic steadiness, which is a superlative musical quality.

To this end, there are several effective teaching methods, such as counting aloud or the use of the metronome. Without some such assistance, 'feeling' will inevitably let the player down, and every teacher should from the very beginning use these resources to ensure that his pupils play in time. It will have been the experience of every musician that for the beginner, and indeed for those more advanced, there are so many musical and technical problems that it is simply impossible to achieve the inner detachment needed for complete control of one's sense of time. Even experienced musicians sometimes 'run away' with difficult passages, and never notice it. Leopold Mozart, too, has something to say on the subject:

> These running notes are the stumbling-block. . . . Many a violinist, who plays not too badly otherwise, falls into hurrying when playing such continuously running, equal notes, so that if they continue for several bars he is at least a crochet in advance of the time.[38]

The only remedy for this so frequent weakness is constant self-education, by counting or by practice with the metronome. Even though the usefulness of the metronome is disputed as an aid to practice (and naturally it should never be more than this), we have found that as a means of checking it is indispensable. Another excellent way to develop rhythmic steadiness is to play chamber music. Piano-duet playing, in particular, is of incalculable educational value. Only those who can play absolutely in time should allow themselves to make conscious deviations in tempo—agogics and rubati.

Of course, playing in time does not mean rattling off a piece with the exactness of a metronome, any more than it means automatically accenting every first beat. Compare Liszt's words:

> I may perhaps be allowed to remark that I wish to see an end to mechanical, fragmented, up and down playing, tied to the bar-line, which is still the rule in many cases; I can only concede real value to playing that is periodic, that allows important accents to stand out and brings out the melodic and rhythmic nuances.[39]

The bar-line must not be felt. One could compare bar-lines with the pillars of a bridge, and the melody with a road that runs over the bridge. If at each pillar one had the sensation of passing over a humpback bridge, this would be a fairly sure sign that the architect was incompetent. Nothing of the kind should disturb the form and inner flow of a piece. Leopold Mozart often referred to a thread, '*il filo*', which runs through any composition and must not be allowed to snap.

However, it is also very important to be clear about the way Mozart constructs his periods. The norm is a symmetrically subdivided 8- or 16-bar period (song-strophe) whose construction is straightforward. But deviations from this norm are much less rare than many musicians assume. For example, in the development section of the first movement of the D major Sonata (K.576) (bar 81 onward) there is a grouping $2 + 3 + 3 + 3 + 5 = 16$. It is amazing that even in a dance movement (the Minuet of the A major Sonata (K.331) there are asymmetrical formations: $2 + 3 + 3 + 2$. Consciously correct interpretation is impossible unless one appreciates these asymmetrical groupings of bars within higher-order formal principles that are regular. For just as in the microcosm, in a $\frac{4}{4}$ bar, the first and third crotchets must be felt to be stronger than the second and fourth, or in a $\frac{3}{4}$ bar the first and third are stronger than the second, so in a group of three bars the accent lies on the first bar and the least weight will, as a rule, be given to the second.

III.   Agogics and Rubato

Audible tempo-deviations within a movement will usually be unnecessary and disturbing in Mozart. Most of his movements have such structural unity that the filigree details can be played at the same tempo as the most excited passage-work. If this sometimes seems impossible, the trouble is usually an excessively quick tempo, which Mozart repeatedly stigmatized as a crude offence against good taste. Yet there are places, mostly in the nature of joins, where even a very steady and musical performer will press unobtrusively[40] onward or else hold back the tempo a little. These subtle variations in tempo we call 'agogics'. The use of agogics is what distinguishes a steady player from an unrhythmical one; a rhythmical player will only vary the tempo to match the sense of the music; an unsteady player varies the tempo indiscriminately.

A good musician will hardly ever vary the tempo within a theme or a self-contained section; the most he will do is to use rubato. The principal use of agogics is to give a natural feeling to the transitions that occur in multi-thematic musical forms (sonata or rondo, as against earlier mono-thematic forms). We see from C. P. E. Bach that this sort of slight agogic deviation is wholly in accordance with eighteenth-century musical practice:

> It is customary to drag a bit and depart somewhat from a strict observance of the bar. . . . This applies to fermati, cadences, etc. as well as caesuras. *Essay*, II, 6, 'Performance', p. 375.

But it would be incorrect to introduce this kind of agogic deviation in all such transitions. They depend so much on the actual 'feel' of the music that one cannot draw up hard and fast rules, but we should like to give a few examples in which we feel that a certain freedom of tempo is necessary.

In the great Sonata in C minor (K.457) the first and third movements sound best if one can do justice to their expressive qualities without altering the basic tempo. (An exception is the recitative passage in the Finale, bars 228–43, where Mozart's own marking is 'a piacere' and then 'a tempo'.) In the second movement, on the other hand, one will make a slight ritardando in the second half of bar 41 (marked 'calando'* in the first edition), as a natural preparation for the return of the first subject. Bars 17 and 58 also demand a certain freedom of metre. The passage from bar 35 to bar 39, which builds up by painful chromaticisms from the distant key of G flat to the dominant of C minor, is the climax of the movement. As the excitement grows, the tempo can press forward a little; then at the climax, to match the distressed tension, it can broaden again and effect the return to the basic tempo.

In such a process of intensification a long 'build-up' is usually followed by a relatively brief release of tension. However, just because in this passage the build-up is fairly long, the accelerando can take its course quite gradually, so that it will not sound forced or obtrusive.

Clearly audible switches of tempo are equally out of place in the concertos: this applies particularly to the orchestra. Mozart must surely have agreed with his father, who wrote in his *Violinschule*:

> Many who have no idea of taste, never retain the evenness of tempo in the accompanying of a concerto part, but endeavour always to follow the solo part. These are accompanists for dilettanti, and not for masters.[41]

In the first movement of the E flat Concerto (K.482) there are places where it seems in order for the soloist to make slight ritardandi, e.g. in bars 117 and 149–51:

*We should again point out that for Mozart the word 'calando' usually meant simply 'get softer', but not 'get slower'.

Note the subtle way in which the transitional notes F–E–E flat (first bar) are repeated in the third bar with a 'composed' accelerando. In this bar there is room for a technical trick which makes the transition sound more organic: one does not prolong the ritardando until the entry of the new subject, but resumes the basic tempo just a little earlier. A slight ritardando is also advisable in bar 247, so that one does not pass too abruptly into the peaceful A flat major passage that follows. Before the cadenza the orchestra can broaden out a little.

The second movement of this concerto is an interesting combination of (free) variation and rondo. In variation form it has always been customary to take particular variations or groups of variations at a tempo different from that of the theme, according to their character. (Within any one variation the tempo must, of course, be strictly maintained.)[42] Although it is not essential to play the energetic second variation (bars 93–124) slightly above the basic tempo of $\flat$ = c. 74, this is quite justifiable. The last bar before the coda (bar 200) is one of the 'joins' at which a ritardando seems desirable.

In the Finale of this concerto one must aim at maintaining a constant tempo. Even if in this movement one makes involuntary tempo-alterations of the kind already discussed, they must be perceptible only to a listener who is following with a metronome. In bar 181 one can introduce a very slight ritardando, since this is a 'lead-back', and then reintroduce the solo subject in exactly the original tempo. Before the pauses in bars 217 and 264 one will also broaden out a little, but not before the cadenza (bar 361), where a ritardando would in fact be disturbing; significantly, the fermata is in this case not over the $\frac{6}{4}$ chord, but over the ensuing rest.

It must be expressly emphasized that all musicians, even the 'steadiest', make slight agogic deviations—that it is, in fact, impossible to mould the musical form of a work of art, which is an organic entity, without agogics. Here we are concerned less with justifying agogics than with their extent. This has varied with different generations of composers and interpreters; Mozart differs from Beethoven and Brahms in the degree of agogics required, Chopin differs from Prokofiev, etc. Similarly, pianists of the older generation, such as Backhaus, Kempff, Schnabel and Fischer, allow themselves many more agogic liberties than those of later generations. Apart from this, individual temperament and personal taste affect the degree to which agogic variations are used.

Though slight agogic variations are indispensable for free, relaxed and expressive playing, audible changes of tempo are not. One should recall Schnabel's reply to the question, 'Do you play in time or with feeling?'— 'Why should I not feel in time?'

Judicious use of rubato is one of the most difficult problems in playing Mozart. In a letter to his father which we have already quoted in part, he wrote:

> What [these people] cannot grasp is that in tempo rubato in an adagio, the left hand should go on playing in strict time. With them, the left hand always follows suit.[43]

This is an unambiguous description of the kind of rubato Mozart demanded in his slow movements: the accompanying parts are to remain steady while the melody makes slight rhythmic alterations for the purpose of expression. There will be a very slight, hardly noticeable deduction from the length of one note, in order that the next shall be slightly prolonged—this produces the accent which the composer may have had in mind. Rubato was not invented by Chopin, as many people nowadays believe. It is an expressive device that has always been in use (no doubt it is particularly associated with vocal music), though the first descriptions of it date from the early seventeenth century; later it was discussed by such writers as Frescobaldi, Froberger and Tosi.[44] It is used mainly in passages of an arioso or declamatory nature.

The essence of true rubato is that the accompaniment remains steady, is not allowed to follow the slight accelerando and ritardando in the melody. To quote Leopold Mozart,[45]

> But when a true virtuoso who is worthy of the title is to be accompanied, then one must not allow oneself to be beguiled by the postponing or anticipating of the notes, which he knows how to shape so adroitly and touchingly, into hesitating or hurrying, but must continue to play throughout in the same manner; otherwise the effect which the performer desired to build up would be demolished by the accompaniment.

He added in a footnote:

> A clever accompanist must also be able to sum up a concert performer. To a sound virtuoso he certainly must not yield, for he would then spoil his tempo rubato.

Today rubato is practically a lost art. Where is the pianist who is capable of playing strictly in time with his left hand, while allowing his right hand rhythmic freedom? The disappearance of this gift is to be regretted, since it was one of the most important elements in lively and expressive performance of early classical works. There are many examples of metric construction in two-, four- or eight-bar periods, which strike us as all too simple, or even naïve, and which only take on life when one uses rubato, loosening the symmetry while not destroying it. Much of the blame for this lies with current teaching methods, which do nothing to encourage the hands to be independent. In teaching beginners, all the attention is directed to absolute simultaneity of the hands, and their independence of movement is neglected, though it is absolutely indispensable for correct rubato.

In the slow movement of the C minor Sonata (K.457), Mozart wrote out a rubato (bar 12, second half):

Without the written-out rubato, this passage would probably read:

The main difficulty in both cases is to get the accentuation right; in the first example the rising melodic phrase is shifted forward by a semiquaver, so that the melodic accents coincide with the unaccented notes of the accompaniment, whereas the turns must not be accented even though they coincide with the rhythmic accents of the left hand. The difference between this and a normal syncopation is that the latter is felt as a contradiction of the prevailing beat, whereas in this case one must if possible be aware of two simultaneous systems of beats, which run alongside each other, unconnected and therefore not contradictory.

One should at first practice as follows:

In this way one will gradually 'grow into' the right way of playing the passage.

In bar 20 of the same movement Mozart again 'wrote out' a rubato, as can be seen from comparing the bar with bar 3:

bar 3:

One essential feature of rubato is that very often the notes on the unaccented parts of the bar are prolonged.

There is another example of a written-out rubato in the Piano Sonata in F (K.332), second movement. In bar 34 and its upbeat the first edition (which appeared during Mozart's lifetime)[46] contains a rubato:

(On the other hand, five bars earlier the thirds are written without any rhythmic displacement, even in the first edition.)

The finest example of a 'written-out' rubato in all keyboard music is perhaps the slow movement of Bach's 'Italian' Concerto. We select two passages to show the way a composer of genius uses this device, though there are many others. Ten bars before the end, Bach replaces—

by:

and three bars before the end the text reads:

Without the 'written-out' rubato it would have to read:

For the most part, composers only rarely wrote out their rubato, not simply because its complicated rhythmic notation took a great deal of time, but because this important expressive effect cannot be reproduced exactly by means of existing notation, which is too crude to register accurately the subtle rhythmic displacements involved in true rubato. All the same, great composers such as Bach and Mozart and especially the Romantics, have constantly sought such a notation. C. P. E. Bach wrote:

> Fig. 178 contains several examples in which certain notes and rests should be extended beyond their written length for affective reasons. In places, I have written out these broadened values; elsewhere they are indicated by a small cross. . . . In general the retard fits slow or more moderate tempos better than very fast ones [op. cit., I, 'Performance', §28, p. 159].

Played:

In Mozart's earlier works, where he hardly ever wrote out a rubato, but certainly often made one in performance, it should be played in this way. But it should be confined to slow movements, and even there, used only in particular passages, for Mozart himself must have used it comparatively seldom as an expressive effect, and it appears that in his later years he made less and less use of rubato. In slow movements from his Viennese period the texture is often too polyphonic, or in homophonic movements the melody too closely bound up with the accompanying parts, for any opportunities for rubato to present themselves. A rubato would be unthinkable in the first subject of the slow movement of the Piano Sonata K.533/494, or at the beginning of the chorale-like second movement of the Piano Concerto K.595. One reason for this move away from rubato was perhaps the development of the piano from an instrument with an evanescent tone to the more cantabile instrument of the 1780's; but the main reason must have been Mozart's own development into a great and mature composer, far ahead of his time.

Even when Mozart wrote out his rubato (as in the examples quoted), his notation is only a cue for the use of the effect, for in fact rubato consists not of any constant syncopation, but of very uneven prolongations, which are too subtle to be reproduced by our notation. Thus Leopold Mozart's words prove true:

What this 'stolen tempo' is, is more easily shown than described.[47]

IV. Some Peculiarities of Rhythmic Notation

On a few rare occasions Mozart still felt obliged to comply with traditional baroque usage. This applies mainly to the performance of dotted rhythms, which in Bach and Handel are often not played as written. Leopold Mozart too, wrote:

> There are certain passages in slow pieces where the dot must be held rather longer than the afore-mentioned rule demands if the performance is not to sound too sleepy. For example, if here

> the dot were held its usual length it would sound very languid and sleepy. In such cases dotted notes must be held somewhat longer, but the time taken up by the extended value must be, so to speak, stolen from the note standing after the dot.[48]

Wolfgang, on the other hand, tended to write this kind of rhythm in the way he wished it played, following one of his father's precepts that the composer should be as exact as possible in notating rhythms, and should in certain cases use the double dot.[49] But there are some exceptions in which the dotted rhythm has to be played rather more crisply than it is written. This is often so in passages where Mozart was writing in the 'old style', under the influence of Bach and Handel, whose music he had come to know through van Swieten. There is a characteristic example in the A major Violin Sonata (K.402), first movement, fifth bar before the double bar:

Both the complementary rhythm and the canon between piano and violin mean that the quavers in the first bar must be played as if double-dotted, and the semiquavers as demisemiquavers.

In the music of the 'ordeals' in the Act II of *The Magic Flute*, it again seems advisable on rhythmic grounds to apply a double-dotted rhythm throughout,[50] making all the anacruses demisemiquavers:

performed:

This view is confirmed by the sketches for *The Magic Flute* (cf. *Oesterreichische Musikzeitschrift*, 1956, p. 447).

There is a similar example in the well-known introductory Adagio from the Adagio and Fugue (K.546), in which a double-dotted rhythm should be played throughout. Again, the rhythmic figure in bar 97 of the third movement of the Duet Sonata (K.521):

should be played:

There are further examples of this shortening of the anacrusis in the A major Symphony (K 201), opening of the second movement, and in the Piano Duet Sonata (K.497), also second movement (up-beat to bars 29 and 96). In Mozart's operas there are a large number of passages where rhythms have to be made to correspond. Here we mention only a few. In *Don Giovanni*, Act I, Finale, last Scene ($\frac{2}{4}$ C major section) the following rhythm constantly returns in the orchestra (p. 283 of the Eulenburg score):

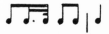

But, according to the score, Don Giovanni has to sing the words 'Viva la libertà' to the dull rhythm ♪ ♪♪♪ ♪| ♩ Here, of course, an adjustment must be made so that the semiquavers are sung as a dotted rhythm. In this same finale, Scene 20, Adagio (B flat section, alla-breve), all the parts have a semiquaver anacrusis ♩ ɤ. ♪♫♫ | ♩ ɤ. ♪♫♫ | ♩

Here again a demisemiquaver should, of course, be played. In eighteenth-century performing practice this went without saying; it was one of the things that were so obvious that few theorists even bothered to mention it. In Türk's very thorough *Clavierschule* of 1802 it is reassuring to find this practice mentioned (p. 404):

> If in passages with several parts there are simultaneous dotted notes of *differing* values . . . then to make them agree better one generally prolongs the longer of the notes by a second dot, thus playing the ensuing note of all the parts simultaneously, i.e.:

becomes: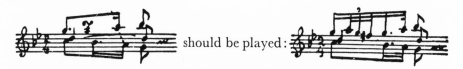

The same is true for Variation IV of the Piano Duet Variations (K.501), bar 2 and corresponding passages:

 should be played:

Here the old edition by Lebert (published by Cotta) gives the correct version in a footnote. Unfortunately, the text of some old editions contains a resolution of the ornament which is certainly incorrect:

In the coda, sixteen bars before the end, the dotted rhythm should again be emphasized in the same way. The turns in the Primo part must be equated with the Secondo's demisemiquavers.

In the Rex Tremendae of the Requiem the rhythm ♩. ♪ again has to be performed as if double-dotted, otherwise there are constant disturbing collisions between the rhythms of the various vocal parts (e.g. at the end of bar 10). There is even a case where the two rhythms are written simultaneously (Larghetto of the Piano Concerto K.595, bars 103, 124 et seq.).:

Here the Eulenburg score correctly alters the piano's rhythm to correspond to that of the other instruments.

One very frequent practice of the baroque, which also occurs occasionally in Mozart, is that one part will have triplet quavers and another normal

quavers, in which case the two rhythms often have to correspond.[51] In the
ensuing example from the Piano Concerto K.482 the clarinets and bassoons
will obviously play their first quaver as an upbeat quaver triplet:

should be played :

A similar adjustment is recommended when the following rhythm occurs:

We see that this supposition is correct if we look at the original notation of
bar 76 of the first movement of the B flat Concerto (K.450); the right hand
of the piano has:

and the third of each quaver triplet is written exactly under the semiquaver.

But it would certainly be incorrect always to equate triplets and dotted
quavers. In the second movement of the Violin Sonata K.296, for example, a
polyrhythm is obviously intended: the third bar proves this:

To end this chapter we would like to say something about the observation and correct performance of the hemiola. The hemiola is an accentual

displacement by which two bars of triple time produce a higher-order 'bar' containing three accents.

The hemiola is often wrongly believed to be very rare in classical music.[52] In fact it is at least as frequent as in Renaissance choral music or nineteenth-century piano music (Schumann, Brahms), even if not as easily recognizable as in fifteenth and sixteenth-century notation, which coloured the relevant notes.

True hemiola occurs when all the parts undergo this change of accent, as in the second movement of the Piano Sonata K.281, bars 24 and 25:

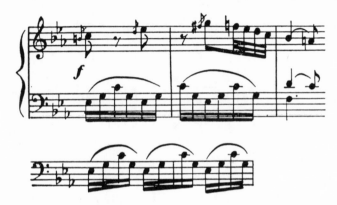

or the second movement of the Piano Concerto K.482, bars 58–9:

These two bars are felt as a hemiola:[53]

The same applies to bars 9–13 of the cadenza of the first movement of the

Piano Concerto K.449, or for some passages in the Requiem ('Hostias', bars 19–20, 'Recordare', bars 18–19, etc.).

There are, however, many cases in which it is hard to say definitely whether a hemiola is felt as such or rather as a syncopation. There are hybrid passages, a mixture of hemiola and syncopation, in which the accompaniment retains its original accentuation while the melody undergoes the accentual displacement that amounts to a change of barring. The theme of the Minuet in the G minor Symphony (K.550) is a case in point:

The attraction of this kind of disguised hemiola is the simultaneous flow of two different rhythms.

There is a wonderful combination of simultaneous barrings, creating a kind of hemiola, in the Act I Finale of *Don Giovanni*, where the stage orchestra plays a contredance in $\frac{2}{4}$ against the main orchestra's accompaniment written in $\frac{3}{4}$.

Sometimes Mozart even gives a hemiola dynamic markings which emphasize its displacement of accents, as in the first movement of the Piano Sonata K.332, bar 64:

In playing hemiolas the shift of the bar-line must be clearly audible, for it is this varied distribution of rhythmic accents that gives the figure its particular interest.

Chapter Three

ARTICULATION

EDITORS of Mozart, particularly those of the old complete edition (*Alte Mozart-Ausgabe* (*A.M.A.*), Breitkopf and Härtel, 1876–86) have often sinned against his spirit, but nowhere more frequently and seriously than in their treatment of his articulation markings; they have made alterations and additions, adding markings and omitting others, without clearly indicating that they have departed from the text found in Mozart's manuscript. Specialist knowledge of this subject is rare.

First of all, the prevailing confusion about the words 'articulation' and 'phrasing' should be cleared up. In music, as in language, 'articulation' means the style of delivery that is necessary to make clear the meaning of a musical or linguistic text, right down to the smallest detail. Thus in music 'articulation' covers the various 'modes of attack' (types of touch on the piano, types of bowing in violin-playing, etc.). Since the end of the sixteenth century, many composers have used various notational signs to show the articulation they wanted—such signs as staccato dots and strokes, or legato slurs. As for 'phrasing': by 'a phrase' we mean a melodic section, such as a motive or theme, which is usually self-contained and which hangs together as a significant whole. 'Phrasing' (an expression first used in the nineteenth century) should only be applied to motivic or thematic figures used in the construction of a melody, and a phrasing mark (slur) is a way of notating the coherence of a musical phrase.[54]

Mozart never used slurs in his music as phrasing marks. They were only added to his texts later by certain editors, particularly Riemann, who published 'phrased editions' full of these markings. They are open to the criticism (which has already often been made) that the inner relationships between melody and rhythm, etc., are far too complicated and intangible to be represented by merely adding a few slurs,[55] which seriously obscure or even distort Mozart's graphic presentation.

The need to mould phrases was obviously recognized in the eighteenth century also. In his tutor, Quantz wrote:

One should be just as careful not to separate what belongs together as to avoid

53

linking together things which, because they are ambiguous, ought to be separated; for much of the expressiveness of performance depends on this.[56]

But it was left to interpreters to grasp the more general relationships, and Riemann's type of enormous slur was not found necessary.

Practising musicians often confuse phrasing and articulation. To prevent confusion, we have tried to avoid this looseness of terminology, and in discussing Mozart's notation we shall refer only to articulation signs; in treating the slurs he used, we shall conform to present-day usage and refer to legato slurs and articulating slurs.

We take Mozart's slurs first. They serve two purposes:

1. To indicate a legato over a fairly long section, which, however, Mozart usually wrote with slurs lasting only one bar each (in accordance with established practice); these slurs are legato slurs.

2. To indicate that two, three or even four notes are to be grouped together 'cutting-off' the last note (i.e. playing it shorter). These slurs are often placed over very short note-values; we call them articulating slurs.

Thus Mozart's legato slurs do not mean that there is to be a break at the end of each slur; this is only so in the case of articulating slurs. It is not always easy to see from the printed page which sort of slur is intended. Musical content is the decisive factor here. This is why many editors have tried to replace Mozart's legato notation by long slurs of a more modern kind.

When such slurs occur in an edition they are usually not by Mozart. It is most important to know this; a slur stretching over more than one bar may sometimes accord with Mozart's intentions, but just as often not. This is because many editors have not merely replaced Mozart's own notation of legato by long modern slurs, but have erroneously added them in many places where Mozart expressly wished to avoid a legato. According to the practice of Mozart's time, absence of any articulation sign meant 'non-legato':

> Normal onward movement is the opposite of both slurring and detaching: it consists of lifting the finger nimbly from the preceding key just before one touches the next note. This normal onward movement is always taken for granted, is never indicated.[57]
>
> For notes which are to be played in the usual way, i.e. neither detached nor slurred, one lifts one's finger from the key a little earlier than the value of the note demands.[58]

It is most important for Mozart-interpreters to know this. There is a very widespread fallacy that Mozart's passage-work particularly needs a constant legato. He does indeed often demand a legato for melodic passages, but for whatever instrument, he almost always wanted virtuoso passage-work played 'non-legato'. At least we have never come across any extended passage of triplets or semiquavers that should be played legato. There is only one type of virtuoso passage for which Mozart favoured long legato slurs—rising chromatic scales in quick tempo, of the kind that frequently occur in cadenzas. It will nearly always be right to play all other such passage-work non-legato or staccato, whether in a violin work or one for piano.

Fortunately we have one interesting proof of 'non-legato' being the main articulation in eighteenth-century passage work. In the former Heyer Collection (now Instrumenten-Museum, Universität, Leipzig) there exists a barrel-organ (Flötenuhr) in good playing order with an 'eighteenth-century recording' of Mozart's Andante in F, K.616 in an abridged version. The many runs in semidemiquavers are played there in a stylish non-legato.*

Elsewhere than in passage-work, Mozart often adheres to an old rule in strict academic counterpoint: stepwise motion slurred, leaps separated. Thus it is seldom right to play arpeggios legato, unless they are in long note-values, as in the Piano Sonata K.570 (which was originally printed as a Violin Sonata by Artaria in 1796).

Examining Mozart's own slurs (that is to say, slurs which occur in his manuscripts and which have definitely not been added by editors), one can distinguish legato slurs from articulating slurs by the fact that they extend over several notes and often end at the bar-line or before the last note. This is disconcerting at first, but is easily explained by the fact that in classical music the use of slurs originated in violin bowing. The slurs in the above example indicate three changes of bow. Only a very bad violinist makes an audible break at a change of bow (the bow should not leave the string), but on the other hand a completely inaudible change is hardly possible, and up- and down-bows are different not merely technically but in their psychology. So it is understandable that at different times Mozart indicated a legato by slurs over half a bar, a whole bar, two bars or in a few rare cases even several bars. The Viennese classical composers, Mozart above all, adopted a notation typical of the violin throughout their music. The rarity of long slurs is an obvious consequence of the limited length of the violin bow.

As an example of these very common single-bar slurs we take the first subject of the first movement of the B flat Concerto (K.595):

*We owe the first information about this valuable source to Mr. Fritz Spiegel, Liverpool, whose studies in this field throw new light on the problem of performance practice in the eighteenth century.

Similarly the F major Sonata (K.332) begins:

These single-bar slurs often have a deeper meaning; they provide an image of
the melody's wave-like motion. Without making a break between the bars,
the pianist's hand should follow this motion, with movements from the
elbow. He should be physically conscious of this swing in and out, which has
about it something dance-like and hovering, a truly Mozartian delight in
movement.[59] In passages such as this, one should try to lift the hand from the
keys a little at the end of the slur, while maintaining a legato with the pedal.

Just as on the violin changes of bow can mean anything from an imperceptible transition to a clearly accented separation, so there are many ways of
articulating passages in the piano works where legato slurs are marked. In
the Minuet of the A major Sonata (K.331), the various possible ways of
playing the legato slur are combined:

At the end of the first bar one should make a clear break, in order to give
sufficient accent to the second bar; at the end of the third bar the break will
be much slighter, and the fourth and fifth bars should be played legatissimo,
since the melodic progression from E to E sharp to F sharp must on no
account be broken up.

To match the sequential repetition in bar 3, the slur ought only to extend
to the second beat (lower C sharp). Perhaps this version, from the first
edition, is a mistake on the part of a printer unfamiliar with Mozart's way of
treating slurs (cf. p. 141). The edition of the Sonata published in the same
year (1784) by Schott, Mainz, only takes the slur to the second crotchet. We
think this is justified on musical grounds.

In almost every cantabile theme it is necessary to link the notes by playing
legato; even when a literal interpretation of articulating slurs would lead one
to lift the hand from the keys, one should not do so. The above quotation
from the B flat Concerto (K.595) is an example where slurs are used as a
symbol of to-and-fro movement. A four-bar slur would do less than justice to
the musical content. There are numerous passages in which Mozart also
seems to have used legato slurs to indicate rhythmic units, perhaps wishing

to draw the performer's attention to the length of certain internal tensions (Sonata in A major (K.331), first movement, Variation V[60]):

Adagio

Perhaps the half-bar slurs are used so consistently in the left hand as a sign that the unit of internal tension is $\frac{3}{8}$ and not the $\frac{6}{8}$ of the preceding variations. If these slurs extended over the whole bar, the performer might play the Adagio a shade faster, to maintain the tension throughout a larger unit.

There is no point in concealing the fact that Mozart's use of slurs was often inconsistent, i.e. that he often used different markings in passages which are musically equivalent. Einstein wrote:

> . . . but the marking of the individual parts is very often inconsistent where uniformity is often required, and quite frequently he binds together in one passage a group of notes which are divided in corresponding passages. . . . In such cases it is not always possible to distinguish sharply between oversight and deliberate intentions.[61]

A good deal of thought has been given to the problem of whether one should 'iron out' these passages. In doubtful cases we think it better to retain Mozart's inconsistent slurs and possibly to refer to them in a footnote, rather than altering Mozart's text. Addition of slurs that were obviously forgotten is another matter, though in such cases the editor must still make it clear that he has added the slurs. In the MS. of the Finale of the D minor Concerto (K.466) bar 143 has a slur over the flute's quavers:

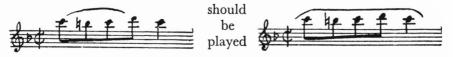

should be played

This also occurs in the oboe part, bar 359, and the piano, bar 367. Obviously these slurs should also occur in bars 151, 306 and 314, and probably also bars 399 and 407. But this kind of reasoning does not apply to the first subject of the movement. The first full bar of the theme does not slur the notes D–C sharp–D, either in the solo entry or the tutti; the theme is written:

But in bars 182 et seq. there is suddenly a slur—

in all the string parts. It would be only too tempting to read this slur into the
first bar. However, if we see how this bar is continued in each case, it becomes
clear that the variation must be deliberate. The sequential treatment of the
theme at the opening of the movement, with its note-repetitions in bars 17
and 19, relies on the fact that the first full bar is played forcefully, hammering
out the notes. In bar 183, on the other hand, the strings have syncopations and
the wind sustained chords, but there is no hammering to be heard anywhere.
Thus the two ways of playing the bar—energetically or rather more cantabile—should be deliberately contrasted. In any case, one must be wary of
coming to premature conclusions by analogy.

Articulating slurs present far fewer problems than legato slurs. Articulating slurs are always short and rarely extend over more than three notes.
Unlike legato slurs, they 'cut off' the last note, i.e. it is to be played softer
and shorter. Often an articulating slur appears in company with staccato dots
or strokes, as in the following typical example (Piano Duet Sonata (K.521),
third movement, bar 7):

Here the semiquavers G and D are cut off, i.e. played staccato.

If an articulating slur is over two notes of equal length, it also indicates an
accent of the first of them, particularly when this is off the beat, as in the next
examples (A major Concerto (K.488), Finale, bars 300 et seq.):

and (C minor Concerto (K.491), Finale, bar 28):

In Leopold Mozart's textbook we find the rule that the first of two or more
notes joined by a slur is to be accented. In section VII, 1, §20, we read:

> Now if in a musical composition two, three, four, and even more notes be
> bound together by the half-circle [i.e. by a slur], so that one recognizes there-
> from that the composer wishes the notes to be separated but played singly
> in one slur, the first of such united notes must be somewhat more strongly
> stressed, but the remainder slurred on to it quite smoothly and more and
> more quietly.

Only in one special case do we find it wrong to make a 'cut-off' at the end of an articulating slur; this is in the common formula:

which is in fact a portamento (anticipatory) resolution of a crotchet accented passing-note.

In passages of this kind the performer should make clear the original relationship of the crotchets—accented passing-note and resolution. For this purpose one should if possible link the two quavers, even using the pedal, and avoid an accent on the crotchet:

Naturally, there are transitional stages between legato and articulating slurs. In the first subject of the A major Concerto (K.488) there is a legato slur in bar 1, whereas in bar 2 those over the third and fourth beats are articulating slurs. We feel that the first slur in bar 2 is a kind of transition from one to the other, and we make a very slight break after it:

There are two possible ways of playing the common formula:

either as a legato slur—

or as an articulating slur:

In such cases we almost always prefer the latter version, which has the virtue of greater clarity (especially in large halls) without sounding too broken-up, for the listener somehow deceives himself into feeling the three notes to be legato. If one makes a true legato, the semiquaver is almost inevitably blurred.

Another passage in which the best result comes from a 'Mozartean' reading as an articulating slur is the theme of the A major Sonata (K.331):

A slur followed by staccato dots does not always have to be taken as an articulating slur. In bars 100 and 102 of the first movement of the E flat Concerto (K.449), it is better to play a legato slur:

But such exceptions are infrequent.

Of course, Mozart knew that his slurs were ambiguous, and in his later works he often tried to find a way round this. In his last period we often find slurs extending over bar-lines, as in the first movement of the B flat Concerto (K.595), bars 108–12, 123–6, 130–1, 263–4: or in the second movement of the same concerto, bars 45, 47 (basses), or in the Minuet of the 'Jupiter' Symphony, bars 9 et seq.:

Earlier, Mozart would probably have written this passage:

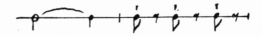

In his Vienna years Mozart also occasionally used long slurs, as in the Finale of the 'Jupiter' Symphony, in which, according to the MS., there is a whole series of four-bar slurs and even one of six bars (362–7); or the F major Concerto (K.459), first movement, bar 358, where he marks a slur seven bars long.

We have already mentioned one peculiarity of Mozart's musical handwriting—he was fond of extending his slurs a little too far, and beginning them a fraction of an inch too soon. This can often be distinctly misleading.

In the first movement of the B flat Violin Sonata (K.454), he wrote the first slur at the beginning of the Allegro in this way:

It would be natural for anyone but the most wide-awake editor to print:

(At the corresponding passage later on, Mozart's omitting this slur entirely does not clarify matters either. But we can tell that this slur must start at the second note, from a knowledge of violin technique, and also from the way bars 100 et seq. (where the figure is developed) are written (clearly!):

This proves that the version of bar 1 given in most editions is correct:

In the Trio of the 'Jupiter' Symphony Mozart again wrote a slur in this misleading way:

This habit of Mozart's when writing down his music has also led to mistakes in some otherwise sound editions, such as the Eulenburg scores. In the A major Concerto (K.488), first movement, bars 59–60 and 301–2, for instance, the slur in the first violins should only extend over two quavers:

And in the Finale of the C minor Concerto, bar 231, the second slur should not start until the right-hand G:

For correct articulation in playing Mozart it is important to know of the old rule that a suspension or dissonance and its resolution must always be smoothly joined, whether the dissonant note is written as a 'long 'appoggiatura, in small type, or written out in notes of normal size. Naturally, it is always the passing-note that receives the accent, and the resolution must be slightly shortened. This rule for playing accented passing-notes is found in C. P. E. Bach (op. cit., I, Part II, I, §7):

> With regard to execution we learn from this figure that appoggiaturas are louder than the following tone, including any additional embellishments, and that they are joined to it in the absence as well as the presence of a slur. Both of these points are in accord with the purpose of an appoggiatura, which is to connect notes.

And Leopold's *Violinschule* says (IX, §1):

> Here now is a rule without an exception. The appoggiatura is never separated from its main note, but is taken at all times in the same stroke.

This rule was so obvious to Wolfgang that he often omitted to write a slur over his appoggiaturas and accented passing-notes. The performer must add the slur:

Knowing this simple but fundamental rule, we can easily work out the articulation of doubtful passages, where the MS. is lost and early editions are faulty. In the theme of the Finale of the C minor Sonata (K.457), Mozart seems to have intended the following slurs:

Thus the theme consists of a series of 'sighing' figures. For teaching purposes, it is a good thing to imagine the theme without its shifts of bar-line, which are akin to rubato:

The individual 'sighs' must not obscure the eight-bar line. Analysis, according to Riemann, suggests a 2 + 2 + 4 grouping, but it would be wrong to put one long legato slur right over the entire theme, as many editors do.

There is only a single exception to the rule that an accented passing-note must be joined to the succeeding note; the rule does not apply when the resolution is delayed instead of occurring immediately after the accented passing-note. According to an old rule of counterpoint it is permissible to leap from an accented passing-note or suspension on to the note below the resolution, or to a consonance, providing the dissonance is subsequently resolved (*cambiata*). This delayed resolution will then be joined to the note immediately preceding it. Mozart used this exception mostly in movements with a polyphonic texture, such as the magnificent F major Sonata (K.533), whose second movement contains the following passage:

Knowledge of this rule also enables one to correct a number of doubtful articulations in the first edition of this Sonata.

It is easy to see that the first two slurs are a quaver too far to the left, that the third slur is rather too long, and only the fourth one reproduced correctly. Since a delayed resolution must not be separated from the preceding dissonance, it follows that in this version the first bar is articulated wrongly. To be correct it should be:

(The rhythmic notation has been modernized.)

One of the particularly attractive features of this passage is that the changes of harmony turn the consonant resolutions immediately into fresh suspensions.

Mozart was very fond of the various staccato markings, which are a type of articulation sign found very frequently in his works. Their notation employs a scale of markings from very short, scarcely perceptible dots to powerful wedge-shaped strokes. There has recently been a great deal of discussion of the exact meaning of these signs.[62] One difficulty is that Mozart's markings can mean different things—at times this even leads to contradictions.

1. They affect interpretation, since they are intended to express all the possible shadings of staccato, from a soft, round, gentle 'separation' of the notes, to a light, pointed shortening of the written value. As early as C. P. E. Bach, we find the demand that staccato-playing should cover a richly shaded expressive range. (I, III, 'Performance', 17, p. 154.)

> Notes are detached with relation to: (1) their notated length, that is a half, quarter or eighth of a bar; (2) the tempo, fast or slow; (3) the volume, forte or piano.[63]

Thus one must take into account the length, loudness and timbre of any particular note, and, equally important, the 'feeling of the piece' (the *Affekt*, as it was called in the eighteenth century). Here both subtle touch and artistic understanding are needed.

2. Mozart also used the staccato marking as an accentual sign, obviously in cases where the only contemporary marking for an accent, *sfz*, struck him as excessively strong, and where in nineteenth-century notation he would probably have written >.

We see from Mozart's MSS. that it is impossible to make a distinction between dots and strokes (or wedges) on a purely philological basis. To attempt to force Mozart's markings into a system based on their appearance and function, and to distinguish 'staccato dots' from 'accentual wedges', is to over-simplify the multiplicity of markings in Mozart's MSS., and to do less than justice to their often contradictory musical meaning, even though one must admit that in preparing an edition this sort of distinction must be taken into account.

When Mozart's strokes or wedges indicate an accent (for he rarely uses a staccato dot in this way), this often carries with it an indication of staccato. In the Trio of the 'Jupiter' Symphony he writes 'accentual strokes' over each of the dotted minims in the first violins (bars 68–75 inclusive):

and again in the Finale, at each forte entry of the first subject:

Here, of course, he does not mean a staccato in the usual sense, but an accent, plus a slight separation of the individual notes.

However, Mozart's articulation signs often mean an accent, which in fact rules out the possibility of their also meaning staccato. Few would claim that the wedges over the bass notes in bars 68–92 of the Finale of the 'Jupiter' Symphony mean that these notes are to be shortened:[64]

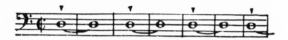

(There is a facsimile reproduction of the MS. of this passage in Volume 9 of the Symphonies in the new complete edition of Mozart.)

The first edition of the F major Sonata (K.533) (Hoffmeister) is full of these accentual strokes over minims, which can hardly mean a staccato (but which may not be from Mozart):

This is also quite clear from the notation of bars 49, 53 and 125, where the stroke is over a tied minim, so that it would be impossible to play it staccato:

In many other later works by Mozart there are wedges that indicate an accent, for example in bar 4 of the Andantino of the E flat Concerto (K.449):

It is hardly surprising that the *A.M.A.* complete edition left out all these markings, which to nineteenth-century editors were incomprehensible. On the other hand, the fact that many earlier printed editions correctly reproduced these markings is a sign of their reliability.

In his *Violinschule*, Leopold Mozart devotes much attention to the combination of slurs and dots (or strokes). This combination signifies that the notes concerned, though played in a single bow, have to be slightly separated. In Wolfgang's piano works, repeated notes are often an occasion on which to use this violinistic way of showing that the notes are to be 'separated', so that they shall sing all the better. Surprising though it seems, the effect intended is the opposite of staccato, and the best way of doing justice to this

combination of legato and staccato, in terms of the piano, is to play both notes
with the pedal depressed (assuming that there is no change of harmony).

Both Mozart's own articulation markings and the testimony of his contemporaries show that non-legato and even staccato, rather than legato, were
the dominant types of touch in his playing. Beethoven described it as 'subtle
but broken-up; no legato'.[65] This criticism, made while Mozart was still
alive, tells us much about Beethoven, who laid much more stress on a
well-blended sound than on transparency. Again, Czerny (who certainly had
much first-hand experience of the Mozart tradition) wrote in his *Pianoforte-
Schule*, Vol. III (1800):[66]

> Mozart's school; notably brilliant playing, more with an eye to staccato than
> legato; intelligent and lively performance.

As we mentioned in discussing legato slurs, Mozart's articulation markings
are often sparingly used, and must at times be supplemented. Leopold Mozart
wrote:[67]

> Similarly, from the sixth and seventh chapters is to be seen how greatly the
> slurring and detaching distinguishes a melody. Therefore not only must the
> written and prescribed slurs be observed with the greatest exactitude, but
> when, as in many a composition, nothing at all is indicated, the player must
> himself know how to apply the slurring and detaching tastefully and in the
> right place.

This also applies to his son's music. Correct articulation, over and above
Mozart's markings, is not as difficult as it looks at first sight. He gives one a
good deal of help. In a piano concerto, intensive study of the orchestral
parts is useful, and for this reason alone a pianist should study not merely the
piano part, but the score, very carefully. Time and again the orchestral parts
contain carefully written-out performing indications which are an adequate
basis on which to add to those in the piano part, as in the E flat Concerto
(K.482), second movement, bar 105:

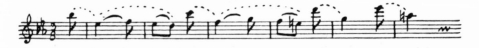

In the piano part there are no slurs from each third beat to the ensuing
strong one, but the accompanying violins have slurs across the bar-line
(dotted in our musical example). Obviously, the piano will also articulate
the phrase in this eloquent way, which is also suggested by the way the
quavers are grouped.

In the next example, from the E flat Concerto (K.449), second movement,
we again find Mozart reluctant to slur across the bar-line. But the motivic
overlapping of piano and violins loses its point unless the piano plays the
three notes C–A–B flat legato.

One should study and learn from Mozart's scrupulously marked piano works, especially those of his maturity. The great A minor Rondo (K.511) is famous in this connection, but the sonatas K.310, 331, 570, 576, the D major Rondo (K.485) or the B minor Adagio (K.540) also show a wealth of articulation that is rare in works by eighteenth-century composers.

In accompaniments, too, Mozart likes to make fine distinctions between legato, non-legato and staccato. In this way he can often lend charm to the least interesting Alberti bass. In the introductory tutti of the B flat Concerto (K.595), we find in bars 16–19:

When this passage is given to the piano later on, the staccato dots can well be borne in mind. In the first solo Mozart placed legato slurs over similar accompanying figures, and here, on the other hand, since there are no slurs one might play non legato or staccato.

There are other instructive examples of the alternation of legato and non-legato accompanying figures in the C minor Sonata (K.457), first and third movements:

(*a*) First movement, bar 23:

(*b*) First movement, bar 59:

(*c*) First movement, bar 74:

(Note the principle of complementarity: in (*a*), irregular and broken-up articulation of the melody is opposed by a peaceful accompaniment, whereas in (*b*) and (*c*) the symmetrical rhythmic figures in the melody are opposed by an accompaniment that is non-legato or staccato.)

Mozart's articulation always sounds natural and never fussy. One must always remember this, when one faces the problem of completing his articulation markings, or when one comes across an edition which seems both fussy and unnatural. In this connection one cannot be sufficiently suspicious of editors, especially when the printed text contains many slurs, and long ones, or even the marking 'legato' which is nearly never authentic (an exception can be found in the 1st movement of K.595).

In general it can be said that wide intervals and rhythmically irregular melodic phrases tend to call for staccato, whereas melodic dissonances (suspensions, passing-notes and changing-notes) should be played legato. Non-legato is mainly to be recommended in passages of a 'neutral' character.

Chapter Four

ORNAMENTATION

Indeed, nobody has ever doubted that ornaments are necessary. This is evident, since one is always coming across large numbers of them. They are, however, indispensable, when one observes their usefulness. They link the notes together, they enliven them, when necessary they give them special emphasis and importance; they lend them charm and thus draw special attention to them; they help to make clear their content—whether this be sad or merry or of any other kind, they always make their contribution; they provide a considerable proportion of the opportunities for true performance, and of the means toward it. A moderate composition can gain by their help; without them, on the other hand, the best melody is empty and monotonous, and its content, however clear, must inevitably appear but indistinctly.*[68]

MOZART's ornamentation is tasteful and distinguished, detailed, but never excessive, elegant and eloquent, refined and yet naïve; it raises even the most banal eighteenth-century formulae to the level of eternal verity.

In his notation of ornaments Mozart again aimed at the maximum of clarity. Even so, many of his embellishments are ambiguous, because as far as ornaments were concerned, he lived in a period of transition. Various things which were a matter of common knowledge in his time, have lapsed into obscurity in the course of the nineteenth century and are overlooked by all too many musicians today. Moreover, Mozart could count on his contemporaries' taste and artistic sensitivity. We are firmly convinced that he left his interpreters a certain freedom in performing his ornaments. It has always been true that strict, inflexible rules exist only in books of theory; art, being alive, constantly produces exceptions, deviations, variants.

Mozart's ornaments consist mainly of appoggiaturas, arpeggios, turns and trills. Whereas in playing single appoggiaturas the most difficult problem is usually one of accent, in the case of compound appoggiaturas we shall be concerned mainly with their place within the metre, i.e. with such questions as anticipation. We shall mention the question of so-called 'vocal appoggiaturas', since these also occur in the piano works. On the other hand, there are few problems in playing the occasional 'intermediate' groups of small notes

*Translation by Leo Black.

69

(*Zwischenschläge*)—scales, etc., so these will not be treated separately. The playing of arpeggios and turns is also relatively simple, whereas trills present problems which are often difficult to solve.

I.   APPOGGIATURAS

(a) Single Appoggiaturas

Appoggiaturas were originally nothing but accented passing-notes. If in the course of the eighteenth century they lost some of this meaning, it is still a very good thing to remember their origin.

Mozart's notation of appoggiaturas is usually based on their real value:

♩ = a minim

♩ = a crotchet

♪ = a quaver (though in this case there are exceptions)[69]

Mozart's use of appoggiaturas shorter than a quaver is inconsistent; he often writes a semiquaver appoggiatura when he must have meant a demisemi-quaver or hemidemisemiquaver, as, for example, in the introduction to the first movement of the 'Prague' Symphony (K.504), bar 17:

which is played:

All the same, the duration of appoggiaturas presents only a few problems, so in the interests of terminological clarity we shall classify them as follows:

    1. Accented—unaccented.

    2. On the beat—upbeat (anacrusic, anticipatory).

There is little to be gained by referring to 'long' and 'short' appoggiaturas, since the difference is only rarely one of length, but rather of whether they are accented or unaccented, on the beat or anacrusic. The only possible combinations are as follows:

    1. Accented and on the beat.

    2. Unaccented and on the beat.

    3. Unaccented and anacrusic.

The fourth combination (accented anacrusic) is ruled out on musical grounds. Thus accented appoggiaturas can only be played on the beat. One further general remark: all appoggiaturas must be slurred to the 'main' note they precede, even when this is not expressly indicated by a slur (cf. pp. 62 and 63).

1. *Accented Appoggiaturas*

This kind of appoggiatura is akin to an accented passing-note. For performance purposes this means that the note-value of the appoggiatura is deducted from that of the ensuing note, which is also played softer. Violin Sonata in E minor (K.304), second movement, opening:

played:

Piano Concerto K.466, bar 85 (solo):

played:

As a rule an accented appoggiatura is the next degree of the scale above the main note. But there are cases in which appoggiaturas leap through larger intervals (third to seventh), e.g. the sixth (Violin Sonata in B flat (K.454), second movement, bar 104):

played:

These accented passing-notes quitted by leap only occur in Mozart's works when they are a repetition of the preceding note (in this case the 'C').

A definite accent is to be given to appoggiaturas that are longer than a quaver, and also in the combinations

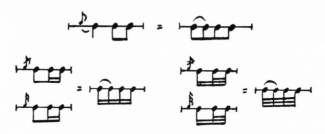

Semiquaver and demisemiquaver appoggiaturas can be either accented or unaccented. It is especially difficult to decide whether any particular appoggiatura is accented or not.

For semiquaver appoggiaturas Mozart had a habit of using the sign ♪, regardless of whether he wanted them played long or short.* It is not generally known that ♪ and ♪, ♪ and ♪ mean exactly the same, and that it was not until the nineteenth century that the transverse stroke came to be used exclusively for the short, 'crushed' appoggiatura.

Semiquaver and demisemiquaver appoggiaturas are always accented and on the beat if they are obviously accented passing-notes, as in the following examples:

Variations for piano K.455, bar 4 (first version):

played:

E flat Piano Concerto (K.271), second movement, bar 34:

* ♪ is merely the south German form of the single semiquaver, and Mozart also wrote it this way as a normal note (i.e. not as a grace-note), as in the song *Ein Veilchen*. (*Translator's Note*: for the English edition of this book the word 'appoggiatura' has been used for all such grace-notes, with or without a stroke through the stem. Although 'acciaccatura' is often used in English to indicate the appoggiatura with a stroke through the stem, this use of the term can create confusion with the form of broken chord also known as 'acciaccatura', and the authors have preferred to follow German usage.)

played:

Two-piano Concerto K.365, first movement, bar 58:

played:

Romanze of the D minor Concerto (K.466), bar 35:

played:

Here an accented semiquaver is to be played, and not (as is too often the case) a quaver. (Mozart did, however, forget to add the transverse stroke on the oboe part.)

The very common figures of this kind:

are played as follows:

here the notes A, F and D are slightly 'cut-off' at the end, i.e. they have to be shortened just a fraction. Other demisemiquaver appoggiaturas which have to be accented are those in bars 9, 13 and 62 of the second movement of the A minor Sonata (K.310):

In the Two-piano Concerto K.365, second movement, bar 67, the appoggiaturas:

can be played as follows:

but according to C. P. E. Bach and Leopold Mozart appoggiaturas of this kind (filling in a descending third) will sound less dull if given less than half the value of the ensuing note:

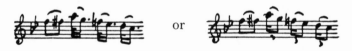

Mozart often tried to indicate this by his notation, writing the appoggiatura as a smaller note value, as at the opening of the D major Rondo (K.485):

played:

(cf. also the second subject of the Finale of the G minor Piano Quartet).

In the MS. of the B flat Violin Sonata (K.454),[70] the introduction to the last movement, Mozart first wrote quaver appoggiaturas, which he later changed into semiquaver appoggiaturas by a transverse stroke (in dark ink). This shows, first, that Mozart was not indifferent to the duration of appoggiaturas, as has been asserted, and also that in this passage he preferred the rhythm known to British musicians as the 'Scotch snap' (Lombardic rhythm). Bars 5 et seq.:

played:

or:

(cf. also the commentary on the example from the second movement of K.365, below).

It is well known that Mozart was fond of these 'Scotch snap' rhythms. They are produced by rhythmic foreshortening of a pair of (originally) equal note values:

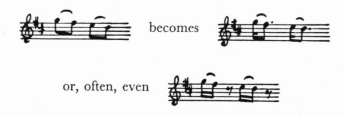

becomes

or, often, even

In playing the two latter examples one must make a clear accent on the short semiquavers, playing the dotted quavers softer.

In the next example it again seems right to play the semiquavers as accented appoggiaturas (K.365, first movement, bar 62, also 72):

should be played:

If in this passage Mozart had intended unaccented, anticipatory appoggiaturas, he would certainly have added staccato dots to the first and third crotchet in the bar.

There is an interesting example in the C minor Fantasia (K.475), bars 31–2.*

Here we suggest a compromise between C. P. E. Bach's approach and the modern one; we would play the appoggiatura G on the beat, but would accent the F sharp, which should sound through; cf. bars 44–5 of the final Rondo K.494 from the Sonata in F (K.533). Our reason for playing the passage in this way is that in such cases the main note is extraordinarily long, compared with the appoggiatura. Our version is in accordance with Leopold Mozart.[71]

In Mozart's early works (till about 1779) one does still sometimes find the old rule that appoggiaturas in triple time are to be given more than their written value. An example occurs in the Finale of the F major Sonata (K.332), bar 64. Bars 63–4:

can be played as follows:

So far as we know, Mozart never applied the baroque rule that when an appoggiatura is added to a note followed by a rest, the resolution comes only at the beginning of the rest.[72] (But one should remember that in J. S. Bach's music this rule was still applicable.)

2. *Unaccented Appoggiaturas*

Appoggiaturas are to be unaccented (short) in the following cases (and here we temporarily leave open the question of anticipation):

*The demisemiquaver appoggiatura goes back to Rudorff's edition. Rudorff had seen a copy with autograph additions, which has since disappeared, and he must have taken this reading from that copy. The quaver appoggiatura in the first edition is certainly a printer's error.

(*a*) When the main note is itself an accented passing-note, e.g. B minor Adagio (K.540), bar 4:

G major Violin Sonata (K.379), Allegro, bar 25:

(in the $\frac{6}{4}$ chord the sixth is, of course, regarded as an accented passing-note resolving on to the fifth).

(*b*) When the main note has a staccato marking (dot or stroke), as in bar 4 of the sixth Variation of the A major Sonata (K.331), first movement:

or the C major Concerto (K.246), first movement, bars 14–15 (first violins):

This is because in Mozart the stroke can be a definite indication of an accent, rather like our marking >.

(*c*) In almost all rising appoggiaturas, e.g. in bar 22 of the first movement of the C major Sonata (K.545):

or the B flat Concerto (K.595), first movement, bar 31, first violins:

'(Also the Sonata K.331, first movement, second variation, bars 7–8, and sixth variation, bars 15–16.) Here again, had Mozart wanted long appoggiaturas, he would doubtless have written them as in bars 8 et seq. of the first movement of the C major Trio (K.548). It appears to have been Mozart's habit, if he wanted this kind of appoggiatura played long, to write it out in normal notes, as in bar 205 of the second movement of the E flat Concerto (K.482):

On the other hand, he wrote the descending appoggiatura small, since here there was no risk of ambiguity. It should certainly be accented.

(d)   Appoggiaturas must be unaccented wherever the main note has a marked accent, since this would lose its effectiveness if preceded by an accented appoggiatura, whereas it will be enhanced by an unaccented one. Opening of the second movement of the B flat Concerto (K.595):

String quartet K.458, first movement, bar 3 (here it is best to play the appoggiatura as an upbeat):

This is also always the case when a semiquaver appoggiatura precedes a minim, as, for example, in the Three-piano Concerto K.242, first movement, bars 53 onward.

It is difficult and often misleading to try at all costs to lay down the law. In problems such as those considered here, much can often depend on the character and speed of the piece, for, as we have said, Mozart relied not only on contemporary notation, but always on the 'taste' and understanding of his interpreters.

The common formula

can be played in a number of ways:

If the semiquavers (or demisemiquavers) after the appoggiatura are on an unaccented part of the bar, then version (1) is usually the best. In his later works Mozart often wrote out this figure in triplets (bars 17, 49 and 101 of the F major Rondo (K.494), but not in bars 98–9). However, one must decide in each particular case, since the character of the piece is an important factor.

In the second movement of the F major Concerto (K.459) from bar 67 onward (and in the corresponding passage from bar 126 onward) there is a sequence in which all the instruments have semiquaver (not demisemiquaver) appoggiaturas, and here one cannot say definitely whether they should be unaccented (short) or accented (long). We tend to prefer the passage played with short appoggiaturas; these strike us as more natural and less forced. Moreover, if Mozart had wanted long appoggiaturas, he could perfectly well have written them out, in accordance with the rules applying at the time:

Either way there is friction with the piano part from bar 71 onward; if the appoggiaturas are short, they clash with the right hand, whereas if they are long they clash with the left. From this standpoint, too, it is more natural if the right-hand of the piano has the accented passing-notes. Finally, according to Leopold Mozart (IX, §18), appoggiaturas should be short when they occur in descending stepwise motion.

One can draw up the following rule for playing short appoggiaturas as listed above ((a) to (d)): a short unaccented appoggiatura is to be played lightly and quickly.* The accent falls on the ensuing 'main' note.

The question, whether short unaccented appoggiaturas should be played on or before the beat, is controversial, and there is no general solution. Contemporary theory contains all manner of rules, according to which appoggiaturas should be accented and on the beat (C. P. E. Bach, Türk),

---

*According to Leopold Mozart (IX, §9) this appoggiatura is to be played '. . . as rapidly as possible'. This seems too general a rule to apply to Wolfgang's music as a whole. In slow movements one finds appoggiaturas which, although unaccented, must not be played too quickly, because of their melodic expressiveness. The first quotation under (a) is an example.

or unaccented and off the beat (J. P. Milchmeyer). Leopold Mozart stands somewhere about the middle, holding that short appoggiaturas should be unaccented, but on the beat.

According to Leopold Mozart, there are two different ways of playing unaccented short appoggiaturas. He holds the unquestionable distinction of having introduced unaccented short appoggiaturas into musical theory. (The accented short appoggiatura had been known for a long time.) In IX, §9 of his *Violinschule* he first treats the unaccented on-the-beat appoggiatura, and later, in §§16 and 18, he deals with the necessity of unaccented upbeat appoggiaturas (which he calls 'passing appoggiaturas'). He gives examples of their use and of how to play them. In between, in §§10–15, he discusses long appoggiaturas from below; but, as already remarked, his son almost always wrote these out in full.

In §9 Leopold says that a short appoggiatura is to be played 'as rapidly as possible', and that 'the stress falls not on the appoggiatura, but on the principal note'. He does not mention whether the appoggiatura is to be played on or before the beat, but the context makes it clear that here he wants it on the beat, since in §16 he sums up what he has written: 'These were purely *Anschlag* appoggiaturas' (i.e. on the beat). He then discusses (in §17) 'passing' appoggiaturas, which are to be played unaccented and before the beat.

C. P. E. Bach also writes of wholly similar examples:

> It . . . is played so rapidly that the following note loses scarcely any of its length. (I, 2, *The Appoggiatura*, 13, p. 91.)

Now, however, in §17, Leopold Mozart adds an example which at first sight has exactly the same content as the first two examples under §9 (filling in descending thirds).

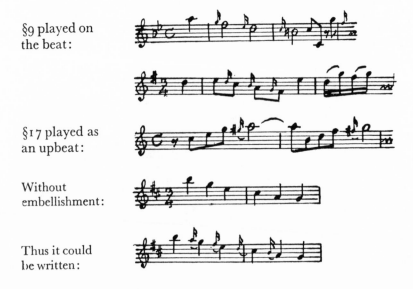

§9 played on the beat:

§17 played as an upbeat:

Without embellishment:

Thus it could be written:

But they are
played thus,
and also best
written so:

Thus it seems that Leopold Mozart still had a few difficulties with the notation of this theoretical innovation. However, he writes, as a commentary on the examples under §17:

> It is true, one could indicate the style by means of a little note, but it would look very unusual and strange. He who wishes to express it in print, sets it down in properly distributed notes.

Apart from this, in §17 he writes the appoggiaturas *before* the bar-line, as against §9, to show that these are to be upbeat appoggiaturas.* It would therefore be quite wrong to rely blindly on the example in §17 and play the appoggiaturas in the D major Rondo (K.485) as anticipations. These appoggiaturas are certainly to be played on the beat (cf. p. 74, last example), for a particular characteristic of Mozart's music is its 'continuity', its rhythmic flow and freedom from jerkiness. If in the opening bars of the D major Rondo Mozart had wanted anticipations, he would have added a further appoggiatura, in order to maintain the flow, perhaps like this:

He would also have written out the appoggiaturas, just as he did, for example, in the A major Symphony (K.201), where he made a clear distinction between written-out anticipations and appoggiaturas written small and played on the beat:

First movement, bar 105, first violins:

(written-out
upbeat
appoggiaturas)

bar 183, first violins:

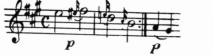

(semiquaver appoggiaturas on
the beat).

*W. A. Mozart never wrote appoggiaturas before the bar-line, as did his father in his example.

Finally, the variant in bar 54 of the D major Rondo is one more sign that he regarded these linking-notes as accented, not unaccented, passing-notes.

Opening, bars 3–4:

Codetta, bars 54–5:

In §18 Leopold Mozart says, furthermore, that one can add

passing appoggiaturas . . . with notes which ascend or descend by conjunct degrees, e.g.:

Without
embellishment:

The manner of
indicating how
to perform it:

Thus it is played,
and also best
written:

So, according to L. Mozart, the above example from the Concerto K.246 should be played as an anticipation, whereas the examples from the Sonata K.545 and the Concerto K.595 (under (c) and (d)) should be played on the beat (and unaccented).

As we see, there are differences of opinion as to the way unaccented short appoggiaturas should be played. A problem of this kind is certainly less interesting to the listener, who in most cases will notice hardly any difference between appoggiaturas on and before the beat, than to the performer, who even in these minor questions needs to know where he stands if he is to be able to concentrate on artistic form at a higher level.* This is probably also the reason why many textbooks and tutors attempt to dispose of all such questions by means of over-simple formulae.

The question here is simply whether one regards a short unaccented appoggiatura as an accented passing-note that has 'degenerated' (i.e. lost its

*In his book, *Toscanini* (New York, 1950), Howard Taubman says that throughout his life the Maestro wrestled with the sliding upward appoggiaturas in the basses at the opening of the Funeral March from the 'Eroica' Symphony.

accent), or as an 'undeveloped' (because very short) upbeat. Whereas some theorists have to this day not accepted Leopold Mozart's innovations, and insist that appoggiaturas should always be on the beat, practical musicians and theorists with a practical approach have always preferred to play them before the beat.

This is seen even in the table given by C. F. Rellstab (*Introduction for Pianists*, 1790).[73]

as it is written   as it is usually played   as it should be played

In his *Clavierschule* (second edition, 1802), Türk also advances an opinion similar to that of Rellstab (pp. 271–83). This is an understandable preference. If appoggiaturas are to be unaccented, then any musician's natural tendency is to play them as an upbeat—it is less trouble, and at first one will almost automatically play them in this way. Leopold Mozart's way of playing them goes against the grain for both performer and listener. For if an unaccented appoggiatura is played on the beat, there is a danger that in

the listener will hear not an appoggiatura played on the beat, but an accompaniment that comes in off the beat (early). It is all too easy to hear not (as intended)

but

All the same, in this case we cannot share the opinion of A. Beyschlag,[74] who regards this effect as grounds for saying that short appoggiaturas should not be played on the beat. On the contrary, much pleasure can be derived, especially in cantabile movements, from this delayed accent; the delay is quite slight, the appoggiatura being played very quickly, and it gives a true rubato—that is to say, an occasional slight veiling of the metre, which prevents any impression of a purely mechanical beat. Melodic feeling is always weakened by too close a tie-up with metre. If all unaccented appoggiaturas, single or compound, were played as anticipations, then the main melodic accents would always coincide with those resulting from the metre, and the result would be dry, inexpressive playing. of the kind that is unfortunately all too common. On the other hand, in passages of a markedly rhythmical character, such as march-like or dance-like movements, there is certainly no objection to playing these notes as anticipations; yet even here there are times when the accent is enhanced rather than weakened by a dissonant appoggiatura on the beat. In bar 22 of the first movement of the Sonata K.545 (our example gives the passage as we would play it):

the accompaniment is indeed so regular that the above-mentioned effect could not possibly occur. There is no definitive solution to the problem, 'to anticipate or not?', nor would one be desirable; but in the examples listed under (a) and (b) above, we mostly advocate anticipation, whereas those under (c) and (d) should mostly be played on the beat.

The following examples seem to show that Mozart himself often played appoggiaturas as anticipations: D minor Concerto (K.466), third movement, bars 64–6:

and 71:

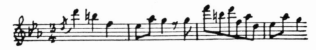

Here, for once, Mozart writes out a typical octave appoggiatura, obviously to emphasize its thematic relationship with the first solo in the first movement. Another example of a written-out anticipatory appoggiatura is in the C minor Concerto (K.491), first movement, first solo, bars 108 et seq.:

Here bars 3 and 4 are obviously a varied intensification of the first two bars. The semiquaver appoggiatura in bar 1 has broadened out and become an expressive quaver anacrusis to bar 3.

A minor Sonata (K.310), opening:

Before the recapitulation of this subject the appoggiatura D sharp is written out in the form of an anacrusic semiquaver:

Here various editors have added the original D sharp appoggiatura: this seems a crude misunderstanding of Mozart's abbreviation 'Da Capo 8 mesur'.

In the G major Violin Concerto (K.216), Mozart writes a (short) demi-semiquaver appoggiatura (bar 16 of the second movement); but in the corresponding passage in bar 39, which is exactly similar, there is a written-out anacrusic demisemiquaver, and this nicely proves that in this case Mozart wanted an anticipatory appoggiatura.

Mozart's notation in the third movement of the 'Hunt Quartet' (K.458), on the other hand, again seems to indicate performance on the beat.

A similar example where one must play the appoggiaturas on the beat is in the third movement of the C minor Sonata (K.457), bars 28–9 and corresponding passages:

In these cases the appoggiatura has to a large extent kept its character of accented passing-note, because the preceding note is repeated. In the Finale of the D major Sonata (K.284), Variation XI, bar 11, there is another example of an octave appoggiatura, which must obviously come on the beat:

Note, however, that this is a variant of bar 3, where the lower A is a part of the melody:

But octave appoggiaturas may often be treated as anticipations. In this case we recommend playing them as follows:

C minor Concerto (K.491), first movement, first solo, bar 100:

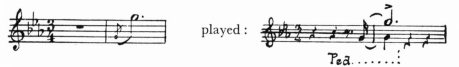

We find that to play the appoggiatura tenuto, at the same time pedalling it, is the best way of making clear the legato that extends over this octave.

Octave appoggiaturas must never be accented. Even in his earliest youth Mozart made a clear distinction between broken octaves with the lower note accented (*a*), and octave appoggiaturas with the upper note accented (*b*): as in the Variations on a Minuet by Fischer (K.179), Variation X, bar 5:

and Variation XI, bar 44:

We feel it is often more important for the sound to be full and smooth than for the upbeat to be separately perceptible. Thus in bar 40 of the Romanze from the D minor Concerto we do not advise playing the appoggiatura as an anticipation:

played in some such way:

This way of playing the bar gives the F of the melody more resonance, so that it can more easily be made to 'sing'. This kind of sustained melody note should be played with an attack like that of a bell, i.e. one should quit the key immediately after the (fairly energetic) attack, and keep the note sounding by means of the pedal.

Although an unaccented appoggiatura can often be made much shorter than an anacrusic semiquaver, we must expressly warn against coldly rattling off these grace-notes. They must always sound like part of the melody.

We have already mentioned that the length of appoggiaturas offers far fewer problems than their accentuation, and that Mozart mostly wrote the note values he wanted played. But at times he obviously indicated the duration of appoggiaturas inaccurately, either on purpose or by mistake.

Thus the length of quaver appoggiaturas seems not always to be exactly fixed. We have already mentioned the introduction to the Violin Sonata K.454, where Mozart (if only after the first performance) made an alteration in dark ink, changing the quaver appoggiaturas into semiquavers. In an older MS. of the variations on 'Unser Dummer Pöbel meint', bar 4 contains a semiquaver appoggiatura which in the later (final) MS. is a quaver. The voice part of the song 'Ein Veilchen' has quaver appoggiaturas in bar 10. To take this literally would produce intolerable clashes with the piano part:

With semiquaver appoggiaturas:

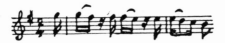

With quaver appoggiaturas (not recommended):

Here the only possible solution is to sing the appoggiaturas as semiquavers. Probably Mozart did not write semiquavers because then, as a result of the clash with the piano part, there would have been a great temptation to make the semiquaver appoggiaturas into anticipations, or to perform them as demisemiquavers. But the accentuation of the appoggiaturas is more important than their duration.

In the Andante of the C major Sonata (K.279) we would regard the quaver appoggiaturas in bars 1 and 43 as coming on the beat, and perhaps a semi-quaver long, for in his youth Mozart was apparently not very exact in indicating the difference of the lengths of his appoggiaturas.

Best played:

The semiquaver appoggiaturas in bar 21 of this movement may well be made short. To play them as quaver triplets would make the rhythm of the passage monotonous, but would not be incorrect.

In exceptional cases semiquaver appoggiaturas can be played rather longer. This is probably the case in the Finale of the B flat Concerto (K.238); in bar 4 Mozart wrote a quaver appoggiatura in the piano part, whereas in the otherwise identical reappearances of the bar he wrote semiquavers. But from the musical flow of the theme one can take it that Mozart can only have intended quaver appoggiaturas in this case.

(b) Vocal Appoggiaturas

A particular form of accented passing-note, with which every educated pianist should be familiar, is the one known as the 'vocal appoggiatura'. As it can also occur in instrumental music, it must be discussed here.

According to a tradition that lasted well into the nineteenth century, this type of accented passing-note is not sung as written. Bernhard Paumgartner writes:

> In Mozart's recitatives, arias and ensembles, the use of the vocal appoggia-tura must be regarded as absolutely indispensable and in Mozart there are many classic passages where failure to use an appoggiatura must be regarded as a crude offence against the style of the music. In Mozart's time, as before and for a long time after, this accented passing-note was used far more than even the most passionate present-day advocates of the appoggiatura might suppose.[75]

This type of appoggiatura is to be used, above all, when in a recitative (and also often in an aria) a phrase (or section) ends with two notes of the same pitch; in this case the first of the two is almost always sung a tone (or a semitone) higher than it is written.

The Marriage of Figaro, Act IV, recitative:

At 'momento' it would also be possible to introduce an upward appoggiatura. The melodic filling-out of the leap of a third, as at*, is particularly important, and it is impossible to excuse the misguided 'faithfulness to the text' that makes singers constantly sing such passages 'as written'.[76]

To show that in arias, too, this type of appoggiatura was clearly to be used (if more rarely), we take as an example Fiordiligi's aria from Act II of *Così fan tutte*, No. 25 (Rondo), bars 3–5 of the allegro moderato (and their later reprise). Here, according to the MS., the first violins are to play:

whereas the vocal part is written:

If, however, there are two notes of the same pitch following a downward leap of a fourth, then the first of them is sung a fourth higher than it is written:

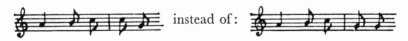

An example from the Act I Trio of *Così fan tutte* (bars 35–7) shows that, even over larger intervals, here the seventh, this kind of appoggiatura is still to be employed. Here the first violins play:

whereas the voices have:

sung:

O fuo-ri la spa-da

Well, out with your sword, then

spa-da

sword, then!

This appoggiatura develops out of the natural melody inherent in the language. If one translates the text as 'So out with your sword, then', it is incomparably more natural to give a musical emphasis to the word 'sword', just as it is wholly unnatural to sing the phrase 'as written', thus giving the main melodic emphasis to the words 'with your'. Naturally, it would not be a good idea to employ the appoggiatura whenever notes are repeated in a recitative. Sometimes this would have a disturbing effect, at others it might be a matter of taste; yet often the appoggiatura is necessary on musical grounds; in the latter cases, its omission either offends against a natural law of melodic writing, as in the formula:

or else results in faulty declamation, as in the example quoted from *Così fan tutte.*

In the eighteenth century the appoggiatura was often used in conjunction with other 'arbitrary' ornaments, i.e. those which could be added at will. A fine example of a decorated appoggiatura occurs in Figaro's famous aria:

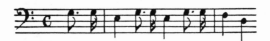

Naturally, the singer will follow the first violins:

first violins:

Figaro:

- ro - - so

Ko - - sen

play, lad

One important rule in performing appoggiaturas concerns places where the composer has indicated an appoggiatura by means of a small note; if a 'long' appoggiatura is placed in front of two notes of identical pitch, then the first of the two notes is in fact *replaced* by the appoggiatura, as in the Countess's Aria, Act II of *The Marriage of Figaro* (Cavatina, Act II, Scene 1):*

*In the Eulenburg score this appoggiatura is correctly resolved, being written out in normal notes.

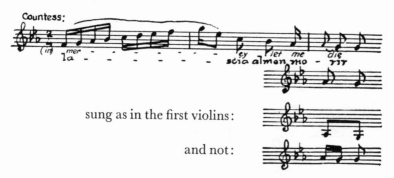

sung as in the first violins:

and not:

But the 'vocal appoggiatura' occurs not only in the vocal music, but often in instrumental works where there are passages of a recitative-like character. Thus we are firmly convinced that in the first movement of the G major Violin Concerto (K.216), bars 149–52 (a typical 'accompanied recitative'), appoggiaturas should be introduced.

Solo violin:

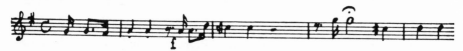

to be played as follows, despite the dissonance created in bar 152:

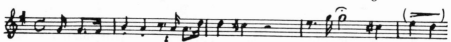

(cf. the wholly similar passage in the Minuet of the 'Haffner' Symphony (K.385), bars 13–16, where, however, Mozart wrote out the appoggiaturas presumably because he could not expect everyone in the orchestra to be equally familiar with this kind of ornamentation.)

Unfortunately, this passage is almost always played incorrectly, because most violinists who try to be 'faithful to the text' play everything 'as written'. In the Finale of the F major Piano Sonata (K.332) Mozart may have intended this kind of appoggiatura (bars 16 and 162):

played:

We base this reading on the next bar but one, where Mozart wrote out his appoggiatura (in this case resolving upward). One could also perhaps play:

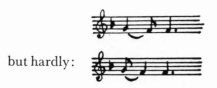

but hardly:

The fact that Mozart wrote out this kind of appoggiatura in the Finale of the C minor Piano Sonata (K.457) (bars 228 et seq.) is an almost improbable stroke of luck, since otherwise we should certainly have the pleasure of hearing the passage played as follows:

And if the solo subject of the D minor Concerto (K.466) came in an opera, it would nowadays be played as follows:

since Mozart would have written it:

The whole of contemporary theoretical literature confirms that there were rules for the introduction of appoggiaturas not written in the text. This eighteenth-century practice was the only reason why Mozart wrote his appoggiaturas as small notes, since otherwise his interpreters would have often added another (long) appoggiatura in front of the written-out one, as in (c) of the next example from Leopold Mozart's *Violinschule*, IX, §3:

(a)

is played thus:

(b)

It is true that all the descending appoggiaturas could be set down in large print and divided up within the bar. But if a violinist, who knows not that the appoggiatura is written out, or who is already accustomed to befrill every note, happens on such, how will it fare with melody as well as with harmony?

I will wager that such a violinist will add yet another long appoggiatura and will play it thus:

(c)

The form of vocal appoggiatura discussed on pp. 91–3 might explain the remarkable fact that in his instrumental works Mozart very often wrote semiquaver appoggiaturas before repeated notes, where, from the point of view of musical expression, he must have meant quavers. Violin Sonata in G (K.301), opening of first movement:

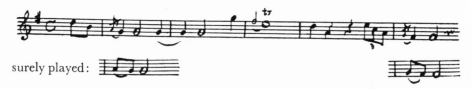

surely played:

If he had written the appoggiaturas as quavers, many players of the time would have played crotchets, as was then the practice.

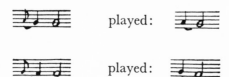

In the MS. of the final Variations of the D major Sonata (K.284), Variation XI reads:

Adagio

In the first edition, published by Torricella at Mozart's own instigation, most of the appoggiaturas are written out normally, and we find:

Adagio

*The slur is not in the MS.

Again, in the Finale of this movement the appoggiaturas must again surely be played as quavers:

(a)

(b)

This (b) is how they are written out in the first edition.

At the opening of the A minor Sonata (K.310) the appoggiaturas in bars 2 and 4 should similarly be played as quavers:

played:

This is how Mozart wrote out the appoggiaturas in bars 10 and 12.

Similarly, in the first movement of the *Kleine Nachtmusik*, bars 11 and 12:

would possibly be played:

Here we must confess that we have got used to the usual way of playing these bars—with a 'Scotch snap' rhythm—and find it very attractive.

As far as we can see, there can be no general solution to the problem of how to play semiquaver appoggiaturas before repeated crotchets. It is indeed true that Mozart usually wrote upward-resolving appoggiaturas not as ornaments but in normal notes, and if we examine some of these cases we may conclude that he did in fact often intend a 'Scotch snap', i.e. accented semi-quaver appoggiaturas.

In the G major Concerto (K.453), first movement, bars 97 et seq., we find the following rhythm:

and in the C major Concerto (K.246), first movement, bars 64 et seq.:

Piano

This seems to justify the assumption that in the G major Violin Concerto, in the first violin solo, he wanted the same rhythm:

i.e. the first beat of bar 2 is: not:

for otherwise he could as well have written out the quavers in bar 2 as in bar 3. However, one must be careful not to draw over-subtle conclusions. Composers have often written similar ideas in different ways, and in most cases they probably meant nothing at all by it.

(c) Compound Appoggiaturas

Mozart usually treated compound appoggiaturas like unaccented single ones. Here again there is no general answer to the question whether or not they should be anticipations. C. F. Rellstab's[77] table, already quoted, shows that in this respect the second half of the eighteenth century was a time of transition.

As early as J. P. Milchmeyer's *Die wahre Art das Pianoforte zu spielen* ('The True Way to play the Pianoforte', which appeared in 1797), anticipation is already unreservedly advocated:

(quoted in Beyschlag, *Die Ornamentik in der Musik*, second edition, Leipzig, 1953, p. 177). Milchmeyer's innovation was energetically opposed by Türk in the second edition of his *Clavierschule* (1802). It is particularly interesting that to refute Milchmeyer, Türk draws on examples from piano works by Haydn and Mozart (p. 272, from Mozart's Variations for Piano (K.264), Variation VIII, bar 24):

(originally an octave lower)

In this case anticipation would give consecutive octaves A–G. The F sharp must therefore be played on the beat and lightly accented.

cf. also pp. 271–2 (§§281, 282).

Since theory usually lags a whole generation behind practice, Milchmeyer's views could in many cases apply to Mozart's music. But in general we would recommend Leopold Mozart's 'compromise solution'—playing short appoggiaturas without an accent, but on the beat. This has a good effect melodically, for the very reason that the accent does not coincide with the strict metre of the accompaniment. Thus a true rubato results. We particularly recommend playing the ornament in this way when Mozart consciously writes in an 'old-fashioned' style.

In the second movement of the Concerto K.453 there is an *Überwurf*, an ornament very popular in the generation before Mozart, but one which he used on few other occasions:

Here we advocate playing the ornament on the beat:

The Andante of the F major Sonata (K.533) is written in three strict parts. In bar 3 and corresponding passages we recommend playing the left-hand compound appoggiatura on the beat, but accenting the main note, so that the ornament is not too unwieldy. In the recapitulation this ornament is written as follows in the first edition:

This seems to support our views. (Moreover, the accented passing-note B, moving to C, only has its full effect if played on the beat.) Similarly, the ornament in the last bar of the Andante of the Concerto K.450 must surely be played on the beat. Leopold Mozart calls all compound appoggiaturas of this kind (including the turn when placed above the note) *mordente*:

> By mordent is meant the two, three or more little notes which quite quickly and quietly, so to speak, grasp at the principal note and vanish at once, so that the principal note only is heard strongly.[78]

There is a remarkable ornament in the second movement of the E flat Concerto (K.271), bars 62 and 68:

To maintain the sequence this would probably have to be played:

The ornament in the eighth bar of the Andante from the E flat Concerto (K.482) is very reminiscent of the baroque 'slide' (*Schleifer*). Here again we would recommend playing it on the beat:

played:

Against the B flat the C creates a dissonance which is very harsh for its time, and the effect of the ornament is in a sense to ease its passage into the listener's consciousness. In most of Mozart's earlier works it will also be right to play such ornaments on the beat, for example in the C major Sonata (K.279), Andante, bars 1, 11, 12, 13.

II. ARPEGGIOS

Mozart indicates arpeggios by a transverse stroke, not by the wavy line nowadays customary. This notation is rightly modernized in all present-day editions.

If the right hand has an arpeggio or an arpeggio-like ornament against a chord or held note in the left hand, we believe that the lowest note of the arpeggio should coincide with the lower part.

One example occurs in the Rondo K.494, bar 59; another is bar 1 of the Minuet from the A major Sonata (K.331):

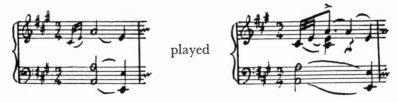

We also recommend this latter reading in bar 11 of the Minuet.

The wide arpeggio in the C minor Concerto (bars 250 and 267 of the Finale) should also be played on the beat:

On the other hand, left-hand arpeggios should often be played as anticipations, as, for example, in the 'Rondo alla Turca' of the A major Sonata (K.331). If both hands have arpeggios simultaneously, as in bar 88 of the first movement of the B flat Concerto (K.595), the ornaments should again be anticipations. (The best way to pedal this passage is to start half a bar ahead and to 'fling' the hands at the top of the arpeggio, which will go on sounding because the pedal is down.)

Among the theorists, J. P. Milchmeyer (1797) advocates playing arpeggios as anticipations, whereas most of the older theorists say they should come on the beat. To prove that arpeggios should not be anticipated, Türk quotes two instructive examples from Mozart's violin sonatas:

Violin Sonata in G major (K.379), first movement, bars 19–20:

Of this passage Türk writes (*Clavierschule*, p. 272):

> Furthermore it would often not even be possible to play this in the way demanded by Milchmeyer. . . . For who could play the broken chord in the time left by the notes immediately before it? The 'forte' added here also shows that the D is to come on the strong beat.

As a second example, Türk quotes bar 98 from the second movement of the B flat Violin Sonata (K.454):

wrongly played (Türk, p. 272).

It is self-evident that the inverted B flat chord must not be anticipated. Thus the bottom D should sound simultaneously with the F in the top part.

On this point Mozart is perhaps less dogmatic than his disciple, Türk. For in the second movement of the A minor Sonata (K.310) he writes out an *anticipatory* arpeggio which, according to Türk, would be 'wrong':

 instead of

III. TURNS

One very frequent ornament in Mozart is the turn: ∿. In studying how to play the turn, it is very useful to know that Mozart often wrote it in the form of compound appoggiaturas or even in normal notes, e.g. in the first piano solo of the B flat Concerto (K.595), first movement, bar 74, or the second bar of the Finale of the E flat Concerto (K.482), etc.

(a) *The Turn Immediately Over a Note*

If the turn is written over a note, then, according to the old rule, it will start with the next note above, thus consisting of three notes, and will be played on the beat. Finale of the B flat Violin Sonata (K.378) opening:

played:

Allegro of the G major Violin Sonata (K.379) opening:

played:

Mozart hardly ever marked any accidentals within a turn. But it is obvious that in major keys the lowest note will be sharpened whenever there is a turn on the dominant, and usually whenever there is one on the mediant. In minor keys one will sharpen the lowest note of a turn on the tonic, and often also of a turn on the subdominant or dominant.

In a quicker tempo, as in the Romanze from the D minor Concerto, bar 21, the turn plus main note will produce four even notes* (here demisemiquavers).

One often hears the turn played as a quintuplet starting on the main note, but old textbooks show that this cannot be justified and it is certainly incorrect stylistically.

Wrong:

*On this point, cf. Schenker, *Ein Beitrag zur Ornamentik*.

However, it is often better to play the turn as an anticipation, particularly when the rhythm necessitates a clear accent on the main note. This is so, for instance, in the Finale of the Concerto K.450, bars 113–17.

played:

The staccato dots over the ornamented notes are authentic and occur even in the first bars of the movement. If one were to play the turns like those in the preceding example:

wrong

this would give the impression of a legato connecting the turn with the succeeding C. But as Mozart indicates that the notes should be separated, the turn must be slightly anticipated.

In the Finale of the E flat Concerto (K.482), bar 180, the main note's rhythmic accent makes anticipation necessary:

played:

To play this passage:

would not sound well.

In the Andante of the same concerto (bar 33) there is a turn written out in small notes:

Here we suggest anticipation:

But a few bars later, the turn seems more satisfying when played on the beat:

The different ways of playing the turn in the last two examples result from the fact that the turn comes at a different point within the metre.

If a group of three small notes occur before a strong beat, they are often the equivalent of a 'turn between two notes' (see later, p. 104). This is shown very clearly by a passage from the first movement of the Piano-duet Sonata (K.521), bar 92:

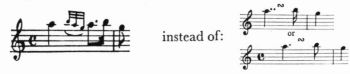

In the theme of the Finale from the G major Trio (K.496) we feel anticipation is more appropriate:

In Variation VIII of the Variations K.613 (on 'Ein Weib ist das herr-lichste Ding') the turn could indeed be played on the beat:

but we believe that if Mozart had wanted this, he would have written out the ornament in normal notes, or in the form ∿, instead of notating it:

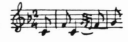

Finally, we should mention another possible way of playing the turn, not mentioned in any textbook and yet often the most elegant solution (also in Beethoven)—a compromise between anticipation and playing on the beat.

This is how we recommend playing the very difficult turns in the flute part of the Concerto K.595, third movement, bars 122 and 261. The advantages are obvious; the figure slips lightly over the bar-line and at the same time the dotted rhythm is preserved:

played:

Fitting these figures into the metrical scheme is less crucial than ensuring that they remain unaccented—they should slip gently on to the ensuing 'main' note, smoothing its path.

In a few exceptional cases it seems right to begin on the main note:

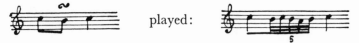

played:

The violins (and basses) of modern orchestras often play the turns

in bars 38 et seq. of the Andante of the *Kleine Nachtmusik* in the following way:

We find this quite acceptable. The historically correct way would be:

It is often impossible to determine exactly whether a turn should be over or after a note. In such doubtful cases we must once again rely on our musical taste. In bar 113 of the C minor Fantasia (K.475), for instance, we should like to think that the turn should be a little further to the right (unfortunately, it is impossible to check against Mozart's MS.), in order to avoid repeating the note B flat, and to make the melodic step of a third clearer:

Again, in the Andante of the E flat Concerto (K.482), bars 153 and 154, this version appeals to us more:[79]

In this connection, we should mention an ornament which is very rarely found in Mozart—namely, the second and third turns in bars 107–8 of the second movement of the E flat Concerto (K.449):

Leopold Mozart calls this ornament a 'half-trill' and, according to him, it should be played before the beat.

(b) The Turn Between Two Notes

If a turn is between two notes, then it always consists of four notes and is usually played as late as possible.

In slow tempi this is played:

(cf. opening of the second movement of the D major Sonata (K.576), where Mozart wrote out this ornament.)

At quicker tempi it is played:

or

At very quick tempi:

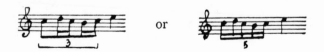

or

(c) The Turn After a Dotted Note

When a turn comes after a dotted note it is played before the dot is reached:

played: 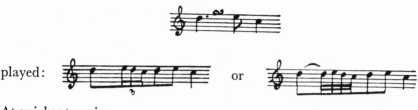 or

At quicker tempi:

This applies equally when Mozart wrote a turn in small notes, as in bar 61 of the first movement of the Two-piano Concerto (K.365):

 played

Adagio of the F major Sonata (K.332), opening:

played: or

In many cases one can also consider making the dotted rhythm sharper:

(cf. pp. 47–9.)

This way of playing the turn after a dotted note is supported by rules which are found in all the contemporary theoretical literature. It is played in this way because the succeeding note must not be accented, as would inevitably happen if it were immediately preceded by the turn. This rule is found, for example, in Türk's *Klavierschule* (1789).

If a dotted crotchet is followed by two semiquavers there are two possible ways to play the turn:

Romanze from the D minor Concerto, bar 4:

One cannot say with any certainty that either of these is exclusively right, but we believe that Mozart may have preferred version (*a*), since in bar 7 of the 'Minore' of the F major Rondo (K.494) he wrote out this ornament in normal notes. Of the two versions, this is the more placid, and the clearer: on the other hand, it can easily break up the phrase, if the quaver is unduly stressed after the triplets. Version (*b*), which is often preferred by present-day performers, only sounds well when the ornament is played a good deal more lightly than the succeeding notes. Otherwise the final semiquavers lose clarity and the listener may be given a wrong impression of the rhythm:

In the middle section of the Andante from the D major Concerto (K.451) we find:

Mozart sent his sister a variant of this passage, with ornaments:

Here one will obviously play:

In the Larghetto of the C minor Concerto (K.491), bar 25, the more placid version is again preferable:

In the Andantino of the E flat Concerto (K.449), on the other hand, version (*b*) may be considered, to avoid rhythmic repetition:

may be played:

or else (as the rule prescribes):

cf. also the notation of bar 107 of the same movement, where version (*b*) is possible:

In bar 13 of the Adagio variation (V) from the A major Sonata (K.331) version (*b*) is perhaps the more likely:

One could, alternatively, play this passage with a double-dotted quaver and demisemiquaver, by analogy with the next bar:

After a double-dotted note the following version is advisable:

or

In the next example Mozart's notation shows how the turn should be played (Sonata K.311, third movement, bar 159 (and also bar 161):

Mozart took remarkable pains to attain clarity of notation in this movement. In bars 21 and 23 he wrote:

and, clearest of all, in bar 163:

Obviously all three ways of notation mean the same.[80]

Finally, we should say that in playing turns one should aim at suppleness and liveliness of expression. One's fingers must react with lightning speed. For this reason the fingering 4313, 4212 or 4321 (rather than 4323) should be used wherever possible.

IV. TRILLS

(a) Beginnings of Trills

Nowadays there are two clear schools of thought about how to begin a trill: the 'unprepared' and 'prepared' schools. The 'unprepared' school begin every trill on the note that carries the trill-sign; their opponents insist that every trill must begin on the note above ('upper auxiliary').

So what do these two kinds of trill look like?

A prepared trill will be written:

according to eighteenth-century practice, without an initial appoggiatura:

according to modern notation:

played:

and is distinguished by a certain acuity and brilliance. It satisfies old-fashioned theorists because it can be analysed as a succession of accented passing-notes and their resolutions:

Its disadvantage is that it can obscure the flow of the melody, since it accents the upper auxiliary (E in the example quoted). For instance, in a rising scale it will anticipate the succeeding note, and this can often rob a line of some of its sense of direction.

The unprepared trill:

does, on the other hand, make the main note (here the D) quite unmistakable, and this eases matters for the listener. But it has a duller effect than a prepared trill, because one misses the acuity of the accented dissonance.

If one uncritically applies to Mozart the theoretical maxims of the second half of the eighteenth century, there is no problem about how to begin the trill: they are unanimously in favour of preparation. As we have said, it was exactly during the second half of the eighteenth century that a yawning gap existed between theory and practice; indeed the theorists are not wholly consistent. Tartini (1692–1770), in a letter, advocates beginning the trill on the main note, but in his *Trattato delle appoggiature* he is in favour of the upper auxiliary.[81] J. G. Albrechtsberger, a contemporary of Haydn, born in 1736, came down in favour of beginning on the main note (this was not known before):

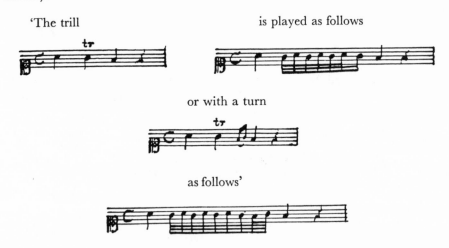

(Piano tutor 'Anfangsgründe der Klavierkunst',[82] which is still in MS.)

According to Leopold Mozart's *Violinschule*, however, the trill in the above example would have to be played:

Albrechtsberger gives only this one example of a trill. (Note that it is given as a rule, not as an exception!) The first printed piano tutor to make the same demand is that of J. N. Hummel, which appeared in 1828. Though Hummel makes out that his rule is completely new, this is doubtless a considerable exaggeration. But the habit of beginning trills on the main note did not become widespread until Czerny, the great piano teacher, came out in its favour in his *Klavierschule*, op. 500, which appeared in 1840. By about 1900 all pianists started their trills on the main note.

Turning from theory to Mozart's works, we find many passages where, in our opinion, one can only begin a trill on the main note. But we feel that these examples, which we shall give later, by no means prove clearly that Mozart began all his trills in this way.* There are numerous cases in which it seems more appropriate to begin on the upper auxiliary. Apart from these, there are very many 'neutral' cases, where either is possible. Much depends on which version we regard as the rule, and which as the exception. So there seems to be no general solution to the problem of the trill, short of the discovery of contemporary evidence of Mozart's own execution of 'trills'.

---

*Nor does the fact that Ernst Pauer, a pupil of W. A. Mozart, junior (1791–1844), is said to have begun all trills on the main note (Beyschlag, op. cit., p. 177). Two generations are too great a lapse of time when the correctness of a tradition is in question. Mozart's son never knew his father at all!

Shortly before this book went to press we were able to listen to an eighteenth-century barrel-organ playing K.616 (see above p. 55). An interesting light is shed on this problem by the way the piece was played. Most of the trills including the first one start with the main note. The fact that this piece was originally composed for a barrel-organ indicates that in all probability this was Mozart's intention. Since there were also a few trills starting with the upper note, our theory, that this was a time of transition and that there was a certain freedom of execution allowed, seems to be confirmed. It should be borne in mind that manufacturers of barrel-organs obviously intended to reproduce a live performance. This barrel-organ, for instance, follows the text most accurately, playing strictly in time yet adding some delicate rubato in the passage-work.

In the following (numerous) cases it seems right to begin the trill on the main note.

(*a*) When in a legato the trill is preceded by the next note above.

1. Two-piano Concerto (K.365), first movement, bar 154:

2. Variations on 'Salve tu, Domine' (K.398), Variation V, bars 11–12:

3. Variations on a Minuet by Duport (K.573), coda:

4. B flat Concerto (K.595), first movement, bar 107 (and 108, 270, 272):

(*b*) When the trill is preceded by three rising or falling notes like a 'slide'. This anacrusic figure grew out of the baroque ornaments C𝅘𝅥𝅮 and C𝅘𝅥𝅮.

1. B flat Sonata (K.333), third movement, bar 200:

2. D major Rondo (K.485), bar 52 (and 135):

played approximately:

3. Variations on 'Come un' agnello' (K.460) (454a), cadenza before the Adagio variation:

(Note the imitation of the initial motive!)

4. Close of the original cadenza for the third movement of the B flat Concerto (K.450):

(c) When the trill is on a dissonant note.

1. E flat Concerto (K.482), second movement, bar 167 (also in 151 and 173 of the same movement):

The friction of the A flat with the suspended G must, of course, be preserved. To begin this trill on the upper auxiliary would have exactly the result which eighteenth-century theory wished to avoid—the accented dissonance would become an unaccented changing-note.

2. Original cadenza for the first movement of the B flat Concerto (K.450):

(d) In trills in the bass. Here the function of the bass as root of the harmony might suffer if one began the trill on the upper auxiliary.*

1. E flat Concerto (K.482), second movement, bar 149 (165, 171). Here case (c) also applies.

2. Variation V of the Variations on 'Salve tu, Domine' (K.398), bars 12–23. See second example under (a) above.

(e) In trills at the end of rising scales.

1. Opening of the original cadenza for the first movement of the Concerto K.365.

*There are organ toccatas by J. S. Bach with written-out trills in the bass; these begin on the main note, probably for the reason given here; the effect of the harmonic root is more important than the charm characteristic of a trill starting on the upper auxiliary.

2. Two-piano Concerto (K.365), third movement, bar 137. Here another factor enters in—Mozart's genius in writing for the piano. To begin the trill on the D would be extraordinarily unpianistic and difficult.

(fingering by the authors).

(*f*) When the trill is preceded by the same note, as a sharply-attacked anacrusis:

1. F major Concerto (K.459), third movement, original cadenza, bar 40. (Also in the C major Concerto (K.467), first movement, bar 382):

If one began this trill on the upper auxiliary the impression would be of an unprepared trill starting a semiquaver too soon.

2. C minor Sonata (K.457), first movement, bars 2, 6, etc.

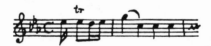

Mozart was fond of these sharply attacked anacruses. (Cf. the two B flats in the first example given on p. 112). But our reading is controversial. Comparing the first violin motif from bars 63–6 of the first movement of the E flat Concerto (K.449) and the notation of the same motive in the original cadenza, two explanations are possible: either the notation in the cadenza is a deliberate variation, or it indicates an easier (shorter) version of the trill, which would then, however, have to begin on the upper auxiliary.

First violin:

Original piano cadenza:

(*g*) In chains of trills, e.g. in the second movement of the Concerto K.482, bars 151–2, 173–6.

To start on the upper auxiliary would obscure the chromatic progression, since in each case there would be two trills beginning on the same note. Case (*c*) also applies here.

(*h*) In the formula

In allegro movements it is possible to play, at most, three notes at such points, if the semiquavers are played in time, as in the second subject of the first movement of the F major Sonata (K.533).

(*i*) Finally, in a number of special cases that are hard to classify:

1. Two-piano Concerto K.365, second movement, bars 47 et seq.

As so often in this concerto, the second piano here (bar 48) 'hands over' the note A flat to the first piano. If the first piano were to begin the trill on the B flat above, the result would be a dissonance which would sound as if someone had made a mistake.

2. Variations on 'Come un' agnello' (K.460 (454a)), Variation VII:

Here it would seem plausible to begin the trill on the upper auxiliary, but for the fact that there has already been a note-repetition in the middle of this run. As it is, the fourteenth and twenty-eighth notes are given a sharp attack and repeated, while the climactic E is reserved for the next bar.

Since there are so many examples of this kind, we can at least deduce that Mozart had a certain preference for unprepared trills. On the other hand, one should not try to build on the fact that in a very few cases he added a short appoggiatura before a trill. Bar 59 of the first movement of the A major Symphony (K.201) is informative in this respect. The first and second violins trill in octaves; in the first violins Mozart has added a short appoggiatura, but not in the seconds! Nor do the first violins have an appoggiatura in any of the subsequent corresponding passages. The only reasonable explanation of this passage is that, although it was obvious that the trills were to begin on the upper auxiliary, Mozart wanted to confirm this explicitly on the first occasion when the trills occurred.

In other passages of this kind one must consider, above all, the possibility of an accented passing-note ('accento con trillo') in front of the trill:

First movement of the B flat Concerto (K.238), bars 47–8 (and corresponding passages):

Second movement of the E flat Concerto (K.271), bar 35:

(Quoted as in the Eulenburg edition. In the Peters edition of this and corresponding passages the appoggiatura is a semiquaver.) Second movement of the C major Concerto (K.246), bars 38 and 104:

Bar 38:

Bar 104:

It is remarkable that these appoggiaturas before trills occur only in works from Mozart's youth (until about 1777). They occasionally appear in late editions of his later works, but here they almost always prove to be longer appoggiaturas that have been read incorrectly, or else arbitrary editorial editions.[83]

We ourselves were greatly influenced over the years by hearing unprepared trills in Mozart performances by great pianists of an older generation; it is well known that habit carries greater conviction than the most watertight arguments. There was a time when we thought it right to begin all trills on the main note. But there is really no reason to go against the general principles of the eighteenth century in the matter of cadential trills.

According to eighteenth-century textbooks this would have been played to give the following harmonic scheme:

And surely it is more illuminating to play accented passing-notes than the unaccented changing-notes that result if one adheres to the nineteenth-century harmonic scheme:

It is interesting that the majority of nineteenth-century instruction books for string players do not show this swing toward unprepared trills. This makes us think that pianists could learn much from good string players. Listening keenly to such performers, one notices that usually they do not accent the upper auxiliary note at the beginning of the trill, but play it as an anacrusis. This seems an inspired compromise; the accent can fall on the main note, but the preceding upper auxiliary allows the trill to begin easily and smoothly. The strings of the Casals Festival Orchestra, for instance, play the first subject of the Finale of the Sinfonia Concertante (K.364), written:

as follows:

However, a pianist will find it almost impossible to flick off the short appoggiatura in this way, when the trill is so short, because of the greater inertia of his instrument's mechanism. When a passage of this kind occurs in the piano works, one should omit the appoggiatura; but when the trill is longer there is no difficulty about fitting the appoggiatura in, and 'it makes a good effect'. Of the three possible ways to play the closing trill in the next example, (b) or (c) will usually be preferable:

But when a trill begins a passage, as in the first piano entry of the Two-piano Concerto K.365, it is best to begin it on the main note.

In the following cases we recommend beginning the trill on the upper auxiliary.

(*a*) If in a melodic run a trill is preceded by the same note (this should not be confused with (*f*) mentioned above).

1. E flat Concerto (K.482), first movement, bars 83–4:

played:

In this case there is another reason for beginning the trill on the upper auxiliary—to ensure the dissonant diminished octave B natural–B flat.

2. Three-piano Concerto K.242, first movement, bar 237:

and bar 243:

Also the third movement of the G major Concerto (K.453), bar 169, but not in the fourth bar of the G minor Piano quartet (K.478): here the note-repetition across the bar-line has a thematic significance, and, moreover, the trill is on a dissonant note (accented passing-note).

(*b*) In a frequently occurring formula which often appears in quick movements when a trill is marked over a quaver upbeat.

1. Three- (or Two-) piano Concerto in F (K.242), first movement, bars 145 et seq.:

played:

or:

2. Two-piano Concerto K.365, first movement, bar 64 (and 281):

played:

3. C major Concerto (K.467), third movement, bars 120 et seq.:

played:

In these cases it would be hard even to fit in quintuplets. If, however, these 'tr' markings occur in the course of rising stepwise motion, and are not over isolated upbeat notes, e.g. in the third movement of the Concerto K.456, bar 77, then we should for once prefer an unprepared trill, so as to make the melodic course clearer.

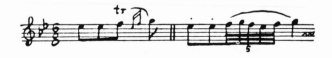

In cases 2 and 3, the trill is played exactly as if it were a turn. The two markings were often interchanged in Mozart's time, particularly in printed editions. In the Finale of the 'Jupiter' Symphony, Mozart for once makes a mistake and writes ∼ instead of *tr* (bar 61). This also applies to the notation of bar 98 of the first movement of the Concerto K.453, where the piano's trills must obviously be played in the same way as the figures on the first violins (and bassoon).

As for how to play trills: naturally, Mozart's trills must usually be played with great sparkle and as rapidly as possible. It is only in the case of long trills in Andante and Adagio movements that one may sometimes begin a little slower, for the sake of expressiveness, and then gradually make the trill quicker, or possibly slow it down a little toward the end. But these two ways of playing trills can all too easily sound affected, and this makes us recommend the greatest caution in varying the speed of one's trills. It is also obvious that trills should be played as clearly and evenly as possible. Speed must on no account mean a loss of precision. Mozart's remarks about the singer Mlle. Kaiser bear this out:

> She still takes her trills slowly and I am very glad. They will be all the truer and clearer when later on she wants to trill more rapidly, as it is always easier to do them quickly in any case.*

In playing most trills we find it indispensable to make a slight build-up or a slight diminuendo, according to the character of the passage. As regards touch, there is a subtle but perfectly audible distinction between the virtuoso 'fluttering' staccato trill and the expressive legato trill. The one is achieved by 'throwing' the fingers from the knuckles, whereas in the other the fingertips never leave the keys. And indeed the mechanism of the modern piano makes it possible to play the same note again before the damper falls back on to the string, so that one can 'tie' a note to itself.

(b) Endings of Trills

Mozart's trills are usually written to end with a turn. It is often highly

*In a letter to his father, 2nd October 1777.

advisable to play one, even when it is not written.* For example, in the theme of the variations from the G major Violin Sonata (K.379):

In the MS. score of the B flat Concerto (K.238) there is not a single final turn written after any of the numerous trills in the first movement. It would be quite unmusical to play all these trills without a final turn.

But here again there is obviously a limit to the degree of artistic freedom left the interpreter. According to an old rule, one can best omit the final turn in descending stepwise motion, e.g. in bar 3 of the second movement of the E minor Violin Sonata (K.304),[84]

played:

Also in the second movement of the Sonata K.533, bar 4:

(Text as in the Hoffmeister first edition. Later editors have falsified this trill marking, changing it to ∿, which would here be equivalent to a short *tr* with a final turn.)

If a trill without final turn occurs in an ascending line, then one must 'cut off' the trill in time, to leave the course of the melody clear, as in bar 152 of the second movement of the E flat Concerto (K.482):

played:

*This rule, which is based on most contemporary theoretical literature, should also be applied to Beethoven, for whom this unwritten turn was often self-evident. For example, in the first movement of the B flat Piano Trio, op. 97, he only wrote turns when they contained an accidental (natural sign or sharp).

But many artists add a final turn here, and this can also be justified:

C. P. E. Bach said that in such cases it was a moot point whether the short notes after the trill should be regarded as a kind of final turn, in which case one should refrain from also adding a normal turn (*Versuch*, 2/III, §13).

There are several possible ways to play the second bar of the C major Sonata (K.330):

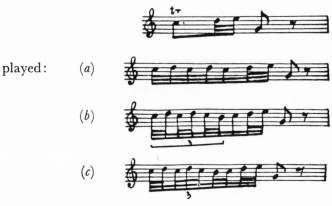

(*c*) appeals to us least, but is not incorrect.

(*c*) The Half-shake (Pralltriller)

Mozart's notation does not distinguish between trills and half-shakes. The marking ∿ is extremely rare in his works (e.g. in the MS. of the Quintet for piano and wind (K.452), first movement, bars 65–7 and 120), and when it occurs in printed editions it is almost always found to be a trill that has been read wrongly. (Mozart often wrote the letters *tr* so hastily that they do indeed look almost like a ∿.)

Thus one has to tell, from the particular trill concerned, whether it is an ordinary trill or a half-shake, and this is not so difficult. A half-shake should simply be played whenever there is no time to play a full trill. It can be played in the following ways:

(*a*) Prepared:

This corresponds to Leopold Mozart's *trilleto* (*Violinschule*, 1787 edition, X §20).

(*b*) Unprepared:

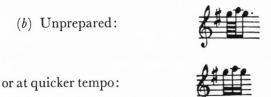

or at quicker tempo:

Version (*b*) is advocated by Marpurg (Tab. 5, No. 1) and Türk (pp. 251 and 273—*Schneller**) among the theorists. Here the first note of the half-shake is to be accented, e.g. in bar 8 of the Finale of the E major piano Trio (K. 542).

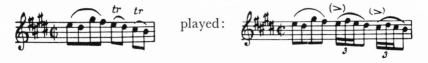

played:

Here a version (*a*) would hardly be feasible technically, and this is enough to make us prefer version (*b*).

In the frequent formula  we recommend making an antici-

pation (what Türk called the *Schneller*), e.g. in the Finale of the Two-piano Sonata K.448, the coda of the Variations on a Minuet by Duport (K.573), the original cadenza for the A major Concerto (K.488) or bar 99 of the first movement of the B flat Concerto (K.595) (and the corresponding place in bar 262):

This is because to play the ornament any other way would disturb the even flow of the semiquaver figure.

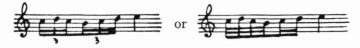   or

alters the original semiquaver rhythm.

However, in such cases one can also play a short appoggiatura instead of the half-shake, and to the best of our knowledge nobody has so far pointed

---

* *Translator's Note:* The *Schneller* (which Robert Donington translates as 'snap' in the article on Ornaments in the fifth edition of *Grove*) was an upper (inverted) mordent, i.e. main note–note above–main note. It differed from the half-shake (*Pralltriller*) in that the latter adds another note (the upper auxiliary) at the beginning.

this out. There are various examples to show that Mozart at times wrote *tr*
when he obviously meant only an appoggiatura, as for example in the Variations on a Minuet by Duport (K.573), last bar but one of Variation IX. Here
there is an appoggiatura. In the immediately ensuing coda, where the same
motive is sequentially developed, there is a *tr*: but it is out of the question to
play this same passage in two different ways. In the A minor Sonata (K.310),
second movement, bar 12, the two last *tr* are unplayable, even as *Schneller*.
But if they are played as appoggiaturas, there results a wholly Mozartean
line, which is identical with the run at the end of the second movement·of the
Piano-duet Sonata (K.521), bar 93. In the latter passage Mozart wrote
appoggiaturas. There is a third example of a trill played as an appoggiatura
in the Finale of the E flat Concerto (K.482), where in bar 573 there is a *tr*,
and in bar 73 (otherwise an unaltered repetition) an appoggiatura.

In the formula , or in slow movements

a half-shake is again usually intended.

G major Concerto (K.453), first movement, bar 1:

played:

or as an anticipation (but this sounds less
well than playing on the beat):

or, best of all, starting on the note above:

In the original cadenza, the Eulenburg and *A.M.A.* editions wrongly
give a final turn. We were able to inspect the MS. of this cadenza, and found
that Mozart did not write a single final turn.
However, in the Andante of the C major Sonata (K.330), bar 15, a genuine
trill seems to be intended:

played:

or:

Also in bar 34 of the second movement of the Concerto K.414:

We believe that in Mozart half-shakes usually begin on the main note. However, there are three possible ways to play the delightful passage from the first movement of the Three-piano Concerto (K.242):

either: (a)

(b)

this corresponds to Leopold Mozart's *trilleto*;

or   (c)

All three sound charming, and all three could certainly be defended on stylistic grounds. Here, much depends on the mechanism of the piano that is used, and on how strong and nimble a particular pianist's fingers are. Version (a) played cleanly will always sound better than (c) played sloppily.

Clearly the problems touched on in this chapter are often very difficult to solve, and demand a great deal of musical sensitivity as well as historical knowledge. Textbooks or practical editions of Mozart often contain summary tables and rules, devised to give an infallible answer to all problems that could arise. It is certainly very convenient for a performer to be able to play ornaments in a standard way, but unfortunately it is often wrong, as we have tried to show. Even if students adhere to these over-simplifying 'rules', a responsible artist will not, must not, find them sufficient!

Chapter Five

THE URTEXT PROBLEM

FOR the beginner at the piano, laboriously seeking out the notes and glad if he can find them, the problem 'Which edition to choose?' hardly yet exists. Only when he is capable of observing tempo and performing indications, and of playing every staccato or legato in the correct way, will he gradually discover that even the tiniest grace-note expresses the composer's personality. And at this stage he should be faced by the question of finding a text that will really reproduce all the minute details of the composer's notation.

The least we can do for a great master such as Mozart is to try to find out his intentions even in the smallest points. An artist does not merely play for the public, who in any case rarely appreciate the extreme subtleties of interpretation and usually have only an intuitive feeling whether something has or has not been played correctly. Aware of his responsibility to the composer and to the whole of our musical culture, the artist is prompted to observe with the utmost exactness the text handed down to him, irrespective of whether anyone praises him for it. This sense of responsibility is, in the last analysis, what distinguishes a true artist from a charlatan who is concerned only with success.

Every musician at some time reaches the point when he starts to feel uneasy about an edition which he has previously accepted uncritically; perhaps an articulation-marking will strike him as odd, or a forte in a passage where he feels he should play softly; it may have been added by some great man such as Arthur Schnabel or Hans von Bülow, whom he has till then respected as infallible—or it may be an obvious printer's error. The natural thing for him to do is to resolve his doubts by consulting other editions; and now he soon makes a depressing discovery. Printed editions of the same work often contradict each other in even the most important questions, and it is almost incredible to see what has been done to a great composer's text, even by such famous editors as Czerny, Liszt, Bülow, Köhler, Saint-Saëns, Ruthardt and others. In Czerny's edition of the B flat Prelude from the first Book of Bach's *Forty-eight* there is an extra bar at the end—'composed' by Czerny—and though Liszt did not add a bar to the end of Beethoven's Sonata, op. 109, he added some very disturbing notes; Bülow distorted Bach's tonal answer (starting on D) in the Chromatic Fantasia and Fugue into a real answer (starting on E), Saint-Saëns' edition of Mozart's A minor Sonata (Durand) often writes the left hand an octave too low, etc. If one is to go at all deeply into interpretative problems, one obvious precondition is an indisputable original text—this is a platitude, or should be, for any musician. If we never knew whether any particular articulation-marking or dynamic indication stems from Mozart himself, how could we possibly do what he wanted? The usual term used nowadays for editions that attempt to reproduce an authentic original text, free from all additions, is 'Urtext edition'. (The fact that the word had to be invented by using the German prefix *Ur*—original, basic—shows in itself that in earlier editions the original text, i.e. the composer's MS., was rarely reproduced.) It can be imagined that after the traumatic experiences outlined above, we flung ourselves voraciously on Urtext editions that promised to reproduce the composer's text either from the MS. or from the first edition. And it is true that many passages which formerly seemed problematical now made sense, as if by magic. We constantly found in the process that though great composers were more sparing with performing indications than the editors of their works, the few indications they did use fitted far more naturally and organically into the overall form than did other people's often well-meaning additions and alterations.

Here we should not fail to mention the efforts of a man who was a pioneer in the purification of texts and the observation of sources: Heinrich Schenker. At a time when it was not yet fashionable to study the manuscripts of great works and use them as the basis of new editions, he laid the greatest emphasis on the importance of sources. Besides producing immaculate editions of texts (such as those of Beethoven's piano sonatas), he was the author of countless papers dealing with errors that had established themselves in performances of great works, and with erroneous readings in editions current at the time. But his particular service was that, realizing the enormous importance of manuscripts, he provided the stimulus to the foundation of the Photographic Archive of the Vienna National Library (also called the Hoboken-Archive, after its founder). This archive has preserved photocopies of many manuscripts whose originals have since been lost, making them available to scholars, and thus to the whole musical world. One example is the MS. of *The Magic Flute*!

Unfortunately there are even many Urtext editions which do not stand up to the demands made upon them by a musician who is really in earnest. Often there are still many errors, distortions of the original and foreign additions (which are doubly dangerous since the unsuspecting student or musician naturally believes that he is using the original text). How else could it happen that two Urtext editions, which, according to their Forewords, draw on identical sources, contain numerous passages where they are not in complete agreement? The only logical explanation would be that the MS. (or other sources) admitted of variant readings (but this is seldom the case), or simply that one or other editor has made mistakes or been careless. And the latter is often the case, as we were obliged to conclude after comparing a considerable number of MSS. and first editions with Urtext editions. It should be said in defence of Urtext editions that many of them have in fact been revised on the basis of comparison with the MS. or first editions; and even if they are not free of mistakes, in these editions the number of mistakes has been considerably reduced.

But there are other editions which make a wholly unjustified claim to the title 'Urtext'. One still comes across the fallacy that the old complete edition published by Breitkopf & Härtel between 1876 and 1886 (*Alte Mozart-Ausgabe*, here referred to by the abbreviation *A.M.A.*) offers an authentic 'original text'; and there are a number of publishers, both in America and England, whose reprints have relied on the *A.M.A.* instead of the MS. (presumably because this was cheaper and more convenient). The very popular *Lea Pocket Scores* of Mozart are described as 'from the "Urtext"-edition', whereas they are a photographic reproduction of the text of the *A.M.A.*, complete with mistakes and, above all, the long nineteenth-century phrasing-slurs, which are quite out of the question.* Again, the editor's Foreword to the Peters edition of the Piano Concerto K.449 says: 'This new edition follows the original text'. But it does not! Here, too, the new edition follows the *A.M.A.*[85] Naturally, this is not designed to clarify the situation for those who buy the score. It would be a good thing if the use of the word 'Urtext' were protected by law, to prevent such misuse.

One cannot blame Breitkopf & Härtel for the mistakes in the *A.M.A.* We should at once add that the revisions of the *A.M.A.* have varied greatly in quality, and that certain groups of works have been quite excellently re-vised. The *A.M.A.* is still exemplary in the matter of correcting pure printing errors. The publishers were the first to become aware of the faulty nature of a large part of their complete edition (the result of the very confused situation prevailing at the time with regard to sources, and of the romanticizing approach of some of the 'editors'); not long after the edition was complete, they were already at work on a revised edition of the piano works—revised according to the MSS. and contemporary first editions. This edition, published in 1895 under the editorship of Rudorff, was the first to use the term 'Urtext', and is still a good edition. If in a few cases it is wrong, this is mostly because Rudorff did not have access to certain manuscripts which have only since been rediscovered.

One can divide into three groups the editions current at the moment:

1. More or less free arrangements. This group includes, among others, the so-called 'instructive editions' of the last century, e.g. Riemann's phrased editions, but also more recent ones.

2. Editions based on inadequate nineteenth-century sources, mostly the *A.M.A.* This group includes most of the printed editions published in the

---

*In the meantime a new edition of *Lea Pocket Scores* has been issued, based on the much more reliable edition of Rudorff (see above), but so far, unfortunately, the footnotes have not been reprinted. According to a personal letter from the publishers, the footnotes will be added in a later edition.

English-speaking territories, the pre-war Boosey & Hawkes edition, *Lea Pocket Scores*, Broude's editions and the *Philharmonia Pocket Scores*.

3. Editions revised according to the MSS. and first editions. Above all we should mention the editions published since the war by Henle, whose editors have been quite particularly scrupulous about reproducing Mozart's original text. Other editions are those of the piano concertos edited by Fischer and Soldan, published by Peters, and those Eulenburg scores which are edited by Blume or Redlich (with the exception of the latter editor's editions of K.414 and 451), and for the solo piano works the edition by Ernst Rudorff already mentioned (Breitkopf & Härtel), the edition of the four-hand piano works edited by Christa Landon (Universal Edition), and the Peters Edition of the piano pieces. The recent edition of the *Sonatas and Fantasias*, by Nathan Broder, published by Theodore Presser, Bryn Mawr, is also a very good Urtext edition. The 'original version' edition published by Edwin F. Kalmus, New York, is a good edition, because it is a photographic reproduction of Rudorff's edition; the only difference is the omission of many footnotes, some of them very important.

For serious study only the editions mentioned under (3) should ever be used. In buying, one can unfortunately not always rely on the publisher's imprint 'Urtext', since, as we have said, group (2) contains some editions which wrongly lay claim to this title, whereas the Eulenburg and Peters editions of the piano concertos do not call themselves 'Urtext' and only mention in their Forewords that these editions aim at reproducing the original text. But forewords, too, are not always to be relied on. Thus the Eulenburg score of the G major Piano Concerto (K.453), which appeared shortly after the war, had an excellent Foreword by Friedrich Blume, but, instead of using his revision of the text, it simply reprinted the *A.M.A.* text without mentioning the fact. This could be seen from the presence of incorrect legato and phrasing slurs taken from the *A.M.A.*,* and, as further proof, Blume's Foreword announces certain revisions which are not in fact present in the text. Only in the recent edition have Eulenburg printed Blume's revised text as well as his Foreword. This edition is marked by the plate-number E.E. 4,866, which appears at the bottom of each page and is not in the earlier edition. It must be said that the publishers acted irresponsibly in this case. Not only can the professional reputation of an editor be affected by the use of his Foreword without the appropriate revision of the text, but when an edition contains a distinguished foreword together with an unrevised text, the customer is likely to be misled. In the new Peters edition of the piano sonatas the Foreword mentions that the first edition was used as the basis of the text of the Sonata K.533/494. Despite this, the text does not agree with the first edition—there are numerous deviations, some of them definite mistakes. (For example: none of the dynamic markings in the second movement

---

*Above all in the first cadenza, for which, according to the Foreword, the MS. had been consulted. A random sample showed that this cadenza alone contained about thirty mistakes! (The MS. of the cadenza is at present in the University Library of Tübingen.)

are in the Hoffmeister first edition, nor are the ties in bars 17–18 and 25–6 of the first movement.)

Even in the editions mentioned as being good, there are many mistakes, ranging from slight and unimportant signs of haste to crude misreadings of the text, and in some cases to an inexplicable failure to consult sources.

We find in the B minor Adagio (K.540) an example of the way crude errors persist from one edition to the next. The Peters Urtext edition, and even the first edition (but not the 'corrected edition' that appeared in 1955) of the Henle text, give a forte in the last bar but one of the coda, whose effect, bursting into the delicate dying fall of the B major ending, is disturbing, in fact unmusical. This Adagio was not printed until 1795, four years after Mozart's death, and, according to Einstein's revision of Köchel, there is no known copy by anyone connected with Mozart, so that the manuscript is the sole authentic source. Fortunately, we were able to consult the MS., which is in a private collection in Stockholm. We were delighted to find that this remarkable *f* is nothing but the tail of a left-hand semiquaver pointing upward:

MS. (as nearly as it can be reproduced):

Reading by the editors:

There is another example of a misreading right at the beginning of *The Magic Flute* Overture. Here every modern edition contains a *ff*. This can hardly be right. When Mozart wrote an alla-breve time signature, he always added a stroke shaped like a *f*. In the first violin part there is a *for*: (which could also possibly be a *sf*) immediately after this stroke. Fortissimo cannot be intended, since Mozart always wrote '*fortiss*' in this case.

It will be seen that after our experiences with the reliability of texts, even in modern editions, we were awake to every possible opportunity of consulting Mozart's manuscripts.[86] It is always an exciting experience to hold in one's hand the manuscript of a work one has often played; and the mistakes already mentioned will be enough to suggest that we made many discoveries, small and large. We would particularly recommend the Henle editions of the solo piano works. As performing editions these have a clear lead over all the others, since the editors have subjected the entire text to a really thorough revision and have made use of all the sources, both long-standing ones and a number which have only been rediscovered in the last few years—some of them of sensational importance. This edition comes nearest to a true reproduction of the original text. Our only comments are on the text of the Fantasia K.475.

It is difficult to revise the text of works whose manuscript is lost, since the editor has to rely on his knowledge of the composer's style to correct all the mistakes in the first edition. We feel that in the Henle edition there are places where the editor's touch has momentarily forsaken him. For example, in bars 8 and 19, and also five bars before the end, the *fp* markings are given incorrectly. On grounds both of musical logic and of comparison with countless similar passages in Mozart's slow movements, one is led to the conclusion that short expressive accents should *not* come on the strong beat.* (The *fp* on *long* notes are discussed on page 23.) It is a remarkable fact that all modern editions have reproduced this passage incorrectly.

The right reading would doubtless be:

(and similarly in bar 19).

In the first edition (Artaria) the *f* is indeed wrong under every first and fifth semiquaver, but the *p* is at least correctly placed under every third and seventh semiquaver for the left hand. There is a similar passage in the second movement of the E major Trio (K.542), bars 40 et seq.

Manuscript:

Incorrect version in most editions:

(Cf. also Sonata KV 310, second movement, bar 11, 22, 25; Sonata KV 457, Adagio bar 31; Concert Rondo D KV 382, Adagio Variation bar 126/127, etc.)

*The accent on the second and fourth (etc.) quaver marks a certain melodic freedom, a kind of rubato that opposes the prevailing metrical scheme.

Another obvious error of the first edition occurs in the second last bar of the c-minor Fantasy: obviously the two last quavers are printed a third too high, for the main part is of course e♭—b (cf. second beat of this bar). In such cases, accompanying parts have to be *under* the main part, such as, e.g., earlier in the Fantasy, bar 105, 107. The correct reading of the second last bar would thus be:

It preserves the dimin. descending Fourth of the preceding motive and is therefore preferable to the usual amendment found in most editions:

(For similar endings cf. also Sonata KV 309, Andante second last bar.)

Only very recently there have appeared two long-awaited Urtext editions of Mozart's variations, a volume published by Henle and the corresponding volume of the *N.M.A.* new complete edition. Henle's edition is to be strongly recommended. However, we feel one or two remarks should be made about the editing of the Duport Variations (K.573).

Since the manuscript of the Variations on a Minuet by Duport is lost, Henle have used as a main source the first edition (*Artaria*, 1792). Unfortunately, some very obvious printing errors in this old edition have been automatically repeated by Henle's editor, who adhered too closely to the first edition. An old MS. copy in the possession of the Gesellschaft der Musikfreunde, Vienna, which has been discovered recently and which seems to derive directly from the lost manuscript, makes it possible to correct most of these errors.

The dynamic markings in the theme and first variation are spurious (the *mf* in bar 13 and the *f* in bar 17 of the theme are undoubtedly not Mozart's).

Theme, bar 23: a *Pralltriller*-sign should be added above the first semiquaver of the right hand.

Variation I, bars 2 and 18: the notes in the right hand, third beat, should of course read G–F sharp–A–F sharp.

Variation V, bars 4 and 20: according to the MS. copy all the appoggiaturas in these bars should be placed one note lower than printed.

Variation VII, bar 15: the notes in the right hand, last quaver, should of course read: F sharp–Second D above middle C.

Variation VIII, bar 12: the concluding notes of the rapid upward run should read: A–B–C sharp–D–C sharp–E–D–C sharp–B.

Variation VIII, last bar but two: on the second beat the left hand has the notes (A)–D–F sharp, and on the third beat A–E–G.

Variation IX, bars 1 and 17: according to the MS. copy, *p* should be added; bars 5 and 21: according to the MS. copy, *f* should be added; bars 5 and 6: there should be a slur over the two F-sharps in the right hand.

Coda, bar 5: as in bars 1 and 3, the left hand should play repeated chords in quavers, not a minim. Bar 21 of the coda should be repeated, thus creating a group of four bars corresponding to the previous group.*

The editors both of the volume of variations in the new complete edition and of the Henle edition include the Variations on Sarti's 'Come un' agnello' (K.460), among the works of doubtful validity and relegate them to a supplement. But we feel this is the result of an obvious mistake (cf. *Mozart Jahrbuch*, 1959, pp. 127 and 140).

Until recently there was no edition of the piano-duet works which aimed at correctly reproducing the original text. This makes all the more welcome the two almost simultaneous publications of these neglected works, by Henle and in the new complete edition,[87] both of which can be said to be agreeably free of mistakes. There are only a few points in which the two editions differ, and here the Henle text is usually to be preferred.

The new complete edition (*N.M.A.*, IX, 24, Series 1) provides a text of the two-piano works which is remarkably free of mistakes.

In 1950 Breitkopf & Härtel published an Urtext edition of the violin sonatas which unfortunately does not wholly deserve the title. It is a reprint, without comment, of an older edition by the same publisher, which is not much better than the Peters edition edited by Hermann. On the other hand, here again the new Henle edition must be praised. In the last bar of the first movement of the Violin Sonata in B flat (K.454), the forte marking should not come till the second crotchet, as we found by consulting the manuscript; otherwise there seem to be very few mistakes. The Peters edition of the 'Mannheim' Sonatas (K.301–306) (Bastiaan) can also be taken as excellent.

But the editions of the Piano Concertos leave most to be desired. Many of the earlier concertos, including the splendid works K.175 and K.238, have not yet appeared in a modern edition,[88] only in reprints of the *A.M.A.*† Comparing the *A.M.A.* edition of K.238 with the MS., we found an incredible number of mistakes: wrong notes (e.g. bar 37), Mozart's MS. staccato markings altered into 'legato', the Finale's alla-breve time-signature changed to an ordinary $\frac{4}{4}$, wrong dynamic markings, incorrect ornaments, etc. The omission of three ties at the opening of the second movement is particularly nonsensical. The text here should read:

(bars 1, 8, etc.) A new edition of this concerto, as of the Concertos K.242,

*Before the discovery of this interesting old MS. copy was known (1959), we had discovered most of these errors by pure analysis. The last error we mentioned in an article printed in *Neue Zeitschrift für Musik*, vol. 11, 1958, Schott, Mainz, which was translated into English and published in the *Music Review*, May, 1961.

†The text of the recent Breitkopf & Härtel editions of these two concertos is identical with that of the *A.M.A.*

246, 413, 451, 453 and 459, is urgently needed. The Peters editions of the concertos edited by Fischer and Soldan are on the whole the best. The piano concertos revised by Blume, which have been published by Eulenburg, are also generally good editions. Blume's revision of the Two-piano Concerto (K.365) is outstanding. On the other hand, the text of Redlich's edition of the Concerto K.414, published by Eulenburg, shows many additions, above all phrasing-slurs in the nineteenth-century manner, which were certainly not in the MS. (lost since the end of the war), and which must be rejected on stylistic grounds, even if (as the Foreword claims) they have been taken from first editions (Artaria, Vienna, and Schmitt, Amsterdam) that appeared during Mozart's life-time—an assertion one doubts. The cadenzas have not been revised at all, although MSS. of them are readily available in Marburg and Tübingen. A sheet belonging to the former Prussian State Library (at the moment in the West German Library, Marburg) contains cadenzas, and also a lead-in* for use in the second movement; this has not yet been printed, and the incipit is not given by Einstein in his thematic catalogue of the cadenzas for the piano concertos (grouped under the Köchel numbers 624/626a). Clearly this lead-in has so far always been overlooked because the Prussian State Library made a mistake in numbering the cadenzas on the sheet. (The supplement to this book contains a facsimile reproduction of this unknown lead-in for the Andante.) The revised editions of the Concertos K.413 and 415 (also by Redlich and published by Eulenburg) seem to be a good deal better than that of K.414.

The Concerto K.449, as we have said, has been reprinted by Peters following the *A.M.A.* text, so that this edition contains numerous mistakes. On the other hand, the Eulenburg score of this concerto, edited by Redlich, can be taken as reliable. As the MS. is at present lost (it used to belong to the Prussian State Library), Redlich's revision is based on the relatively reliable text of the first edition published in 1792 by André in Offenbach. Some passages in André's edition do, however, seem to contain printing or editor's mistakes—for instance, the following passage in the first movement, bar 130 (and 277): the slur should only extend over two crotchets. In Mozart's manuscripts the end of a slur hardly ever coincides with a staccato dot, as is the case here.

In bar 350 one should add an E flat. At the end of the cadenza the turn has been wrongly omitted. The MS. of the cadenza has been preserved and is easily accessible; it shows that the trill is to be introduced as follows:

Translator's Note: The German word *Eingang* seems never to have acquired a standard translation. I hope that 'lead-in', despite its slight air of the colloquial, will be acceptable as an exact and compact equivalent.

In bar 66 of the third movement the following reading would be more correct (cf. the introductory tutti):

In bar 187 of the third movement the turn should be over the first note, to correspond with bar 59. In bar 329 of this movement there must be a printer's error; the third in the right-hand (second beat) should be G–B flat.

We found a few further mistakes (obviously made by the printer) in the Eulenburg score of this concerto:

First movement

Bar 13. The first viola double-stop should be D–B flat.
Bar 153. The slur over the last two crotchets in the piano part is certainly not right.
Bars 162–8. Are these legato slurs really Mozart's?
Bar 212. The pianoforte has a *p* on the first beat.
Bar 260. The 'legato' marking is certainly not Mozart's.
Bar 273. Here the piano should have slurs over the whole bar, as in bar 126.

Second movement

Bar 104. The last note of this bar in the first violins should of course be a D.

Third movement

Bar 40. The legato slur over the final quavers of the piano part can scarcely be Mozart's.
Bars 63 and 66. The 'legato' marking is not Mozart's.
Bar 178. A minim G should be added to the piano part to correspond to bar 170.
Bars 242–5. Again the legato slurs in the piano part are not Mozart's.

Of the editions of the Concerto K.450, both the Peters edition edited by Fischer-Soldan and the Eulenburg score edited by Blume are good. K.453 has already been discussed. The new revision of K.451 (Eulenburg) makes practically no use of old sources, and is therefore in no way reliable, whereas the same publisher's edition of the Concerto K.456 is good. A new revised edition of the Concerto K.459[89] is urgently needed. At the moment there is not a single good edition on the market—for example, in all editions bar 234 of the first movement wrongly has a D on the first beat, instead of the F in the MS.* The best editions of the Concerto K.467 are those of Peters (Fischer-Soldan) and Eulenburg, but in the case of K.482 Eulenburg's score and Neue Mozart Ausgabe are to be recommended. N.M.A. restored correctly two missing bars in the first movement (bars 282–3). (Here we should mention a small mistake in the Eulenburg score: the piano in the second half of bar 220 of the first movement (piano part) is not Mozart's, but an unnecessary addi-

*For a discussion of editions of the Concertos K.466[90], 488 and 491, see the remarks on their interpretation, pp. 243 et seq.

tion by the editor.) The best scores of the last concertos, K.503, K.537 ('Coronation' Concerto) and K.595 are again those of Eulenburg, though they are not free of mistakes. As regards two-piano editions, however, there is only one good edition of any of these three, the Peters edition of the Coronation Concerto (Fischer-Soldan). Thus it is all the better that the *N.M.A.* are shortly to publish these last concertos, and their editions should surely be the last word in textual correctness.

We should briefly mention some important mistakes in the Eulenburg scores of the Concertos K.503 and K.595. In the first movement of K.503 the second trumpet in bar 26 should have G, not E as in Eulenburg's score. The G produces a complete C major chord, with the notes of the horns, whereas the printed E doubles the third, so that the fifth G is missing. (For another mistake in this concerto, see p. 142.) We do not understand why the Eulenburg edition of the B flat Concerto (K.595) does not restore the seven bars in the exposition of the first movement, which have been omitted from all editions since the *A.M.A.*—this despite the fact that in the Eulenburg Foreword the edition is said to have been revised on the basis of the MS. and first edition.[91] In both these sources there is an insertion between bars 46 and 47: the chromatic upsurge of bars 352–8 from the final tutti is added. There is no doubt that this 'cut', which, moreover, produces very un-Mozartean lines in the first and second violins, is the work of a foreign hand, since otherwise it would at least be made in the first edition published by Artaria four months before Mozart's death. In the second movement of this concerto, according to the manuscript, the left hand should play an octave lower from the middle of bar 104 until the end of bar 106, thus avoiding the consecutive fifths between first violin and piano found in almost every existing edition.

Here we cannot discuss some other slight deviations. Since the manuscript of the cadenzas is still missing, the text of the first edition should have been given, not that of the *A.M.A.*, which as usual contains many slurs, some of them nonsensical.

Apart from the concertos mentioned, the Concert Rondo K.382 has also been published in a good edition by Eulenburg. The only mistakes in this otherwise excellent edition seem to us to be the legato slurs in bars 17–22, left hand, bars 41–56 (over the triplets) and again from bars 153 and 169 onward. The remarks about these in the editor's report are wide of the mark. The bass octave at the opening of the cadenza should start in the preceding bar.

Another delightful Concert Rondo in A major (K.386), has only recently come to light. In 1958 the authors, assisted by Charles Mackerras, started to collect the pages of this hitherto unpublished piece, which were scattered throughout the world, and to reconstruct those parts that were still missing, using an old arrangement for piano solo made before the piece had been literally cut to pieces. In 1938 Alfred Einstein had already attempted to re-write the piece. Working from two pages only, he arrived at a version quite different from that originally scored by Mozart. The reconstruction by Paul Badura-Skoda and Charles Mackerras will be published in 1962 by Schott, Mainz (Germany).

Since the *A.M.A.* is still the only available printed edition of some of these concertos, we should point out some of its most important mistakes.

1. The word 'legato', which the *A.M.A.* attaches to practically every semi-quaver or triplet passage in quick movements, is not authentic and should be disregarded. The same applies to legato slurs over more than two bars—they are almost always additions by a foreign hand.

2. In the slow movements of the piano concertos in D minor (K.466), C minor (K.491), D major (K.537) and B flat (K.595), the *A.M.A.* has arbitrarily changed the alla-breve time signature into **C** and thus created confusion in the matter of choosing a tempo. The alla-breve stroke is again missing in the last movement of the B flat Concerto (K.238) and the first movement of the F major Concerto (K.459).

3. Most of the articulating slurs in the *A.M.A.* are spurious. Mozart's

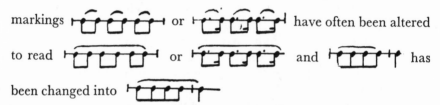

markings   or   have often been altered to read   or   and   has been changed into

In passages with mixed articulation (combination of legato and staccato) the tendency of the *A.M.A.* is always to reduce the amount of staccato arbitrarily. For example, in the B flat Piano Concerto (K.238), first movement, bars 17–20:

First violins, MS.:

has been changed in the *A.M.A.* to:

In writing dotted notes it was an old custom, which Mozart followed, to write the dot only at the beginning of the extra duration of the note. The slur in brackets in the second bar (which is wrong) is only added in the corresponding passages later on.

4. Many of the turns at the ends of trills in the *A.M.A.* are spurious. As far as we know, Mozart only rarely wrote out turns, and never in such passages

as

However, the *A.M.A.* tends to add turns as follows:

for example, in the Concerto K.449.

For practical new editions of works by Mozart, the following factors should be borne in mind. An edition should aim to reproduce Mozart's original text. The only authentic sources for this are manuscripts, copies with additions in Mozart's hand, and first editions that appeared during Mozart's lifetime. If any one of these sources is available, then all later editions are valueless for the purpose of revision, and should not even be called upon for purposes of comparison, since this can easily mean that mistakes, once introduced, can be perpetuated. When the manuscript is lost, and a first edition appeared during Mozart's lifetime (e.g. the Sonata in F (K.533), the Fantasia K.475, etc.), this is the edition which counts as the most valuable source and must definitely be used as the basis of the new edition. In the rare cases where there are differences between different manuscript versions of a work, or between a manuscript and a first edition which was obviously or supposedly corrected by Mozart, the editor must first choose one or other version of the text, after thorough examination of the style of the passage, and then add all the important deviant readings in small print and footnotes. It is not good enough for a new edition to run together parts of various versions, without comment, including in a version based on the manuscript passages from the first edition, and vice versa. A good Urtext edition without an editor's report, however short, is flatly impossible. But even if for any reason it is not practical to include an editor's report, the edition should at least indicate which source(s) have been used for each piece or sonata.

We should expressly reject the practice, which is unfortunately widespread, of resolving Mozart's ornaments within the main text. Mozart's notation of ornaments should always be retained, and problematic resolutions given in small notes above the stave or in a footnote.* There are strong objections to the Eulenburg scores' practice of resolving appoggiaturas 'where there is no doubt as to how they were played', and writing them out in the main text. Here the editors are skating on thin ice, and it is not long before mistakes occur. Incorrect resolution of ornaments can often mean distorting the text, as in the following case: in bar 97 of the C major Piano Concerto (K.503), first movement, Mozart's MS. contains an appoggiatura written as follows:

The Eulenburg score resolves this appoggiatura, wrongly, to our mind:

The reason why this mistake is so damaging to the musical sense is that the whole charm of bars 96–8 rests in their triple repetition of the accented F, with a different upbeat figure each time. Moreover, it is quite wrong to resolve an ornament into normal notes without also adding the necessary

*It will be obvious that this does not apply to Mozart's way of writing the semiquaver appoggiatura ♪, which is better written ♪.

slurs, as, for example, in the B flat Concerto (K.595), first movement, bars 15 and 249 (cf. p. 60 on this point). Mozart's notation is as follows:

Eulenburg's score gives the following incorrect resolution:

correct version:

Printed editions should as far as possible reproduce any special features of notation that appear in the MS., such as the way horizontal stems are grouped, the way the notes are distributed between the two staves, tails pointing up or down, etc. Naturally, there is no objection to the practice of writing out in full those passages in which the MS. uses abbreviations for repeated figures. One major problem for editors is how to supplement Mozart's signs for articulation. Where there are repeated motives, for instances in sequences, Mozart often wrote slurs and dots or strokes only at the outset. According to Leopold Mozart's *Violinschule*, 'one must then continue with them until a change is indicated' (I, iii, §17, footnote). It is interesting, however, that in many cases Mozart obviously did not want the articulation 'evened up' in this way, and wanted a motive played differently on its reappearance. This is certainly so in the Finale of the F major Concerto (K.459), where the characteristic motive is marked with dots instead of slurs when it reappears after the cadenza.

In any case, editors should make it clear that the markings they have added to 'even out' the articulation do not stem from Mozart, since the composer's inconsistent notation can on occasion have been intentional.*

Editors are faced by a particular problem when they come to reproduce in printed form Mozart's staccato markings. From a practical point of view, there are only two alternatives: either one restricts oneself to a single sign representing both Mozart's dots and his strokes (wedges)—it does not much matter whether one chooses a stroke or a dot—and has recourse to a wedge-shaped sign only in the rare cases when Mozart's marking seems to have a special accentual significance; or else the editor ventures on too thin ice by trying to interpret Mozart's markings, perhaps using a dot for a fairly soft, 'round' staccato, and the stroke for a sharper, more energetic one. In this case he will certainly have at times to weigh philological arguments (based on

*On the subject of supplementing dynamic markings, see p. 20.

Mozart's notation) against musical ones, and choose subjectively. For there are many cases in which the outward appearance of a sign in Mozart's MS. clashes with its musical significance, for the simple reason that he happened to be using a faulty quill whose point had spread. Since in any case one cannot reproduce in print the great variety of nuances in Mozart's staccato markings, it is perhaps more sensible not to attempt to make oversubtle distinctions, and to use only *one* marking for all staccati. However, the foreword should mention the many different ways in which this single marking can be interpreted (cf. pp. 63–6).

It goes without saying, of course, that editors of Mozart's works should be thoroughly familiar with the special characteristics of his style and notation. For example, considerable powers of intuition are often needed to determine where his slurs are to begin, since the MSS. do not always make this clear. Einstein made the important remark that Mozart usually wrote his slurs rather too long, particularly the short ones.[92] It is often also necessary to know the details of the way Mozart wrote down his works, if one is to revise his text reliably. Mozart composed horizontally, i.e. he usually wrote out the melodic parts and the bass first, writing in the 'filling-out' parts later.[93] For example, in the opening tutti of a piano concerto he would first write down merely the first violin and bass, then write out the piano part from its point of entry to the next tutti, then again only the violin and bass, and so on till the end of the movement. Often the first draft also hints at entries of important subsidiary parts. Naturally, it also sometimes happened that in making the final copy he slightly altered his original idea, as, for example, in the Concerto K.503, first movement, bar 31.

First version
(crossed out):

Final version:

Mozart's 'horizontal' way of writing down his works sometimes produces contradictions between the different parts in vertical section. An example occurs in bar 111 of the first movement of the 'Haffner' Symphony. In the first version, the second bassoon has a remarkable B at this point, which in the first half of the bar produces an unsatisfying doubling of the dominant seventh (first violins), and in the second half a note that clashes with the harmony. Moreover, there are consecutive fifths between the first bassoon and the violas. In the second version Mozart corrected this second-bassoon B to C sharp, and gave the first bassoon E sharp–D. This got rid of the consecutive fifths between first bassoon and violas, but unfortunately it produced new consecutive fifths with the first violins! The well-known Mozart conductor George Szell makes the first bassoon play E sharp–F sharp (doubling the second violins) at this point. There are, however, some conductors who defend the first bassoon's D, finding it harmonically stimulating.

Writing mistakes are in fact rarer in Mozart's MSS. than in those of other composers, but they are not wholly absent. It is well known that Mozart wrote down the C minor Concerto (K.491) in great haste. It is 'Beethovenian' not only in character, but in its graphic appearance, which is unusual for Mozart. Some passages are practically illegible, because three different versions have been written over one another. Thus it is understandable that there are more problematic passages in this concerto than in any other of Mozart's works. In one case there must certainly have been a mistake on Mozart's part; in the Larghetto of this same concerto there is an obviously unintentional clash of two different harmonic ideas, which, strangely enough, has never been altered or mentioned as problematic in any editions we have come across. Here the wind instruments have a most beautiful harmonic variant, which was not present when the piano part was written (earlier).

Second movement, bar 40:

Piano:

Wind
instruments:

The bassoon part proves that this is a mistake, since it is impossible as a tenor part (it produces parallel fourths with the piano bass on the second and third quavers). Thus it was obviously intended as a bass-line. To take this passage at its face value would mean quite un-Mozartean part-writing (e.g. an ugly doubling of the F on the second quaver, and parallel sevenths between bassoon and piano). Here the piano part must be altered to fit the orchestral parts.[94]

In the first movement, bar 319, the piano part has a D flat, whereas the second oboe has a D. Three bars later a natural sign is missing before the first oboe's A. Both the (necessary) flat in bar 319 and the forgotten natural in bar 322 have been added to the manuscript by someone else (André?) in red ink, but only in the first oboe, and not in the piano part.

Another obvious mistake of Mozart's, which has so far always been overlooked, occurs in the third movement of the C major Concerto (K.503), bars 58–61. In bar 60 there are two simultaneous seventh-chords (G major, II[7] and V[7]). Naturally, the left hand of the piano must be adapted to fit the strings' harmony, since it is unthinkable that Mozart should have intended a chord containing all the notes of the major scale.[95]

Mozart appears to have made a mistake of a different kind in the Cavatina from *The Marriage of Figaro*, 'Se vuol ballare'. In old orchestral parts belonging to the Vienna State Opera the bassoons enter two bars earlier than in any printed score, and musically this makes far better sense than the original version. In *Figaro* there is also a passage where something must be added to the rhythmic notation. In the MS., Scene 10 of the second Act Finale, bar 322, the violas have a rhythm written as follows:

|(𝄴) ♪ 𝄾 ♫♫ ♫| (hemidemisemiquavers)

At the same time the basses and bassoons have

|(𝄴) ♪ 𝄾 ♫♫ ♫| (demisemiquavers)

a rhythm which also occurs in the first violins in the preceding bar. In these bars one must naturally correct Mozart's notation to match the *abbreviated* way of playing the rapid run—this has been discussed in the chapter on rhythmic notation (pp. 47–9). The Eulenburg score (p. 305) gives the following reading, which is unacceptable:

♪ 𝄾 ♬♬ ♪.♪

In such cases the editor should indeed leave Mozart's text alone but unquestionably add the correct reading in a footnote.* One must be very careful in correcting mistakes. Are there not many passages which Mozart's contemporaries took for mistakes, and which were later seen to be bold harmonic strokes?

We should now say something about the so-called 'Vienna Sonatinas'. In 1931, Schott, Mainz, (and later also Universal Edition, Vienna) published under this very arbitrary title arrangements of the five Divertimenti (Serenades) for two clarinets (bassett horns) and bassoon, K. Supplement 229 and 229a (K.439b). As early as 1805 the publisher Artaria published arrangements of these divertimenti as *Sonatines pour le Pianoforte*, and also brought

---

*Part-writing in general should be treated with far more sensitivity. In the Sanctus of the Requiem, Süssmayer introduced ugly delayed consecutive fifths between the first and second violins. It is hard to understand the fact that no conductor has yet had the courage and initiative to correct this utterly un-Mozartean part-writing, on the analogy of the numerous similar passages where descending first inversions occur in other works of Mozart. Here we should strongly recommend to conductors the superbly successful attempt by Wilhelm Fischer to complete the Lacrimosa (printed in the *Mozart-Jahrbuch*, 1951). In this attempt Fischer showed extraordinary powers of intuition and great knowledge of Mozart's style, and certainly made a better job of it than did Süssmayer, who was concerned only to complete the fragmentary work as quickly as possible. Two other good reconstructions are by Ernst Hess (Zürich) and Marius Flothuis (Amsterdam), still unpublished.

out a number of pieces from these same divertimenti in an arrangement for two violins and 'cello.

There is no intrinsic objection to arrangements of unknown masterworks that are scarcely ever played in their original instrumentation. Quite the opposite—one welcomes arrangements of fine works which are capable of filling a gap in musical literature; after all, there are not so many easy piano works by classical composers. Transposition of these pieces to different keys is also a good idea, since the original movements are all in B flat, presumably because they were written for B flat clarinets.

On the other hand, to publish these sonatinas as if they were original compositions was to mislead the public. One looks in vain on the title pages of the Schott editions (Catalogue No. 2,159) for any indication which works by Mozart are involved; on the contrary, they are marked 'Die Wiener Sonatinen . . . "Originalklavierausgabe" ' [sic]!

Apart from this, the arrangement is not really successful. For example, no genuine piano piece by Mozart would use piano figures like those in the right hand of bar 11 of the opening movement of the First Sonatina, a passage which is for that matter not at all easy for beginners to play. The arrangement also makes some very arbitrary alterations, such as a pointless upbeat in the Adagio of the First Sonatina, harmonic changes in bar 2 of the Fourth Sonatina, not to mention many performing indications which distort the sense of the music. The many odd and unmotivated changes in the order of the individual pieces are equally to be deplored. The four-movement form of the First, Second and Sixth Sonatinas is quite against Mozart's practice, for he never wrote sonatas in four movements. It is almost comic to see how the very first movement—the opening movement of the First Divertimento (according to Mozart) becomes the last movement of the Sixth and last Sonatina (according to the arranger). Add that it is in sonata form. . . .

But naturally 'Five Serenades by Mozart, arranged as easy piano pieces' would be a much less attractive financial proposition for a publisher than 'Six Original Sonatinas'. At the very beginning of the nineteenth century Mozart's first biographer, Niemetschek,[96] came out very strongly against this kind of commercial exploitation:

> Arrangers and music dealers are now making a great deal of mischief with his works, and the public is often misled, and the name of this great composer is greatly damaged. In the first place, many a shoddy work is passed off under his name, which is quite unworthy of his genius; and even more frequently unauthorized arrangers patch together piano pieces out of his larger works, which they then sell as original works, and which are necessarily far below the standard of his other piano compositions.

Two years after completing his great biography of Mozart, Hermann Abert published an essay, 'The State and Tasks of Present-day Mozart Research',[97] in which he said that the question of purification of texts was 'one of the most urgent'. Although there have since been great advances in this field, there is still much to be desired, as we have tried to show. It is therefore most heartening that a new complete edition of Mozart's works has been planned and is already in production. To judge by the scrupulously worked-out instructions given by the publishers to their editors, and the revision of the volumes that have already appeared, this edition ought really to satisfy all the demands such an edition must face. It must be hoped that at a time when ample money and idealism are devoted to bringing out complete editions of far less important composers, a complete edition of Mozart's works will not have to be prematurely discontinued from lack of public interest or financial difficulties.

Chapter Six

SOME TECHNICAL QUESTIONS IN THE PIANO WORKS

'WHEN I play Mozart,' a well-known artist once said, 'I have a pleasant tingling feeling in my fingers, as if they too, were delighted by his music.' This is no accident; Mozart was a born pianist and composer for the piano, and his piano works 'lie well' under the fingers. He was, however, not attracted by virtuosity for its own sake—he tended to avoid unnecessary technical difficulties. He was amused by Clementi's passage-work in thirds, which at that time were difficult to play: 'but he sweated over them day and night in London', he wrote:[98] and his works contain neither trills in thirds nor anything else of the kind. Certainly the great simplicity of his piano writing creates major problems, paradoxical though it may sound, and these often defeat even the greatest pianists. 'The hardest thing is to be simple' is a saying particularly applicable to Mozart's music.

A pianist must be in control and command of his fingers if he is to play Mozart's single melodic lines cantabile and expressively, and give a really even flow ('like oil') to his legato passage-work, which should sound like a melodic line played quickly, and his tingling 'con-brio' passages. For 'non-legato', which occurs so frequently, the fingers should be kept as curved as possible. One's touch should be clear and sparkling (*jeu perlé*); this is best achieved by slightly drawing in the fingers, so that they tap the keys like little hammers. But here the wrist should always be kept pliable; it should follow the play of the fingers, i.e. in phrasing it should be quite free to take part, just as it should follow the movement of a violin bow. It is particularly important to keep the whole body free of tension, relaxed, shoulders free of strain, the neck muscles relaxed. Mozart's finely developed sense for every kind of naturalness often made him criticize a player's posture:

> All that I can say about the daughter of Hamm, the Secretary of War, is that she undoubtedly must have a gift for music, as she has only been learning for three years and yet can play several pieces really well. But I find it difficult to give you an idea of the impression she makes on me when she is playing. She seems to me so curiously affected. She stalks over the clavier with her long, bony fingers in such an odd way—[99]

as he wrote to his father from Augsburg. In the following ironical report he makes an even sharper criticism of an unnatural posture:

> Anyone who sees and hears her play and can keep from laughing must, like her father, be made of stone.* For instead of sitting in the middle of the clavier, she sits right up opposite the treble, as it gives her more chance of flopping about and making grimaces. She rolls her eyes and smirks. When a passage is repeated, she plays it more slowly the second time. If it has to be played a third time, then she plays it even more slowly. When a passage is being played, the arm must be raised as high as possible, and according as the notes in the passage are stressed, the arm, not the fingers must do this, and that too with great emphasis in a heavy and clumsy manner. But the best joke of all is that when she comes to a passage which ought to flow like oil and which necessitates a change of finger, she does not bother her head about it, but when the moment arrives, she just leaves out the notes, raises her hand and starts off again quite comfortably—a method by which she is much more likely to strike a wrong note, which often produces a curious effect. She may succeed, for she has great talent for music. But she will not make progress by this method—for she will never acquire great rapidity, since she definitely does all she can to make her hands heavy.[100]

Without elasticity, one's tone will not 'carry'. Only a relaxed singing tone can penetrate to the heart of the listener.

Lightness of touch is so important because present-day pianos, as we have said, have a tone that is basically too full for Mozart's music. To make legato scales as clear on a modern instrument as on a Mozart piano, one must often play non-legato: and a 'non-legato' on the old instrument must nowadays be played 'staccato'. There are, incidentally, endless possible nuances in staccato playing, all the degrees in a scale from a gentle separation of successive notes

to a sharply cut-off, very short attack. In the Piano Concerto in A (K.488), second movement, e.g. bars 10 and 21, a very soft staccato is appropriate.†

One should also aim at a bright timbre, without, however, trying to force the brightness by hard, 'glassy' playing. A hard touch does indeed make the tone of a modern piano brighter (richer in overtones), but it also makes it uglier, since at ff level many non-harmonic overtones take part in the vibration process. To list the physical reasons for this would take us too far afield. In any case, excessively hard touch gives the impression of a certain brutality, which is quite out of place in Mozart.

Naturally, the various kinds of touch should be practised separately. Exercises such as those given in Cortot's *Principes rationnels de la Technique pianistique* and *Editions de Travail* can be strongly recommended. Their use must, of course, be supervised by a teacher in the course of individual tuition.

---

* *Translator's Note*: 'Stein', the family's name, means 'stone'.
† Cf. pp. 261, et seq. on this point.

Piano technique is based on a small number of constantly recurring principles such as finger action (staccato, legato), the passing-under of the thumb, trills, octaves, chords, etc. We will try to provide a few hints on each of these points.

1. *Finger Action*. For a 'tingling', non-legato touch the fingers should be kept as curved as possible—this has already been mentioned. To develop the concentrated force that is often needed, the best exercises are those where repeated notes are played (the remaining fingers may perhaps rest on the keyboard):

and similarly for the left hand, gradually increasing the speed. In doing these exercises it is important to keep the wrist loose. The natural tendency to let it become stiff and cramped in doing this kind of finger exercise must be resisted from the outset. It is best to move the wrist up and down in smooth waves while doing these exercises.

Whereas staccato playing is based on distinct finger attack, legato playing should rely above all on finger pressure. Legato playing is often made easier by keeping the fingers flat, sometimes almost stretched out, as if the finger tips wanted to stroke the keys. One very useful device is to 'tie' the notes; one note is not released as the next one is struck (or rather 'depressed', since a full piano tone results from pressure and not from sudden force), but is prolonged a little, e.g.:

played:

In quicker legato passages it is also possible to make a double 'tie':

played:

True legato playing however, requires not merely this kind of 'tie' but also conscious support by dynamic gradations, e.g.:

B flat Concerto (K.595), first movement, first solo:

Fingers flat! 'Tie' the notes! It is particularly important to play the semiquavers in bars 2 and 3 smoothly and not too fast.

First movement, bar 100:

Only if the second note of each descending fourth (G, E, B, etc.) is played noticeably softer than the others will the impression of a legato be given. Good legato playing, too, finally depends on the ability to imagine the sound that is to be produced. A player who can feel a melodic line will invariably have a better legato than one who regards legato playing as a mere task to be carried out mechanically.

2. *Scales and Arpeggios.* To play these without bumpiness, elasticity of the wrist and lightning reactions in passing the thumb under are essential. The best position for the hand in playing scales is a 'diagonal' one, i.e. the arm is held at an acute or obtuse angle to the keyboard; the third finger reaches farthest inward, and the elbow should move ahead of the fingers. This also applies to extended arpeggios.

Exercises such as these have been found useful: Lightning preparation of the next note:

Thumb exercises:

Scales for the two hands together should also be practised with dynamic gradations:

Fingering is a special problem in Mozart; one should wherever possible avoid having to call upon the 'weak' fourth and little fingers:

In playing Mozart it is better not to apply the old teaching rule that the thumb and fifth finger are to avoid the black keys. There are many passages which can only be played evenly if one uses 'unorthodox' fingering—for example, E flat Concerto (K.482), first movement, bar 176 (modern fingering above the stave, orthodox fingering below):

bar 258:

The orthodox fingering makes the hand unsteady because the thumb is passed under more often.

Concerto K.488, first movement, bar 281:

third movement, bar 151:

3. *Trills*. Some pianists 'are born' with a powerful trill, others have to prac-
tise for years before they can trill properly. The latter may find these
hints useful. Above all, trills must be even. A slower trill is preferable to
a quick, bumpy one. There are a number of exercises that have proved
useful (to be played without accents, quite evenly):

These are admittedly only preparatory exercises. For the trills in
Mozart's works we recommend the following fingerings: 1/2, 1/3, 2/3,
2/4, 3/5. But here there is certainly a good deal of room for individual
preference.

To make a trill 'vibrate' with the desired speed, it is a good idea to let
the whole of the hand shake slightly to and fro, from the elbow, at the
same time carrying out the necessary quick finger movements. Thus the
weight of the arm may help to add power to a forte trill.

4. *Octaves*. So-called, 'broken octaves' are very frequent in Mozart:

Such octaves must 'rotate' from the elbow, and often from the shoulders.
(The fingers are in this case kept in a fixed position and hardly move.)
It is a pity that many teachers pay too little attention to this movement.
The following exercise is very useful:

During the rests one should lift the arm high (at least eight inches above the keys). The wrist must be able to vibrate from the elbow, lightly, loosely and quickly. The exercise can also be played in sevenths:

Not till these can be managed without any trouble should one try the exercise in octaves.

There is often a tendency to reach the upper notes too soon. It can be countered by such exercises as this:

In Mozart we often also find *legato octaves*. These cause a lot of trouble. Sonata in A (K.331), first movement, Variation III:

To play the upper part smoothly is not enough. There will only be a true legato feeling if the thumb, too, plays smoothly. The thumb has to be very mobile to play 'tied to itself' in this way. It is very important that the lower part of the thumb should be active. The thumb should leave each individual key as late as possible and then take hold of the next with lightning speed, but without making an accent. The gap between each pair of notes must be kept as short as possible.

As an exercise, complete melodies should be played with the thumb only!

One curiosity should be mentioned—double glissandi occur in Mozart. They are the merest exceptions (glissando in sixths at the close of the Variations K.264, and octave glissandi in the second original cadenza for the second movement of the Concerto K.453),* since he obviously had little use for this type of virtuosity.

As we have already said in the chapter on Mozart's sound, his music often contains closely-spaced chords in the lowest register of the piano; these sound full and round on a Mozart piano, but distinctly unpleasant on a modern instrument. We would recommend occasional alteration of such passages so

---

*The authenticity of this cadenza is, however, doubtful.

that they at least sound bearable. If the fifth is omitted from the chord in the second movement of the C minor Sonata (K.457), bar 53:

the resulting sound is already a good deal more agreeable. Moreover, the D (third) should be played softer than the other notes. Better still, one can omit the third:

At the opening of the development of the slow movement of the A minor Sonata (K.310) these accompanying chords occur:

Here Mozart had in mind a full, warm accompaniment (like the sound of low strings), but on most modern pianos this passage sounds ugly rather than full. If in the first bar the third is transposed to the octave above, the result will certainly be much more like the sound Mozart intended. But one must be able to span a tenth with the right hand:

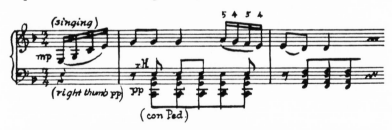

The original version only sounds well on some concert grands which are tuned to produce a particularly bright, clear sound.[101] Unison passages such as the opening of the C minor Fantasia (K.457) often sound much too thick on the modern piano. It is usually a help to play the left hand a good deal softer than the right. At the opening of the C minor Sonata we favour a powerful forte in the right hand, with a mezzo-piano in the left.

The soft pedal should not be used too much. The bad habit of depressing this pedal automatically for all soft passages is far too widespread. The soft pedal does not simply make the instrument softer, but alters its timbre, usually in a way that hinders the production of a good tone. A good pianist should be able to play even *ppp* without using the soft pedal.

There are frequent pedalling problems in playing Mozart. Resonance, and thus better tone, can often be obtained by using the pedal, so there is often something to be said for using it discreetly in cantabile passages, obviously with frequent changes of pedal. There is a fine example of such a passage in the G major Piano Sonata (K.283), second movement, bar 11 (also bars 12 and 34–5):

Here the articulation indicated (slur from G to G, right hand) is hardly possible without the aid of the pedal.[102] But since the pedal thickens the sound, it should at times be avoided. Too much pedal is also a hindrance in phrasing. Above all, rests in the course of a melody should on no account be covered up because the pianist has omitted to take his foot off the pedal. We would particularly warn against this frequent mistake. The correct pedalling for the following figure is:

and not:

Incorrect pedalling makes all the notes sound as if they were marked 'tenuto'. There is a passage in the Duport Variations (K.573), bar 8, which must be pedalled as follows:

It also goes without saying that in staccato or non-legato passages the pedal should as a rule not be used.[103] Interesting problems of pedalling are raised by the arpeggios common in Mozart's works. It would be absolutely wrong to play all such passages with the pedal down; this would in many cases make the sound far too thick. But there are passages in Mozart where the piano should be let off the leash and allowed to make a noise; here the pedal will obviously be needed. The dramatic climax of the first movement of the C minor concerto, where the piano opposes the entire orchestra (bar 332 onward), is such a passage. Others include the stormy arpeggios in the C major Fantasia (K.394), bar 46 (cf. p. 11), which sound even more exciting on a Mozart piano than on the modern instrument, and the passage in the C minor Fantasia (K.475), where the sound shoots like a rocket from the lowest notes of Mozart's piano up to the highest register:

Four bars before this, there must be four changes of pedal to a bar, so that the phrasing is not obscured:

But this dramatic use of chords is not frequent. In arpeggios the main aim is usually a pleasant sound (e.g. the E flat Concerto (K.449), second movement, bars 103 onward):

In passages of this kind the combination of staccato or non-legato touch with pedal produces magical effects of sound. Frequent changes of pedal prevent the sound from becoming too thick. One can introduce some very pleasing pedal effects, which Mozart doubtless intended, at the end of the original cadenza for the A major Concerto (K.488):

But there are many arpeggios which sound best with hardly any pedal, since they occur in passages where a slender sound is most appropriate. Examples of such passages are found in the Concert Rondo in D (K.382), bars 41–56 (according to the MS.):

or the Piano Sonata in F (K.533/494), first movement, codetta:

The sparkling quality of these figures can only be properly brought out if the pedal is not used. So that the sound does not become too thick, the left hand must again be a good deal softer than the right. Furthermore, the interplay of the parts rules out the use of the pedal in the passage that immediately follows the last example.

Mozart-playing demands a pedal technique that uses very exact and frequent changes of pedal. To ensure the slenderness of tone that is the most important prerequisite for playing Mozart, it is better to use too little pedal than too much. In playing Mozart one must above all avoid anything that would mar the clarity, translucency and evenness of one's playing, the quality that contemporary aesthetics called the 'clarity of musical language'. We would end with a quotation from Schubart's *Ideen einer Aesthetik der Tonkunst*:

> The second quality of good musical performance is: clarity. What one cannot understand cannot go to one's heart. Thus one must give a sharp contour to every musical comma, indeed to every single note; practise detaching the notes (for nothing is clearer than staccato playing): never murmur when one ought to speak out; and in playing, be particularly diligent in attaining a rounded tone.[104]

Chapter Seven

'TASTE' AND 'FEELING'

It is well-known that Mozart was an outstanding pianist—not only a supreme artist, but a great success with the public. At a very early age he had learnt how to overcome every technical difficulty and could therefore devote all his attention to the real problems of interpretation.

> He [the pianist Richter] plays well so far as execution goes but as you will discover when you hear him, he is too rough and laboured and entirely devoid of taste and feeling. Otherwise he is the best fellow in the world and is not the slightest bit conceited. When I played to him he stared all the time at my fingers and kept on saying, 'Good God! How hard I work and sweat—and yet win no applause—and to you, my friend, it is all child's play'. 'Yes,' I replied, 'I too had to work hard, so as not to have to work hard any longer.' Enfin, he is a fellow who may be included among our good clavier-players. . . .[105]

This is one of the many passages in Mozart's letters in which he discusses good performance, constantly using the words expression, feeling, 'gusto' or taste. In one of his letters he praised the Italian violinist Regina Strinasacchi as

> a very good violinist. She has a great deal of taste and feeling in her playing.[106]

and in another he gave his sister the following advice:

> I should advise my sister to play them [Myslivecek's sonatas] with plenty of expression, taste and fire and to learn them by heart. For they are sonatas which are bound to please everyone, which are easy to memorize and very effective when played with the proper precision.[107]

Mozart's opinion of Clementi was not very flattering:

> Clementi is a *ciarlatano*, like all Italians. . . . What he really does well are his passages in thirds; but he sweated over them day and night in London. Apart from this, he can do nothing, absolutely nothing, for he has not the slightest expression or taste, still less feeling.[108]

And elsewhere:

> Apart from this, he has not a farthing's worth of taste or feeling; he is a mere *mechanicus*.[109]

Clementi, on the other hand, greatly admired Mozart:

> I had never before heard anyone play with such spirit and grace.[110]

Clementi's praise is in line with the general opinion of his contemporaries. Dittersdorf reports a conversation with the Emperor in his autobiography.[111]

> *Emperor*: Have you heard Mozart play?
> *Dittersdorf*: Three times already.
> *Emperor*: Do you like him?
> *Dittersdorf*: Yes; all musicians do.
> *Emperor*: You have heard Clementi, too?
> *Dittersdorf*: Yes.
> *Emperor*: Some prefer him to Mozart, and Greybig is at the head of them. What do you think? Out with it!
> *Dittersdorf*: Clementi's playing is art simply and solely; Mozart's combines art and taste.
> *Emperor*: I said the same.

Leopold Mozart said that rubato is 'more easily shown than described', and this is even more true of 'feeling', a very broad term which defies rational formulation. All the same, we shall try to say a little about the art of expressive playing, an art that Mozart must have possessed to such a high degree.

As has already been frequently mentioned, Mozart's notation only hints at how the music is to be performed. For example, his dynamic markings are only general indications; both thought and feeling are needed to judge how loud a forte should be. But loud and soft are usually less important than a feeling for melody and for tension and relaxation. Not one note in a melodic curve must be stiff or lacking in life—each note must stand in a correctly judged relationship to the whole. Every note in a graded dynamic process has its own degree of intensity. Here is a rather bold attempt to make a graph of this dynamic oscillation which is so important in the presentation of all melody: C minor Concerto (K.491), first movement (shown over page).

When harmonic, rhythmic and melodic accents coincide, there is a risk that the metre may be excessively emphasized: the music may seem to lumber from one group of bars to the next, or even from one bar to the next—and this is at all costs to be avoided. But all great composers have had a masterly way of displacing the melodic accents in relation to the harmonic and rhythmic ones. This sort of displacement is difficult to determine rationally. There are countless harmony textbooks and numerous essays on rhythm, but never yet a good textbook on melody, since both in creating and in reproducing melodies we depend to a great extent on our artistic instinct (which can, of course, be astonishingly sound). The few rational and really applicable rules—such as the rule that a suspension must be accented and its resolution

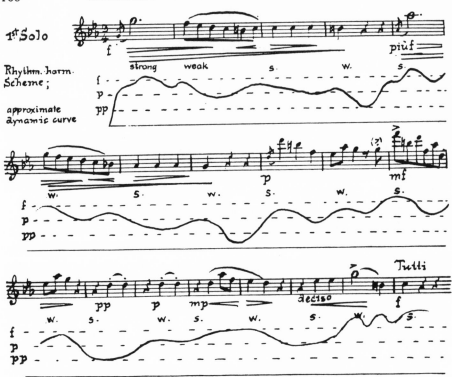

unaccented—depend not only on melodic principles, but also on those of harmony and rhythm.

In the following example (theme of the D major Rondo (K.485)) we find a quiet period of twice eight bars:

It is obvious that from the rhythmic and metric point of view bars 1, 3 and 5 are 'strong', bars 2, 4 and 6 'weak'. Examination of the harmony gives a similar scheme:

But it would be wrong to play the first and third bars as melodically 'strong', i.e. accented. Here our artistic instinct demands that bars 2 and 4 (above all, 4!) should not be played 'weaker', but on the contrary a shade 'stronger':

If the accents come on the metric 'strong points' (bars 1 and 3), this theme loses its charm and even sounds banal. One could, of course, play bars 1 and 4 'strong', 2 and 3 'weak'. From bar 5 onward the melodic accents fall into line with the harmonic-metric scheme, so that two melodically strong bars (4 and 5) are adjacent.

This tendency for melodic tension to increase in the second and fourth bars is a common feature of Mozart's cantabile themes. Examples of themes built on this principle occur in the Piano Concertos K.453, first movement, first and second subjects; K.459, first movement, first subject; K.467, all themes; K.482, all themes in the first movement, etc. One could almost call this a stylistic principle.

It is difficult to bridge the gap between instinctive feeling for melody and conscious observation; but there have been constant and often successful attempts to do so. Eighteenth-century textbooks, which are indeed particularly concerned with melodic expression, contain a few rules (most of them rather primitive) for giving form to melodic lines. Quantz, for example, requires harpsichordists to play 'the various notes that require emphasis . . . with more liveliness and force'.

> This applies to long notes that occur amid shorter ones, also the notes at the opening of a principal subject: and above all dissonances.[112]

And Leopold Mozart says:

> Generally the accent of the expression or the stress of tone falls on the ruling or strong beat, which the Italians call Nota Buona . . . if the composer has indicated no other expression[113] (e.g. syncopations). . . . In lively pieces the accent is mostly used on the highest note, in order to make the performance

right merry. So it may happen here that the stress falls on the last note of the second and fourth crotchet in simple time, but on the end of the second crotchet in $\frac{2}{4}$ time; especially when the piece begins with the up stroke. For example:

But in slow, sad pieces this cannot be done, for there the up stroke must not be detached, but sustained singingly.[114]

In Mozart one should pay particular attention to the very frequent accented passing-notes and suspensions. The rule that the resolution is to be sung or played softer than the dissonance (which should be slightly emphasized) must be strictly observed.

Mozart often adds an extra expression mark in passages of this kind, to show the correct accentuation: B flat Piano Trio (K.502), first movement, bars 52–3:

No good musician is likely to make the mistake of cutting off the final quavers so that he unintentionally accents them.

A parallel can be drawn between the resolution of accented passing-notes and a fundamental rule of rhetoric. In English, as in German and Italian, the accent falls as a rule on the last syllable but one: *m/other, m/utter, m/adre*, etc. The accent on the first syllable automatically means that the unaccented one must be pronounced as a light, short sound. The same applies to the resolution of accented dissonances; the rule of tension (dissonance) and relaxation (consonance) demands that the dissonance should receive an accent, and the resolution the opposite of an accent, represented in prosody by a sign which is unfortunately unknown to musical notation, but which could do good service to indicate 'weak syllables': the sign ◡.*

There are, however, exceptions to this rule, when 'higher considerations' demand just the opposite, i.e. accentuation of the resolution, as in the A major Concerto (K.488), first movement, bar 126 (and 256):

*We are grateful to Mr. Leo Black for pointing out that Schoenberg used such a sign (e.g. in the Piano Suite, op. 25).

Here the melody must soar firmly upward; a diminuendo would break up the line and thus be out of place. There is another exception in the Finale of the Concerto K.466, bar 103:

Here again the resolution E must be accented; otherwise, being so much shorter than the accented passing-note(s), it will not be heard at all.

If two notes are joined by a slur, *in general* the first of the two should be played louder, even if it is not an accented dissonance or suspension (cf. p. 58 of this book). Again there is an exception to this rule; in upward leaps of more than a third, the second note is often to be played louder than the first, as in the following passage from the E flat Concerto (K.482), third movement, second tutti:

Unless there is a slight accent on the top E flat, the passage sounds dull and colourless.

There is a simple and well tried device for clarifying the articulation of a theme; one adds a text, if possible one that seems to express the feeling of the music. Just as a reciter respects the rise and fall of the language, making appropriate gradations, so the notes of a theme must always be in the right rhetorical relationship to one another. When one looks at a theme such as that of the A major Sonata (K.331), as printed in the first edition, one cannot decide on philological grounds whether Mozart wanted the slurs to be over the first two or the first three notes (the MS. being lost and the first edition inconsistent). If we try to imagine this tune with words added, we may think something like this:

Lasst ver- trau- te Weis' er- klin- gen, Lasst uns froehlich Mozart singen!
Sing and play, don't care who hears us? Mozart's music always cheers us!

In this case it is, of course, clear that we can only slur the first two notes of the first bar. Anyone trying to find a good text for the version with a slur over the first three notes would find it extraordinarily difficult and would stop trying after a little while. Addition of a text brings to light a number of important points, and these lessons can then be consciously applied, with a good effect on one's playing. One realizes that the first four bars hang together, and also that the quavers on the third and sixth beats must be played a good deal more lightly than the strong beats. It also follows quite obviously that the fourth bar (the word 'always') contains the dynamic climax of the phrase. Correct declamation will prevent the carelessness that makes many pianists play the (feminine) ending of this phrase too loud. Thus the addition of words can be a useful pointer to correct interpretation.

In a letter to a young colleague[115] the late pianist Dinu Lipatti very rightly remarked that a good musician will concentrate on the weak beats, since the strong ones have a favoured position within the bar and can look after themselves. For this reason many composers have used accents to ensure that notes on weak beats receive the right degree of emphasis. Mozart, too, often wrote expressive accents over notes on weak beats, as in bar 7 of this same theme (K.331, first movement):

or in the C minor Fantasia (K.475), second Allegro, bars 29–31. But even where Mozart did not mark an accent for notes on a weak beat, they are still often the ones the player has to emphasize, e.g. Finale of the A major Concerto (K.488), bars 129 et seq., 151 et seq.:

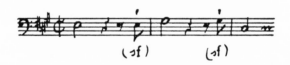

In such passages, where the tempo is quick, the short notes must definitely be accented, otherwise they will not be heard at all.

In the second subject of the first movement of the Piano Concerto in E flat (K.482), the quavers are usually 'thrown away', and cannot be heard clearly enough:

For the same reason, in quick rhythms such as

(C minor Concerto, third movement), the semiquavers, despite being partly resolutions of dissonances, must have a perceptible accent if they are not to be inaudible. The same applies to accompanimental rhythms, such as:

(bars 21 and 29 of the same movement). The accent should come, not on the dotted crotchets, but on the quavers. The above example from the D major Rondo is another in which the quavers (in bars 2 and 4) should not be 'swallowed'.

Repeated notes often occur in Mozart's music, and there is a very great risk that they will be played lifelessly. Here one must know what kind of 'emotion' ('*Affekt*') they are intended to express. In cantabile passages one should make it a principle hardly ever to play two successive notes of the same pitch in exactly the same way. In this case the note-repetition has some particular expressive purpose, and the notes must be made to speak, i.e. given dynamic shading and above all not unduly shortened. For instance, this is how the theme of the second movement of the D major ('Coronation') Concerto (K.537) should be played:

(The first note should be *p*, the second a little softer, the third rather louder than the second, but not quite as loud as the first, the fourth roughly as loud as the first and the fifth somewhat louder.) The note-repetitions in the first movement of the D minor Concerto (K.466) should also be played 'expressively', though in this case with passionate expression and a slight crescendo to build up tension. Another common mistake is to make repeated notes too short. Pianists are particularly liable to fall into this trap. There is a passage in the C major Fantasia (K.394) which should rightly be played as follows:

and not as if there were staccato dots over the right hand:

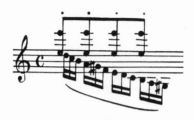

In contrast to these 'expressive' note-repetitions, there are 'playful' ones whose whole charm lies in their lack of accent, their complete evenness, with no dynamic gradation. We would number the Allegro theme of *The Magic Flute* Overture among these, or the main theme of the third movement of the 'Coronation' Concerto:

The notes should be played short, 'tapped out', with considerable inner tension.

One can also add the first eight bars of the D major Concert-rondo (K. 382), and much the same goes for the repeated notes in bars 5 et seq. of the first movement of the Piano Trio in C major (K.548):

This theme, however, depends not only on its rhythm, but also on a specifically melodic element, so that the interpreter is right to avoid making these notes absolutely regular. Bar 6 has the effect of an ironical courtesy; it is as if one were transported to the world of *The Marriage of Figaro*. This crop of

Gs must always be savoured to the utmost. The quaver rests between them are very important and must on no account be shortened—just as throughout Mozart's music the *rests must never be neglected*! To underline the humour of this passage, one can in fact delay the beginning of bars 6 and 8 by a fraction, and make the Gs slightly shorter than their written length:

The 'breathing-space' before the bar-line, as suggested, must be so short that there is no question of holding up the even flow of the metre. Such hesitation, 'pausing for breath', is very important throughout Mozart's music, which is so strongly influenced by vocal writing. This kind of 'breathing-space', a slight caesura, is often in place before the entry of a new subject, as in the second movement of the E flat Concerto (K.482), bar 124, before the flute-motive enters. Without such a caesura, the succeeding C major section would lack the necessary feeling of restfulness at its very outset. But it would be a great mistake to make this kind of caesura in the middle of a cantabile theme, thus breaking up a melody which should be felt as a unit, an extended curve. Great interpreters have always known how to spin a smoothly-curving thread, to mould the alternations of musical tension and relaxation so perfectly that formal sections can make their full effect as self-contained units. To make an unmotivated ritardando is one of the worst offences against good taste. We have heard a well-known violinist play the first solo in the Adagio of the G major Violin Concerto (K.216) as follows:

not merely once, but every time it appeared! Set any words you like to this phrase, following the rhythm—for example, 'My comfort and my treasure'—and the result, if the above phrasing is followed will always be the same: 'My comfort and maaaaaa . . . i treasure'. Even a tenor in an operetta could not get away with that! It is very depressing that such offences against healthy musical sensitivity are only very rarely noticed either by the public or by the critics. Mozart would have had a word for it; '. . . he has not a farthing's worth of taste or feeling'. But the daily Press were almost unanimous in their praise of this violinist's 'expressive' playing. Incidentally, as has been said before, it has always been known that the development of a sound feeling for melody can be greatly assisted by adding words to clarify passages where the flow of musical tension is obscure.

Naturally 'feeling' is not limited to the shaping of melodies: rhythm and harmony, too, serve expressive ends. In Mozart, melody, harmony and rhythm interpenetrate in a unique way. We must, unfortunately, forgo a detailed investigation of Mozart's rhythm, since this would make our book too long, and we shall also have to limit ourselves to a few suggestions on the subject of harmonic expression.[116]

There are already 'romantic passages' in Mozart in which the expressive effect results less from the melodic lines of the individual parts than from the sound they make together. This seems to be the case, for example, in the codetta (epilogue) of the first movement of the G major Concerto (K.453):

Every listener at first takes the G sharp in the second bar as an (enharmonic) A flat. Thus one expects some such progression:

and is very surprised when the supposed A flat unexpectedly resolves on to an A. In the coda (bar 332) the effect of this passage is enhanced by a counterpoint in the wind. The second movement of this concerto, which has an unprecedented range of modulation, also produces some unexpected turns of harmony. The lead-back in bar 86 from G sharp major (dominant of C sharp minor) to C major, within four bars, is one of the boldest and finest modulations Mozart ever wrote. The C major has the effect of a revelation; 'and there was light'—

Here it is best to broaden the tempo, to allow the harmonic intensification its full effect.

The Finale of the C minor Concerto is another place where Mozart achieves most powerful harmonic effects by enharmonic twists:

Any string player would adjust the intonation of the F sharp in bar 234 to make it a little higher than the G flat in the previous bar. Pianists, alas, cannot adjust their intonation to emphasize this kind of expressive point. They have to be content with accenting the F sharp in its function as leading-note to the ensuing G.[117]

In bar 6 of the Adagio of the A major Concerto (K.488), the right hand has a B sharp as an accented dissonance before a C sharp; here again the ear may be enharmonically misled into thinking this is a C (minor third on A). Though one cannot entirely prevent this aural illusion, it would again be in order to accent the B sharp. At the moment of resolution the wideawake listener will correct his mistake 'retrospectively'.

The accompaniment also has an expressive function. For example, the hammering chordal accompaniment of the first subject of the A minor Sonata (K.310) (first movement) is vitally important in giving the theme its passionate character. The chords must be played absolutely evenly, with firm dynamics and rhythm.

Alberti-figures, which are so much favoured by Mozart, may underline the lyrical character of a theme (as in the first subject of the A major Concerto (K.488), first movement), but can equally well delight one by the way they bring out the piano's ability to sparkle (Three-piano Concerto (K.242), third movement, bar 132):

In the first case the Alberti-figures will be played gently and legato; in the second, staccato. When lyrical themes are played legato, some of the notes of the Alberti-bass can often be 'tied', i.e. the key is depressed longer than is indicated in the score, e.g. B flat Concerto (K.595), first movement, bars 79–80:

played:

or the opening of the C major Piano Sonata (K.545), first movement. This way of tying certain notes is certainly in accordance with Mozart's intentions, as is shown by passages from chamber works with piano, and piano concertos, where this kind of Alberti-figure is supported by sustained chords on the other instruments. This is also nicely proved by a passage in the Finale of the A minor Sonata (K.310). In bar 21 Mozart wrote the accompaniment as follows:

but at the corresponding point later, from bar 195 onward, he omitted to indicate that the bass part is to be prolonged (though the passage should certainly be played in just the same way as the earlier one):

(Naturally, this kind of tie should only be made in passages where the accompaniment is in two or more implied parts, not in single-line accompaniments such as that in bars 233 et seq. of this movement.)

If the accompaniment is written in quiet chords, as in the theme of the Variations from the A major Sonata (K.331), one must make sure that they are unmistakably softer than the melodic line. The overall impression of a certain degree of loudness is the result of the combined dynamic levels of the various parts. The secret of singing piano tone lies not least in the fact that the melody is played one degree louder than p ($c.$ mf) and the accompaniment a degree softer ($c.$ pp)—without becoming inaudible, of course. The bass line should often be slightly emphasized, while the middle parts must keep in the background.

Music is, of course, not a play of absolute forms; it does more: it expresses the whole world of human experience. In his operas and vocal music, above all, Mozart leaves us in no doubt that he is concerned with human expression:

I advise you to watch the expression marks—to think carefully of the meaning and the force of the words—to put yourself in all seriousness into Andro-
meda's situation and position!—and to imagine that you really are that very
person. With your beautiful voice and your fine method of producing it you
will undoubtedly soon become an excellent singer, if you continue to work in
this way.[118]

In Mozart's opinion the instrumental accompaniment as well as the vocal
line has a part in the depiction of extra-musical moods:

Let me now turn to Belmonte's aria in A major, '*O wie ängstlich, o wie feurig*'.
Would you like to know how I have expressed it—and even indicated his
throbbing heart? By the two violins playing octaves. This is the favourite aria
of all those who have heard it, and it is mine also. I wrote it expressly to suit
Adamberger's voice. You feel the trembling—the faltering—you see how his
throbbing breast begins to swell; this I have expressed by a crescendo. You
hear the whispering and the sighing—which I have indicated by the first
violins with mutes and a flute playing in unison.[119]

There are countless examples of this kind in Mozart's music. One need only
think of the trio from the first Act of *Così fan tutte* ('Soave sia il vento') in
which the violins unmistakably depict the gentle undulation of the waves.

In the piano music this direct relationship with an experience expressible
in words is not immediately apparent. But one finds figurations from Mozart's
operas, similar moods and experiences, throughout his music.[120] In the C
minor Fantasia (K.475), bars 49 et seq., Mozart writes an excited figuration
which returns almost literally in the second Act of *Così fan tutte*:

C minor Fantasia:

Così fan tutte:

In the opera the orchestra plays this motive at Ferrando's words, 'In qual
fiero contrasto, in qual disordine di pensieri e di affetti io mi ritrovo'.

One may take it that the wholly similar bars in the Piano Fantasia are
intended to express the same mood (helpless despair on the part of an individual faced by an unexpected turn of fate).

One could draw countless further parallels between Mozart's vocal and instrumental music. In this connection, it is interesting that Mozart took over many emotional symbols from baroque music without altering them.[121] The best-known example of this kind must be the song of the Armed Men in the second Act of *The Magic Flute*; Mozart wrote this after the manner of Bach, as regards not only its technique, but also its spirit, which is akin to that of Bach's chorale preludes.[122] It is not so well-known that Mozart always gives the dotted rhythm of the old French overture the meaning it had in the seventeenth century: he uses it as a symbol of majesty, solemnity, e.g. in the 'Qui tollis' of the great C minor Mass, the 'Rex tremendae majestatis' of the Requiem or the introductory chords of *The Magic Flute* Overture.*

The Phrygian cadence:

was counted as a symbol of the deepest tragic expression long before Mozart. He also used it frequently, usually intensifying the harmony by sharpening the sixth (augmented sixth chord) when he intended it to have this effect: e.g. the aria 'Ach, ich fühl's, es ist verschwunden' from *The Magic Flute*, where this harmony twice occurs at the words 'ewig hin der Liebe Glück' ('Happy dream, 'twill ne'er come true'), the second time as an augmented sixth with the fourth added:

This chord has a similarly tragic import in the instrumental works, where it constantly occurs, as in the E flat Concerto (K.482), first movement, bar 138:

or in the Finale of the C minor Concerto (K.491), bar 219.

*This kind of dotted rhythm also occurs at the beginning of the second act of *The Magic Flute* after the March of the Priests. These anacrusic semiquavers are unfortunately almost always played too slowly and heavily. The tempo is 'adagio', alla-breve, i.e. not too slow an adagio. If quietly moving minims are beaten, the upbeats will be played fairly short.

Many musical symbols can have a number of different, if related meanings. Triadic fanfares, for example, are a symbol of both *joie de vivre*, vitality, and of heroism and triumph. In Figaro's aria, 'Non più andrai', all these meanings are combined. A similar mood is expressed in the first subject of the Sonata for two pianos (K.448) (first movement), or of the C major Trio (K.548).

Like all great creators, Mozart knew how to exploit every expressive resource available in his time. But in his day feelings were expressed far more subtly than nowadays, and men's reactions to emotional stimuli were far stronger. One generation will be moved to tears; the next will give an appreciative smile, and the third generation may say, 'A bit pretty-pretty, don't you think?' To draw an analogy: whereas once a smart tap was enough to let loose a flood of feeling, nowadays one often needs a hammer-stroke. There are passages where Mozart could 'make an effect' so that all his listeners were carried away:

> . . . just in the middle of the first Allegro there was a passage which I felt sure must please. The audience were quite carried away—and there was a tremendous burst of applause. But as I knew, when I wrote it, what effect it would surely produce, I had introduced the passage again at the close—when there were shouts of '*Da capo*'.[123]

Nowadays similar means will produce in us only a pale reflection of their original effect. Harmonic strokes, such as chromatically descending diminished sevenths and other bold modulations, usually have little effect on ears that have been dulled. People often talk about Mozart's 'beautiful harmonies', even when they have been listening to a rugged, eerie work such as the C minor Concerto. Did not even Schumann refer to the G minor Symphony's 'floating Grecian grace'?

This alteration in the public's aesthetic reaction must necessarily have an effect on the way Mozart's works are played nowadays. One has, it seems, to emphasize emotional effects for modern listeners, who are thicker-skinned, and to draw the important psychological outlines with broad strokes, particularly in the serious, 'confessional' works. How far can or may the performer go in doing this? The question is one as much of personality as of good taste. It will do Mozart's music no harm to play it forcefully, just so long as one respects its innate limits, so long as one brings out its clarity and beauty, its pure architectonic qualities and above all its moral stature. Mozart is a great composer, and one must not be afraid to play him on a large scale; to present him as a 'little man', a kind of marionette, is a misinterpretation of history that will never do him justice.

The 'simplicity' which later generations have often held against Mozart is only apparent. His contemporaries were far from finding his music too simple —on the contrary, they found it too complex and varied.

> He is unquestionably one of the greatest original geniuses, and I have never yet met with any composer who had such an amazing wealth of ideas; I could

almost wish he were not so lavish in using them. He leaves his hearer out of
breath; for hardly has he grasped one beautiful thought, when another of
greater fascination dispels the first, so that in the end it is impossible to retain
any of these beautiful melodies, [124]

as the composer Dittersdorf wrote about Mozart's compositions. He often
disconcerted his hearers by his unheard-of boldness. Rochlitz has handed on
a well-known anecdote to the effect that shortly after the first Viennese performance of *Don Giovanni* a society of artistic amateurs, the Musikkenner der
Kaiserstadt, found the work overloaded, chaotic and unmelodic.[125]

We have mentioned the need for 'large-scale' interpretation, but this must
not be confused with coldness or stiffness: nowhere are these less in place than
in Mozart's music, which has more grace and charm than anyone else's. By
'charm' we mean the gift of being able to smile even when the situation is at
its most hopeless—and this is a gift that is very difficult to communicate,
particularly by means of written words. It is quite distinct from pathos, but
also from mere superficiality. There is a story which typifies the essence of
Mozart's personality; it concerns the way he sometimes tried to counter the
poverty that oppressed him:

> Mozart and his wife were dancing energetically about the room. When
> Deiner asked whether Mozart was teaching his wife to dance, Mozart laughed
> and said, 'We are simply keeping warm, because it is freezing and we cannot
> afford to buy wood.' Deiner at once hurried out and brought some of his own
> wood. Mozart took it and promised to pay well for it when he had some
> money.[126]

Even Mozart's tragic or melancholy works should not be played completely
without charm, though grace and charm will naturally be less prominent in
the C minor Concerto or the Jupiter Symphony than in the *Eine kleine Nachtmusik*. Obviously, charm is indispensable in all his works where grace and
high spirits predominate, such as the *Eine kleine Nachtmusik*, or the Concert
Rondo (K.382), where an interpretation will stand or fall mainly by its charm
(or lack of it). These hints, like those given earlier, will only be useful and justified if they are really understood, i.e. applied with discretion. One of the things
that distinguishes a good artist from a bad one is an ability to draw the line,
to tread the razor's edge between too much and too little. Mozart, a born
enemy of all exaggeration, was without parallel in this art of striking a
balance, and the interpretation of his works is therefore the acid test of good
taste.

This 'balance' is indeed one of the main reasons why Mozart-playing presents so many difficulties, despite the simplicity of his musical language. For
Mozart had a keen sense of the natural. He rejected all bombast and exaggeration, in fact he got a good deal of amusement from it. This is a bond
between him and present-day humanity. (The nineteenth century, with its
plush curtains and its love of hollow pathos, found Mozart's directness and
naturalness hard to appreciate. His humour aroused indignation, as when he

wrote canons on 'indecent' texts, and people seriously considered destroying his 'compromising' letters to his young cousin, Bäsle!) Mozart always tried to ensure that he would be readily understood, avoided complexity and ostentatious expenditure of energy:

> You know that I am no great lover of difficulties. He [the violinist, Fränzl] plays difficult things, but his hearers are not aware that they are difficult; they think that they could at once do the same themselves. That is real playing.[127]

In fact he was proud if he succeeded in making his own compositions appear easy:

> These concertos are a happy medium between what is too easy and too difficult; they are very brilliant, pleasing to the ear, and natural, without being vapid. There are passages here and there from which connoisseurs alone can derive satisfaction; but these passages are written in such a way that the less learned cannot fail to be pleased, without knowing why.[128]

In choosing texts to set, he particularly looked for simplicity and naturalness.

> The ode is sublime, beautiful, anything you like, but too exaggerated and pompous for my fastidious ears.[129]

His amusing remarks about the affected playing of Nanette Stein[130] are well-known: she pulled too many faces and made too many unnecessary movements for his liking. He was especially adverse to unnatural vibrato on the part of singers:

> Meisner, as you know, has the bad habit of making his voice tremble at times, turning a note that should be sustained into distinct crotchets, or even quavers—and this I never could endure in him. And really it is a detestable habit and one which is quite contrary to nature. The human voice trembles naturally—but in its own way—and only to such a degree that the effect is beautiful. Such is the nature of the voice; and people imitate it not only on wind-instruments, but on stringed instruments, too and even on the clavier.* But the moment the proper limit is over-stepped, it is no longer beautiful—because it is contrary to nature. It reminds me then of the organ when the bellows are puffing.[131]

And he also criticized the singer Raaff:

> Raaff is too much inclined to drop into the cantabile.[132]

Cantabile quality is naturally one of the main things Mozart demanded of his interpreters:

> And who is not aware that singing is at all times the aim of every instrumentalist; because one must always approximate to nature as nearly as possible,

---

*'Clavier' meant clavichord at the time; on this instrument a vibrato (*Bebung*) was possible—in fact, easy.

as Leopold Mozart wrote in his *Violinschule*.[133] And Wolfgang wrote to his father from Mannheim:[134]

> In my last letter I forgot to mention Mlle. Weber's greatest merit, which is her superb cantabile singing.

This is no surprise, coming from a great composer whose music is so essentially song, for whom 'melody is the essence of music. . . .'[135] 'Let every note sound and be free within the framework of the law which, unwritten, lives in every true musician', as Edwin Fischer wrote in an essay on Mozart.[136] Here, as in his relentless opposition to mechanical, lifeless playing, he was in agreement with one of Mozart's contemporaries, Schubart, who wrote in 1789 in his *Aesthetics of Music*:[137]

> Quite apart from any mechanical ability—the ear, the winged fist, dexterous fingers, steady rhythm, feeling for the instrument, sight-reading, and all the rest of it; no soloist should dare to come before the public unless he has creative energy; unless he knows how to transform the notes into so many balls of fire; unless he can inspire the accompanying players as well as his listeners, and—in fact, unless he can summon up the spirit to burn in all ten of his fingers.

Chapter Eight

IMPROVISED EMBELLISHMENTS

IN his textbook *On the True Art of Playing Keyboard Instruments*, C. P. E. Bach described the *Manieren*, a term then applied to all ornaments, and divided them into two major groups. In the first group he included all ornaments—

> which are indicated by conventional signs or a few small notes; in the second are those which lack signs and consist of many short notes.[138]

This division is justified not only logically, but historically. The signs for 'prescribed' ornaments came mostly from the French *claveciniste* school, while Italy, as we know, was generally acknowledged to be the home of 'arbitrary', i.e. improvised, decoration. It is this second group of *Manieren* which we shall discuss here, investigating the extent to which they should be used (if at all) in playing Mozart's music.

Nowadays it is more than ever necessary to deal with the problem of embellishments, because they are one field in which the last few decades' passion for 'faithfulness to the text' has caused a break with interpretative tradition. No eighteenth-century performer would ever have hesitated to embellish a theme if it recurred a number of times, nor would he have dreamed of 'sticking to the text' when playing a passage which was obviously a mere sketch, a melodic or harmonic skeleton of the kind that so often occurs in old manuscripts. If Mozart, when pressed for time in writing down a concerto movement, omitted to fill in a passage he had sketched, he could be certain that contemporary performers would not misunderstand him, would realize that 'something was missing'. He could, however, be equally certain that nobody knew how to vary a theme as beautifully as he did; this is why in Mozart's music (unlike that of his contemporaries) we find a welcome attempt to write out as much as possible, and to rely as little as possible on his performers' talent for composition. Take one glance, for example, at the slow movement of a Mozart piano sonata, and compare it with a similar one by Kozeluch or Abbé Vogler: you will find a profusion of notes that leave no room for doubt: Mozart's works usually contain exact and complete embellishments, and often there is nothing left for the performer to add. Any note that one might add would merely paint the lily and make nonsense musically

The relationship between Mozart and his contemporaries was like that between J. S. Bach and his; almost all Bach's contemporaries (including Handel) relied a great deal on their interpreters' talent for improvisation, and hardly one of them ever took the trouble to write out a movement with such full ornamentation as did Bach in, for instance, the slow movement of the 'Italian' Concerto. Thus Mozart encountered the same criticism as Bach in his time: his works were held to be too complicated and full of notes. 'Far too many notes, my dear Mozart', was Joseph II's famous comment on *The Marriage of Figaro*.

There is further support for the view that Mozart was reluctant to let anyone else embellish his works; for one thing, despite his dislike of writing out music, not only did he usually take the trouble to write out his own embellishments for a theme repeated during a slow movement (e.g. the A minor Rondo (K.511)), and to write out recapitulations in their entirety if they were to be varied, etc.; in his concertos he also wrote out the cadenzas and lead-ins, or else put them down on separate sheets. If for once, in hastily writing out a work, he had not found the time to vary a theme when it was repeated, he would later make it his business to devise some such variant. This is seen from his letter to his father of 9th June 1784, in which he writes:

> . . . there is something missing in the solo passage in C in the Andante of the concerto in D. I shall supply the deficiency as soon as possible and send it with the cadenzas.

The melody, in its unembellished form, is:

A decorated version of this passage has now been discovered in the Abbey of St. Peter, Salzburg, a monastery with which the Mozarts were in close contact; in the third edition of Köchel's *Catalogue* (p. 824) Einstein has mistakenly called this version a manuscript. Are these bars really a copy of Mozart's own embellishment of the passage, which he promised his sister in the letter quoted above, or is this surviving sheet merely an attempt by one of his contemporaries to embellish the passage? The question must remain open.[139] In any case, the discovery of this tiny variant is a great stroke of luck, since it is the first contemporary evidence that this kind of passage was regarded as needing embellishment; moreover, much can be learned from comparing the plain and embellished versions:

In treating the problem of embellishment, we face fundamental questions: 'When may we, or must we, add notes?', and also 'How many, and which notes may we add?' To answer the first question, it is important to start by making sure which of the eighteenth-century rules we know to have pre-scribed embellishment at some points and forbidden it at others. Investigations have shown that in practice the following types of embellishment were permitted: all types of embellishment or figuration could be applied to themes in slow movements, observing certain conditions; some fermatas were a cue for improvisation (but this brings us to cadenzas and lead-ins, which will be treated separately); finally, the performer had to fill out passages where the composer had used abbreviations or merely provided a sketch—these can occur in both slow and quick movements. In the case of this latter group, necessary additions to the text, one is not so much 'embellishing' in the true sense as completing bars that were incompletely written out.

Eighteenth-century performers loved to add embellishments, particularly in slow movements. 'The quicker the movement, the more parts it has, the lower they lie, the more instruments there are playing, and the larger the hall, the fewer the ornaments'.[140] Türk, discussing the question 'When to decorate?', wrote as follows:

> only a general remark, that one may indeed make occasional alterations in the repeat of an Allegro, or in similar cases: but major additions are most often appropriate in an Adagio.[141]

Leopold Mozart's *Violinschule* also says obliquely that allegro movements do not offer opportunities for embellishment; a much-quoted paragraph runs as follows:[142]

> Many succeed so far that they play off with uncommon dexterity the most difficult passages in various concertos or solos which they have practised with great industry. These they know by heart . . . so long as they play an allegro, all goes well: but when it comes to an adagio, there they betray their great ignorance and bad judgment . . . the embellishments are in the wrong place, too overloaded, and mostly played in a confused manner; and often the notes are far too bare and one observes that the player knows not what he does. . . .

There is another indication that embellishments are appropriate only in slow movements; most of Leopold Mozart's examples of embellishment contain figurations which could only be played satisfactorily at a slow tempo. Since even Leopold Mozart and Wolfgang's contemporaries regarded the decoration of quick movements as exceptional, in Mozart's own music embellishments will only be in place in slow movements, if at all.

Nowadays it is hard to get any idea of the extent to which embellishments were used in Mozart's time. The quotation from Leopold's *Violinschule* clearly points to a general assumption that performers would add embellishments in passages that required them. Moreover, there is an informative passage in a biography, by Schnyder von Wartensee, of two musicians who met Mozart in Mainz in 1791. Philip Carl Hoffmann expressly emphasizes that when Mozart played the Adagio movements of his piano concertos they were less plain and simple than would appear from the written-out piano part; he would embellish them gently and tastefully, now in one way, now in another, as his genius dictated from moment to moment.* This was still so even a generation after Mozart, as we see from the arrangements of Mozart's works by such composers as A. E. Müller, P. C. Hoffmann or N. Hummel. Nor, as we know, had Aloys Fuchs, Köchel's predecessor, any inhibitions about embellishing Mozart's themes.[143] But whenever contemporary discussion of musical performance touches the subject of embellishments there are constant warnings against their over-frequent use. We know of Leopold Mozart's repeated complaints about musicians who 'embellish and befrill a piece right foolishly out of their own heads'; and elsewhere he writes:

> Many imagine themselves to have brought something wonderfully beautiful into the world if they befrill the notes of an Adagio Cantabile thoroughly, and make out of one note at least a dozen. Such note-murderers expose thereby their bad judgement to the light, and tremble when they have to sustain a long note or play only a few notes singingly, without inserting their usual preposterous and laughable frippery.[144]

In his autobiography, Dittersdorf also regrets that not only 'masters such as Mozart and Clementi', but also those less-gifted venture to improvise in this way so that—

> You never hear the sound of a piano at a concert without knowing that you will be regaled with every sort of twist and twirl and turn.[145]

Although Dittersdorf and Leopold Mozart complained that the interpreters of their time went too far, they would certainly have been equally horrified at the thoughtless or over-cautious ways of present-day performers, who often reproduce merely the bare skeleton of the music. Without linking notes to bring it to life, 'the best melody . . . becomes empty and monotonous', as C. P. E. Bach said,[146] and this is also true in exceptional cases in Mozart's music.

The question, 'Where and how is one to add embellishments?' does, however, demand of the interpreter a highly developed sense of responsibility. Fortunately, there are many works in which Mozart has provided precious illustrations of his method of embellishment, and these should be most carefully studied.[147] For example, much can be learned by comparing the MS. of the Piano Sonata in F (K.332), with the first edition. In the Adagio the printed edition shows radical additions to the recapitulation, as compared with the version in the MS. This is also true of the Eleventh Variation (Adagio) in the Finale of the D major Sonata (K.284). Many editions usefully juxtapose the two versions, to make comparison easier; this is done, for instance, in Rudorff's edition:

*Cf. Adam Gottron: 'Wie spielte Mozart die Adagios seiner Klavierkonzerte', p. 334, *Musikforschung*, 1960.

Sonata in D (K.284), third movement, Adagio-Variation:

Sonata in F (K.332), second movement, bar 21 onward:

These examples are interesting pointers to Mozart's own way of adding embellishments.[148] The figurations are not overloaded, the number of extra notes is small. Thus the melodic content of the simple version is still fully effective when embellished. Such comparisons indeed show how sparingly Mozart used embellishments, and how strongly the contours of the original melody emerge even in the decorated version. In this respect there is clearly a difference between Mozart's embellishments and those by, for example, Hummel, who often introduced turns of phrase which actually invert the rise and fall of the melody, who did not hesitate even in allegro movements to alter practically every passage, and whose embellishments are surpassed for prolixity only by those of Hoffmann. Hummel's embellishments may be borne in mind as hints (there are neat ideas, for example, in the second movement of the D minor Concerto, bars 40–67, also in bars 126–34), but nowadays the incorporation of all his suggested embellishments, as they stand, would be emphatically rejected:

Bar 122 (not previously altered):

Bar 40:

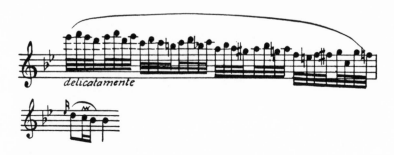

delicatamente

As for Hoffmann, it is enough to compare the embellishments (see p. 178) for K.451, which are probably genuine Mozart, with a passage from the second movement of the C major Concerto (K.467), which as originally written happens to be identical with the beginning of this passage.[149] Where Mozart added only a single note, in Hoffmann there are twenty-four! 'Befrilling' of this kind is certainly not what Mozart intended.

The varied recapitulations in the second and third movements of the C major Concerto (K.415) also throw interesting light on Mozart's embellishments (cf. bar 50 onward, third movement, with bar 221 onward); the varied recapitulation in the Andante of the B flat Violin Sonata (K.454); and the Adagio of the C minor Sonata: here it is interesting that a recently discovered copy of this sonata with handwritten additions gives the recapitulation in unaltered form; here, again, Mozart seems to have added to the work for the printed edition, as against the MS. (which has since disappeared). For it is less than likely that the additions in the printed edition are by anyone but Mozart himself. The finest example of written-out embellishments in Mozart's music is certainly the A minor Rondo (K.511), in which the theme is repeated ten times; every single time it is slightly varied. These few examples are enough to show the reserve with which Mozart used his command of embellishments, and how seldom he introduced any noticeable variation before the third bar of a theme. There is an even richer fund of information about Mozart's embellishments—passages in the slow movements of his concertos where the piano takes over a melody that has previously been given out on the strings or wind instruments. This ornamentation of themes when repeated by the piano amounts to a stylistic principle, which must have arisen less from the evanescent tone of the piano than from the natural need for an expressive intensification. This observation in turn justifies the reverse assumption: that wherever, in repeating an orchestral idea, the piano part is definitely meagre, something is very probably 'missing', as Mozart put it.

Embellishment also seems in place where a rhythmic motive appears twice or more in identical form. There is an interesting example of this in the C major Concerto (K.503). It is obvious that from bar 96 onward Mozart made a completely new sketch for the first solo, having rejected his original version as too conventional; he then carefully made a fair copy on a sheet which he then inserted into the full score. It is even possible that Mozart used the sketch, which has been preserved,[150] merely to settle the layout of the bars on the extra sheet. In any case, the later, final version is six bars longer than the original one. The first five bars in the sketch run as follows:

On the other hand, in the fair copy stuck into the MS. it is:

If we look at Mozart's three groups of piano works: those for solo piano, chamber works with piano and piano concertos, we see that opportunities for embellishment are most frequent in the concertos. Mozart was able to have most of his piano sonatas printed during his lifetime, and this must have been the principal reason why on the whole there are amazingly few places where one can add embellishments. The more we ˙wrestle with the problem of possible additions to works of this type, the clearer it becomes that embellishment is nowhere really necessary.

The same applies to the chamber works with piano, where it is in any case hard to add anything, since the members of an ensemble can never know how their partners are going to improvise.

The piano concertos contain by far the most passages where notes can or must be added, partly because Mozart usually had no opportunity to publish them, and also because he wrote them out for his own use and in great haste. Here one can both embellish 'thin' passages and complete bars which are obviously only sketched out. And at times 'can' becomes 'must'.[151]

In the MS. of the 'Coronation' Concerto the accompaniment is missing from the piano part almost throughout, but Mozart obviously did not intend the work to be a concerto 'for the right hand alone'. Here the accompaniment must, of course, be supplied, and most published editions include André's suggestions for completing the piano part. But it is also quite possible that in the first movement, from bar 265 onward, Mozart intended a slight variant in the sequential repetitions of the motive from bars 263-4, and that in the second movement of this concerto he wanted bars 59-61 to be varied. On the other hand, the themes of the Two-piano Concerto (K.365) contain beautifully written-out variants when they recur, but there is an illuminating reason why here Mozart took the trouble to put everything down in full: he could not take it for granted that two players would match each other in the embellishments they added.

During an allegro the prevailing movement in the piano part may suddenly break off for no apparent reason, and such passages must also usually be completed. Material to fill them out must of course sound as much like Mozart as possible, and can only be regarded as successful if the listener does not notice that anyone else but Mozart has contributed.

We should now like to give a few hints as to the form that embellishments should take, in the few cases where this seems necessary.

In the third movement of the E flat major Concerto (K.482) there is a whole series of bars which are merely sketched out, e.g. bars 164–72. Here, after seventeen bars of written-out semiquaver movement, Mozart wrote a further nine bars which contain only long notes, as a framework.

These bars will sound extremely strange unless they are filled out, perhaps as suggested here:

These embellishments go slightly beyond the compass of Mozart's piano in bar 4, but we see no objection. To avoid doing so, one can play the passage as follows (a version analogous to bars 334–42 in the Finale of the B flat Concerto (K.595).[152]

In the 'andantino cantabile' of this same movement (bars 218–53) Mozart again only hints at the piano part. This can be seen at a glance from the mere fact that except in bar 249 the piano part doubles the first violins exactly. One could conceivably play the piano part as it stands—as in most performances—but this is most unlikely to have been Mozart's intention. It is unheard-of for the solo instrument in a piano concerto to be cold-shouldered for three minutes and made to follow the violin part blindly—particularly during one of the most expressive passages in the entire work. Also it is quite out of keeping with Mozart's style to reduce the amount of figuration when a phrase is repeated, instead of increasing it (cf. bars 240 and 248). Whereas in bars 238–9 the rests in the top part are filled out by quaver figures on the first bassoon, literal interpretation of the corresponding passages (bars 246-7, 250–1) would leave wholly unmotivated rhythmic 'gaps'. Finally, in bars 248–9, there are slight differences between the piano and string parts which are a sketchy indication that the two are not to be identical.

The question, 'Just *what* is missing?' is much harder to answer, but here too there is guidance, e.g. in a very informative comparison with the A flat major section of the Larghetto of the C minor Concerto, which closely resembles this Andantino in its construction.

In both cases a clarinet melody in A flat major is repeated by the piano, accompanied by the strings. In the C minor Concerto the piano part is discreetly ornamented when it repeats the theme. We have already seen that Mozart does not alter the first two bars, and this also applies in the present case. So in the 'andantino cantabile' of the third movement of the E flat Concerto the embellishments should not begin till the third bar at the earliest:

bar 226

or:

or, to be still more cautious, only in the fifth bar:

In the second part of the melody the embellishment should if possible be still more discreet. We feel that all our suggestions for embellishment represent a maximum of addition; if they err, they are too much rather than too little. The peaceful character of this beautiful Andantino must not be endangered. If in bars 242–5 one is not to start doubling the violins again, one can add a trill, as at the opening of the piano solos in the Andante of the Concerto K.365. From bar 246 onward the harmonic and metric construction also reminds us of the second movement of K.365, bars 89–94 and 99–101, which are in fact richly ornamented. Bar 241 onward:

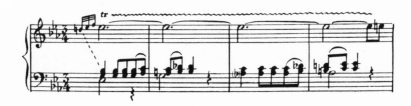

(The left hand doubling of the melody in the first four bars of the above example may appear rather bold, but this kind of doubling is very frequently found in Mozart—cf. the Concert Rondo K.382, bars 97–120.)

Finally, bars 346–7 and 353–6 of this movement need filling out:

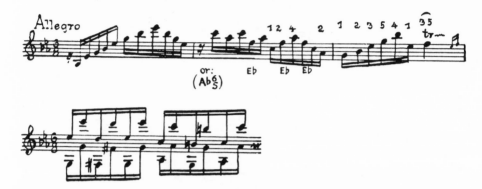

On the other hand, the unison passage with the flute and horn at the final return of the rondo theme (bar 387 onward) does not require completion by passage-work, for this kind of 'farewell' often occurs in Mozart's later works (cf. the C minor Concerto (K.491), second movement, bar 74 onward, or the B flat Concerto (K.595), second movement, bar 103 onward). Here there is in any case an intensification because of the altered instrumentation and harmony (e.g. bar 299).

In the second movement of the A major Concerto (K.488) the passage beginning at bar 80 may also need filling out.[153] Analysis of this passage shows that from bar 76 onward the piano solo is an (intensified) variation of the preceding tutti. In the bars from 81 onward, which correspond to the melodic climax of the tutti, the piano figuration stops for two bars and the piano part contains merely leaps of a fourth and a fifth, such as are otherwise found almost exclusively in the bass. The quaver movement in the middle parts, so characteristic of the tutti, also breaks off abruptly in bar 80 to give way to a new dialogue between the left hand of the piano and the basoon. Finally, from the point of view of tone-colour we find that in the second half of each bar the piano is covered up by the first clarinet. Certainly a Mozart piano, with its much weaker tone, would have been quite inaudible in the second half of each bar if the passage had been taken at its face value. Once more we can find in another of Mozart's works a model on which to base our completion of this passage: in the Andante of the C major Concerto (K.467). Here, from bar 12 onward, the first violins have a descending sequence of fourths and fifths, which is built very similarly, though it is more interesting from the rhythmic and compositional point of view:

But when later, from bar 45 onward, the piano takes up this motive, it plays (of course!) figurations, filling out stepwise the rising leaps of a fourth:

Applying this to our example, one might try the following version:

Too flourishing an embellishment, however, might distract the listener's attention from the above-mentioned dialogue in the low register.

It would be theoretically possible to play a two-part version of bars 81 et seq., by analogy with the preceding tutti; but we can take it that in this case Mozart would probably have written out the variant himself:

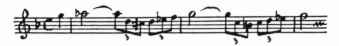

The ensuing passage, bar 85 onward, has such pathos and earnestness if left undecorated (particularly without this kind of embellishment!) that it is best to leave it alone. It is slightly reminiscent of Pamina's aria 'Ach, ich fühl's' from *The Magic Flute*, at the words 'So wird Ruh' im Tode sein'.

It is well known that the D Minor Concerto is another work which Mozart only finished writing down at the very last moment, and that on the day of the performance a copyist was still writing out the orchestral parts. This makes it easy to understand why here again Mozart could not spare the time to write out the variant repeats of the theme: very probably he improvised variations at the performance, since the opening motive of the Romanze occurs thirteen times. It is also striking that whereas there is not a single ornamentation of this motive in the piano part, the orchestral repetitions of the theme show slight variations. Thus it is not until the second entry of the melody that it is doubled an octave lower by the bassoon; on the third repetition of the theme in the orchestra the horn has a new counter-subject, and at the end the first violins a slight embellishment; and on its fourth entry the rhythm of the last bar is varied:

original version:

violins bar 141:

It is natural that in playing this movement a gifted musician will also add carefully to the piano part when the theme is repeated. For example:

Bar 119:

We know, too, that the C minor Concerto (K.491) was written in a parti-cular hurry—hastily, in fact, as we see from the MS., which is full of corrections and in places illegible. So it is not surprising if in this work some passages are only sketched out. For example, in the third movement bars 141–6 are written as follows in the MS.:

Obviously the crotchets in the left hand in bars 142–4 should have been written out as scales, and should be played in that way. This has been done in the best editions of the Concerto (Peters, Steingräber, Eulenburg, etc.[154]) To be consistent, however, the left hand's quavers in bar 145 should be dissolved into semiquavers in some such way as this:

It is interesting to see how Mozart tried to save trouble in writing out a similar passage a few bars later. Wherever he did not want straightforward scales, he wrote out the semiquavers: elsewhere he used abbreviations.

Naturally, this passage has to be completed in the appropriate way, as is in fact done in most printed editions. The only other question to be left open concerns the quavers in the third bar. They may either be embellished in the same way as in bar 145 or else played as written. To be 'faithful to the text' here, playing the notes in Mozart's sketch, would give a rather odd rhythmic structure.

The notation of bars 261–2 and 467–70 in the first movement of the same concerto is very reminiscent of the first example quoted above from the E flat Concerto. Although one could conceivably fill out these bars in some such way as this—

we feel that in the first of these two passages the original text is somehow more powerful and heroic.

It would indeed be grossly wrong to fill out all Mozart's wide leaps. Mozart was particularly fond of directly juxtaposing high and low registers, and these enormous leaps are a stylistic feature which often give his music an incomparable feeling of breadth. We would mention only the opening of the 'Haffner' Symphony, with its theme that reaches out through two octaves, or the pathos of the violins' leap in bars 8 et seq. of the Andante of the C major Concerto (K.467):

But Mozart's boldest and widest leaps are those in the Finale of the C minor Sonata (K.457), third movement, bar 301 onward:

(according to the MS. The first edition transposed the bass notes up an octave in bars 304–8). Not until the late works of Beethoven does one again find such expressive use of the rapid contrast of notes in the highest and lowest registers of the piano.

But let us return to the C minor Concerto. The second of the passages mentioned above is remarkable, since in all probability the first of the enormous leaps is to be filled out, and not the second.

For the completely regular accompaniment in the first six bars (sighing motives on the woodwind, sustained notes for the left hand, crotchets on the strings) suggests that the sequence is also to be continued in the right-hand figurations, perhaps like this:

The altered accompaniment in bars 7 and 8 suggests that the leap is to have pathos, to be played possibly unembellished, giving a rise in the emotional level through its contrast with the foregoing passage-work.

Another possibility would be:

Finally, we should mention a remarkable passage from the B flat Concerto K.595, bars 161–2 and 232–4 of the first movement. It is strange that Mozart should have left these two 'gaps' in the score of this work, which is written out most beautifully and which was, moreover, printed in his lifetime. Certainly something must be added here. Note the steady diminution: in bar 157 a semibreve, in bar 158 two minims, then four crotchets, eight quavers and suddenly nothing at all for two bars—only a legato slur over

three octaves, which is unplayable! The only plausible explanation is that
here Mozart did not want to be tied to any one version, and in fact there is
a whole series of good ways to fill out this passage, e.g.:

or perhaps best of all:

On the other hand, the theme of the Larghetto of this concerto is like a
chorale. To 'befrill' the peaceful, even notes of the chorale when it is repeated
later would be to mistake the character of this movement completely: it is
unique among Mozart's concerto movements, and nothing like it was written
again until the Adagio of Beethoven's 'Emperor' Concerto. This is another
reminder that excessive and irresponsible use of embellishments must be
avoided at all costs. Only in passages which are obviously sketchy should one
carefully make additions. Mozart's melodies, unadorned, are still utterly
Mozartean. The basis of any modest additions to them must be painstaking
study and knowledge of his style, and the necessary sympathy with his music.

Chapter Nine

CONTINUO PLAYING

NOWADAYS we no longer doubt that in performing his piano concertos Mozart at times used the piano as a continuo instrument. Time and again, in tutti sections, he scrupulously wrote out the bass part in the piano, or marked it 'col basso' on every page. This 'col basso' marking is indeed not in itself enough to prove that Mozart wanted a continuo part, i.e. that the piano was to play chords to fill out the harmony. For it is well known that Mozart also used this abbreviation on countless occasions for other instruments, such as the violas or bassoons, which could certainly not play a harmonic continuo part. But there is a whole series of markings which show that at least until the Concerto K.415 Mozart expected a continuo part in the tutti. This is proved by the following facts:

1. The four early Concertos K.37, 39, 40, and 41 contain a number of passages in Mozart's own hand with a written-out continuo. In this connection, the way his notation of the continuo developed during the composition of these concertos is very interesting. In the first movement of the first concerto the bass part of the orchestra is carefully entered in small notes in the piano part, and detailed figures added. In the second movement, too, there are figures, and the piano part even contains indications of the chords that are to be played before the pause in the tutti. At the end of the Finale, however, Mozart already uses the marking 'col basso', as in his later concertos, and omits the figures. In the next three concertos he usually writes 'col basso', and adds a few figures here and there.

2. The manuscripts of the three Concertos K.238, 246, and 271, which form a group stylistically, contain a carefully figured bass throughout, though not in Mozart's hand. It has often been assumed that this figured bass is by Leopold Mozart. Whether or not this is right, it is certain that only an expert could have written the figures and the many 'tasto solo' markings. We were able to examine the figures in K.238 for ourselves; those for K.271 are reproduced in an edition published by Peters. The scrupulously written figures in these three concertos appear to have

something to do with the fact that it was intended to publish them in Paris. In his letter of the 11th September 1778, Mozart wrote to his father that he wanted to have these three concertos engraved. In the end they were not published.

3. The three Concertos K.413–15, which were published in Vienna by Artaria in 1785, are also carefully figured in the first edition. It is quite possible that Mozart supervised their publication. But the reason why concertos were published with figured bass at the time must have been principally that concertos were not published in score—only the parts were engraved. Naturally, the solo piano part would not be enough to show the player the orchestral harmonies.

4. The most important information about Mozart's continuo playing is doubtless the Salzburg copy of the Concerto K.246. This copy, which was not rediscovered till 1920, contains a continuo part for the tutti sections, written in Mozart's own hand. This is a valuable source which tells us not only that Mozart played a continuo part, but also how he played it. There is no historical material that throws any light on continuo in the concertos after K.415. The reason for this deficiency is certainly that nearly all Mozart's later concertos remained unpublished, so that there was no reason to figure the bass. Mozart played these concertos himself and was therefore often content to leave the piano part incompletely written out. Only K.595 was printed, in the year of Mozart's death. In the first edition 'col basso' is written on each page, but there are no figures. It would, however, be premature, to say the least, to conclude that the lack of figures in this last concerto proves anything about Mozart's ideas on continuo in the later concertos. It is more than likely that at the time the work went to print (summer, 1791) Mozart was too taken up with composing *La Clemenza di Tito*, *The Magic Flute* and the Requiem to be able to attend to the publication of this concerto. If he had had more time, he would probably also have filled in the obviously incomplete passages in the first movement, bars 161–2 and 322–4, as he did in many other works where the printed edition contains numerous additions to the 'original'. Early editions of these concertos, from the period directly after Mozart's death, again contain figured piano parts.

The historical reason why continuo playing came into use was the lack of written-out middle parts in most of the seventeenth- and early eighteenth-century music. As a result these middle parts had to be improvised on a harpsichord, organ, lute, etc. in order to give the pieces a harmonic structure. In pieces with complicated harmonies which could not be guessed, the composers indicated the harmonies by the figured bass which might be considered as a very practical kind of shorthand. Apart from filling in the harmonies, the continuo instrument also added tone colour, much in the same way as the harp and organ still do in romantic orchestral works (R. Strauss, *Also sprach Zarathustra*). With the development of the inner parts in the preclassical and classical period, particularly as the viola became an instrument in its own right in string quarters or orchestral pieces (instead of merely doubling the bass line), there was no further need to provide the basso continuo on a keyboard instrument. Thus the basso continuo lost its *raison d'être*. Yet, as is well known, it was retained for many decades. One reason for this was the tradition of conducting the orchestra while playing continuo.[155] Even Haydn conducted his symphonies in London from the harpsichord, although his orchestral harmonies are never incomplete and the sound of the harpsichord is not needed.

In the course of the nineteenth century continuo playing died out, and the *A.M.A.* unfortunately omits all the continuo indications from Mozart's concertos—this has done a certain amount of harm.*

There are indeed valid objections to using the piano as a continuo instrument in modern performances. Orchestral standards have improved, and the piano no longer needs to add 'support'. Quite the opposite; a few particularly sensitive listeners will be disturbed by the clash between the piano's tempered tuning and the pure intonation of the orchestra. Above all, the piano has come to sound thicker, and is far less able to blend with the orchestra than was the Mozart piano with its slender, silvery tone. Since the larger modern orchestra has in any case a fuller sound than that of 180 years ago, it is understandable that most musicians are reluctant to make the sound still thicker by adding a continuo part on the piano. On the other hand, it is wrong to object to a continuo on the grounds that in Mozart's concertos the orchestral harmonies are always so sonorously laid out that the composer cannot even have wanted the piano to play a continuo part. After all, there are many orchestral works of Bach and Handel in which the harmonies are equally complete and sonorous.

Despite these objections to continuo in Mozart, there are naturally a number of thinly scored passages in the piano concertos (such as those in which the texture is limited to two parts, a melody and a bass), and in some of these it is not only possible, but very desirable to fill out the texture discreetly on the piano. Here are some examples:

B flat Concerto (K.456), second movement, bars 196 et seq.:

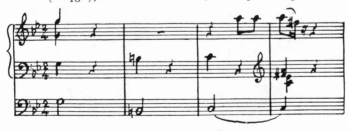

---

*Here is one example of the countless omissions in the *A.M.A.*: in the recapitulation of the first movement of the D minor Concerto the piano starts playing the bass figures only at bar 261—both in this famous edition and all the other editions based on it. But Mozart's intentions are absolutely clear: the piano is also supposed to double the 'celli from bar 254 onward. According to the manuscript, the piano also has to play in bars 12–114 and 285–7.

(cf. H. F. Redlich's Foreword to his edition of this concerto, published by
Eulenburg).

played :

A typical 'thin' passage of this type occurs in the first movement of the
Concerto K.450, bar 26 onward.

One would hardly find a two-part passage of this kind in one of Mozart's
symphonies. The main reason why it is felt to be 'empty' is its markedly
homophonic character. (In contrapuntal passages such as the opening of the
Finale of K.449, two-part writing is not in the least disturbing for a short
time.) Here, however, the effect is much improved by adding a continuo
part:

A major Concerto (K.488), third movement, bars 50–2:

Possible
continuo
part:

The fact that at the end of the movement (bars 506 et seq.) Mozart filled out the harmony with a decorative piano part seems to prove that in this passage he did not want merely an 'empty' two-part orchestral texture. One could, of course, say that these two empty bars give a correspondingly stronger effect to the ensuing tutti outburst, but this is not a very convincing argument, for in bar 52 the only instrument playing the very important B (the dominant seventh) is the second clarinet; so here too the piano has to reinforce the harmony. In bars 250–61 the piano should again play at least the bass line.

We have made many practical experiments in this matter of continuo playing, and have played the concertos both with and without continuo. From considerable experience we would advocate a discreet addition of continuo during the tutti sections. The piano should certainly never play throughout a concerto, from the first note to the last. Even Mozart, who conducted his concertos from the piano,* can scarcely have played a continuo part all the time, since his hands must sometimes have been occupied in conducting. According to Schönfeld's *Jahrbuch der Tonkunst* (1796):[156]

> A conductor at the piano must make still more energetic movements (than a conductor leading the orchestra), so that he often has to work with his head, hands and feet for the sake of the tempo and the beat, and it is not seldom that he is obliged to interrupt the piano part altogether, in order to cleave the air with both arms.

Mozart must also certainly have been guided by the size of the orchestra accompanying him. When the orchestra was small, it would have been more in need of support from the piano, and could also be controlled more easily without stopping playing, so that the pianist could concentrate on the piano part.

As we have said, nowadays it is usually less necessary to reinforce the bass line than it was in Mozart's day. There is no need to reinforce a bass that is

*According to contemporary practice the orchestra was conducted either by the leader or by the solo pianist—in this case Mozart. (Cf. Mozart's letter of 11th September 1778: 'I want to conduct at the fortepiano.')

purely accompanimental, and in many cases this is not even possible (cf. the quick repeated notes in the first tutti during the finale of the D minor Concerto). It is only in forte entries that the bass may be doubled, even in octaves, as in bars 302–5, 362–5 of the first movement of the C minor Concerto (K.491).

There are, however, numerous passages in Mozart which perplex even the most fervent advocates of continuo-playing; passages where it is quite impossible to find any chords for the right hand that will not mar the musical structure. The opening of the D minor Concerto is a good example of this type. Chords played on the first beat would break up the strings' syncopations in a very unsatisfactory way, and there is no question of doubling the syncopated chords, since this would obscure the contrast between solo and tutti— a contrast that is most important in this particular concerto. The opening of the A major Concerto (K.488) is so like chamber music that a continuo part would merely sound clumsy. In the fourth bar it would be quite impossible to find a chord to go over the D in thé bass. The same applies to the third subject of this movement. Wherever the orchestra has a suspension (as in the second movement of the Concerto K.488, bars 14–19 and 51–2) there is again nothing the pianist can do with his right hand, except to add pointless doublings. In all such passages as this, Mozart certainly only played the bass part with his left hand, and conducted with his right. Nowadays there are usually more 'cellos and basses, so that one can often well do without this doubling of the bass line.

The second movement of the E flat Concerto (K.449) begins with a bare fifth in the orchestra. Thus at the very outset one can play a soft chord on the piano (as in the later recapitulation of this theme). In the ensuing eight bars, however, it is neither necessary nor desirable to supplement the harmony; not until bar 10 should one start playing a continuo part again, to match the exactly similar passage from bar 89 onward, where Mozart himself wrote out the chords:

There is another opening bar (that of the first movement of the Concerto K.459) in which the piano can well add the third of the harmony, as later in bar 9 (first horn and first bassoon), but in this latter case it is not advisable to play a whole chord on the first beat. The third has such a delightful effect when it enters in the second half of the bar that it should not be anticipated.

On the other hand, in the development and at the end of this movement (before the cadenza) it is not only desirable but indispensable to fill out the texture on the piano. From bar 196 onward the woodwind and strings alternate with chords over a bass that moves in descending fifths. Whereas the woodwind chords are complete, the strings are in two parts only, since Mozart here uses the violas to strengthen the bass. There can hardly be any doubt that here the right hand of the continuo must complete the harmony in some such way as this:

Similarly, the piano must complete the harmony in bar 249 of the third movement of the E flat Concerto (K.482), where Mozart himself filled out the incomplete harmony of the strings with two five-part chords on the piano.

In the two concertos in minor keys, and also in other concertos, the relationship of piano and orchestra is markedly dualistic: there is strong contrast, which would naturally be weakened if the piano were constantly to play in string passages (in wind passages Mozart in any case meant it not to play). Here is an example from the development section of the first movement of the C minor Concerto:

In such cases as this, the piano must blend with the orchestral tutti so that the listener does not even notice it as a separate element in the overall sound.* Thus in Mozart's piano concertos the piano has two quite distinct and contrasting functions; that of a solo instrument, which opposes the orchestra in a 'concertante' way, and that of a versatile orchestral instrument, which here and there has to support and enrich the texture.

In his continuo-playing Mozart adhered to the following rule: the piano should only play when the lowest strings play the bass line; thus whenever the violas (or in wind passages the bassoon) take over the bass line, there is to be no continuo part. There are, however, occasional odd bars where the left hand of the piano must stop playing, even though the lower strings play the bass (K.456, first movement, bars 129 et seq., K.595, second movement, bars 127–9). After final trills the piano bass switches to playing the orchestral bass, as in the first movement of the Concerto K.459, bar 189, where the MS. runs as follows:

*In a wholly similar passage in the first movement of the Concerto in E flat (K.449) (bars 188–203) Mozart writes rests for the piano during the two-bar tutti passages, and we would recommend this solution in the case mentioned above.

The better the orchestra, the less continuo one should play! In polyphonic string passages, such as bars 143–8 of the first movement of the A major Concerto (K.488), one should in any case not play, since it would only adulterate the sound of the strings. Too little is better than too much! Sometimes it is appropriate simply to double the bass in octaves, as in bars 185 et seq. of the second movement of the Concerto K.482, and in the examples quoted later from the C minor Concerto. Wherever one plays chords, one should try to give them as bright and slender a sound as possible; for instance, one can play staccato without any pedal:

A major Concerto (K.488), third movement, bars 210–29:

In realizing the continuo, it is better not to double any of the orchestral parts, particularly the woodwind parts. The orchestral harmonies are to be enriched, but not made excessively thick by unnecessary doublings.

Even in solo passages Mozart occasionally added chords which fill out the harmony like a continuo, as in bars 88–90 of the first movement of the D minor Concerto:

If the semiquaver figurations were given to another instrument, such as the violin, one would play the chords with the right hand and the bass notes with the left. As it is, one is forced to leave out either the bass notes or the chords.

Friedrich Blume's edition (for Eulenburg) is the only one that has so far taken note of the way this passage is originally notated. Blume's explanation in his Foreword is, however, not quite correct. Mozart's notation is quite easily explained by the fact (already mentioned) that for his concertos he used his own pedal keyboard,[157] playing the lowest notes with his feet. As far as we know this is the only passage in which Mozart included these pedal notes in the piano part of the score, presumably because here they support the bass, which is otherwise present only on the timpani, and therefore not very distinct. It is a pity that these very important notes have to be omitted nowadays. In recordings or broadcasts, when the listener does not see what is happening, one can have these important notes played by the violinist who sits nearest the bass notes of the piano.

There is another important guide for continuo playing in Mozart; in some of his concertos he wrote *ad libitum* wind parts, i.e. these concertos can be played with strings only (or even with a solo quartet).[158] In these cases the wind parts are for most of the time merely a written-out continuo, and one may safely assume that when the works are played without wind instruments the piano must take over this function, at least in all the passages where the wind fill out the harmony. In these works the wind are used sparingly and the part-writing for them is very skilful; this again reminds us that 'filling-in' harmonies should not be used too often. If these concertos are played with wind, the piano will only add to the texture where Mozart would have written a fuller wind texture if more instruments had been available; as for example in the first movement of the E flat Concerto (K.449), bars 16 onward, which can be played like this (naturally in the same rhythm as that of the oboes):

Very similar guiding principles can be deduced from a study of the two piano quartets and the Quintet for piano and wind instruments (K.452), which are laid out in a very 'concertante' style. In the piano quartets the strings play the part of a miniature tutti, and it is clearly seen that Mozart almost always makes the piano play where the tutti is marked *f*, whereas it does not play where the tutti is piano. In the dialogue at the opening of the G minor Piano Quartet, it is striking that the piano takes part on both sides; possibly one could take this to mean that he also wanted the piano to play at the opening of the E flat Concerto (K.271), since the two passages are constructed in exactly the same way. Again, since he lets the piano play in the noisy 'final tutti' of this quartet, he may have wanted something similar in the closing passages of his concertos. The figured bass of K.238 and 271 provides useful indications that he wanted the continuo used only sparingly; and, finally, his original cadenzas allow one to draw a few conclusions, since habit sometimes led him to write out the right hand's continuo chord in the

introductory pause bar; one such exception occurs in the first movement of
the B flat Concerto (K.456):

This naturally means that in the preceding bar the piano has to double the
first and second violins an octave lower:

Mozart very often introduces his cadenza not with a $^6_4$ chord, but with octave-
doublings of the bass note (e.g. Concertos K.382, 414, 488, etc.), and this
again suggests that in the preceding tutti he would only have played a few
chords, confining himself for the most part to doubling the bass. The most
natural way to play the bar before the cadenza of K.488 is:

One special case remains to be dealt with. There are many passages in
which there is a bass note on the first beat, followed by repeated accompanying chords, usually in quavers. Whether such passages occur in solo or tutti,
we would strongly dissuade pianists from adding a chord over the bass note
on the first beat. To do so would thicken the texture unnecessarily. The
result would be not unlike the way a waltz is often played on a bar-room
piano:

In fact it is hardly ever necessary to add chords to fill out the harmony in solo
passages. They are superfluous because Mozart entrusted the harmonic support of solo passages to the orchestra, apart from any other reason.

In solo passages without orchestral accompaniment, as in most of the first
solo entries in the concertos, there will be no question of adding any harmonies, and this also goes for the solo piano works. Bars 85–7 of the first solo

in the Concerto K.482 are often 'filled out' in this way (added notes written small): but this robs the passage of all its lightness and gaiety.

Finally, we shall attempt to draw up a few generally valid rules for continuo playing in Mozart, taking as our guide his own realization of the continuo in the C major Concerto (K.246):

1. Obviously the continuo must stop playing when there are rests in the left-hand part. There is no need to be bound by rests in the right hand, which Mozart habitually wrote at the beginning of a movement. This is how Mozart wrote out his realization of K.246, ignoring the rests added by the copyist.

2. In passages of 'chamber' or contrapuntal character one should play 'tasto solo'.

3. Single accented dissonances or suspensions in orchestral parts played forte are better not doubled (e.g. K.246, first movement, bars 7–8: here the piano plays the resolution chord). In chains of accented dissonances or suspensions, above all those played piano, one should, however, play 'tasto solo', perhaps adding an occasional octave doubling (K.246, second movement, bars 1–3): there are suspensions of this kind at the opening of the second movement of K.449. The reason for this is illuminating: to double the dissonance produces undesirable mixtures of timbre, while to play the resolution chord produces friction which can be ugly.

4. The top part should as far as possible not be doubled. Nor should middle parts be doubled for more than a short space. Bar 17 of the second movement of K.246 is very informative here; Mozart thought out a new middle part for the continuo.

5. The continuo should only be in three or four parts, and should never be decorated or quote thematic material. (Themes and figures in the bass are the only exception.)

6. In unison passages the right hand must obviously not play chords, but should double the bass if it plays at all (cf. first movement of K.246, bar 36). This also applies when the wind instruments have sustained pedal notes (cf. opening of K.449).

7. In forte passages where the whole orchestra is used, a continuo is only necessary if important harmony notes lie very deep or are weakly

scored (cf. first movement, bar 13, also bar 12). Practical application of this principle leads us to advocate the addition of chords in bar 52 of the Finale of K.488, where the second clarinet is the only instrument playing the seventh of the important dominant seventh chord.

8. Solo passages should on principle never be filled out. There is not a scrap of proof that Mozart ever added chords in solo passages. (This has nothing to do with embellishment of the melody; the solos in the slow movements lend themselves particularly well to embellishment.)

9. Mozart's continuo is never 'strict' in the baroque sense. For example, in the second movement of K.246 the continuo in the first tutti contains offbeat chords, while there are rests over the notes in the bass.

(By the way, all good continuo players do the same.)

10. In the concertos from K.450 onward there is steadily less opportunity to introduce a continuo. In the later concertos one should be very sparing and careful in making this kind of addition.

A good player 'accompanies with discretion', as C. P. E. Bach remarked.[159] This applies particularly in playing Mozart. One cannot give a strong enough warning against making too frequent and loud additions. Better no continuo than one that spoils the texture by making it too thick!

Chapter Ten

THE PROBLEM OF ACCOMPANIMENT

IT is unfortunate that in modern performances of Mozart's piano concertos the collaboration between soloist and orchestra often leaves much to be desired. This is because many musicians have little feeling for Mozart's style, and also because the relative forces involved are often the wrong size; moreover, the orchestra often play from parts which have been badly edited. Most orchestras still use the old parts published by Breitkopf & Härtel eighty years ago—parts that contain innumerable nonsensical phrasing and expression marks added by an unknown arranger. The same publisher's scores are more recent and much nearer the original text. Unfortunately, many conductors accept this discrepancy between score and parts with stoical indifference, although almost every bar contains some inaccuracy in the orchestral parts. Bars 20 et seq. of the Finale of the D minor Concerto is a particularly crass example of arbitrary alteration by the editor of the orchestral parts: Mozart's MS. and most scores have:

The Breitkopf orchestral parts have:

The editor, over-keen on consistency, obviously did not realize the difference between an accented passing-note resolving downward by step and a leap of an octave from a harmony note.

It is the same in all the concertos. If the soloist wants to have a satisfactory accompaniment, there is rarely anything for him to do but to go through every single part, making corrections with a red pencil, unless he prefers to take his own correct set of parts with him on his travels.

But the unreliability of orchestral parts is not the only reason why orchestra and soloist so rarely play well together. Many deficiencies are the result simply of bad habits ingrained over many generations. Present-day conductors and orchestral players often show terrifying ignorance of the simplest facts about the instruments Mozart used. They often do not know that, for instance, 'Horns in B flat' means in present-day language 'Horns in B flat alto', since there is not a single example in Mozart of the use of horns in B flat basso. In his early works he took this high crooking so much for granted that he never bothered to write 'alto' at all.[160] It is no joke to hear the horn parts in the second movement of the D minor Concerto played an octave too low. When Mozart divides the 'cello-bass line, the upper part is automatically to be played by the double basses, since they always play an octave lower than written. This often leads to misunderstandings, as in the second movement of the E flat Concerto (K.482).

One bad habit of orchestras when playing Mozart's concertos is to play too much of the accompaniment staccato. Mozart's notation makes a clear distinction between staccato and non-staccato, as one can see by examining the bar 11 of the Romanze from the D minor Concerto:

First violin
(non-staccato)

Second violin and
viola (staccato)

Basses (legato)

It is not right to make the first violin quavers as short as those in the second violins and violas.

Mozart's accompaniments always have something to say, and not one note of them should sound empty or inexpressive. In the first movement of the same concerto it is very important to play the string chords in bars 348-9 fairly weightily, 'non-staccato':

The same applies to the quaver accompaniment in bars 104–6 and 323–6 of this movement.

Mozart often writes:

Nowadays this is often wrongly taken for an ordinary short staccato and played with insufficient expression. It is in fact nothing but another way of writing a soft staccato in crotchets:

Chordal accompaniments in repeated quavers, as in bars 40–60 of the Romanze from this concerto, are nowadays often played 'spiccato'; in other words, one hears forty bows hitting the string, but not the notes. Even simple accompaniment figures, such as those in bar 63, should be made to sing, and not unduly shortened:

It is not only in playing quavers that one must beware of cutting off the notes too soon; this also applies to single crotchets, as at the ends of phrases.

D minor Concerto, first movement, bars 112–14:

The crotchets, particularly the last one, should not be cut off abruptly, but firmly held (tenuto).

Excessive use of staccato is probably the result of an awareness (admirable in itself) that Mozart is usually made to sound too thick, so that the accompaniment often drowns the solo instrument. This is indeed a constant danger, but playing staccato is not the right solution. Mozart chose a much more natural way out; in earlier times it was the habit to use only a quintet or quartet of strings to accompany the piano's solos. This was absolutely necessary, because the Mozart piano had such a small tone. Wind solos were also sometimes accompanied only by solo strings, as in bars 198–9 of the first movement of the B flat Concerto, where Mozart first wrote 'solo' against all the strings, later crossing this out in the bass part and leaving it only in the violins and violas.[161] This example also shows clearly that Mozart's marking 'solo' refers to the accompaniment, which is then to be played by single instruments.

In a letter to the publisher Sieber in Paris, Mozart offers him the Concertos K.413, 414 and 415 for publication, and adds the remark:

> . . . this letter is to inform you that I have three piano concertos ready, which can be performed with full orchestra, or with oboes and horns, or merely a quattro.[162]

In the case of the Concerto K.449, Mozart again emphasized that it could be played 'a quattro', i.e. as a piano quintet (he used the phrase both in entering the work in his thematic catalogue and in a letter to his father on 15th May 1785[163]). Even though the louder tone of the modern piano and the increased size of concert halls usually rule out performance with single strings, it should be enough to use between two and four desks of first violins (five at the most), and the other strings in proportion—this is quite enough even for Carnegie Hall. It is sheer nonsense to use fifty or more musicians to play repeated chords as an accompaniment to the piano's cantilenas. One only has to try giving the accompaniment to a few string players who are capable of a smooth, pleasing soft tone, and one will see that the effect is incomparably better and more natural.

The modern piano's increased volume of tone is a very distinct advantage from the point of view of collaboration with an orchestra. The Mozart piano's forte was just loud enough to be audible if the accompanying orchestra played piano, and its fortissimo was about as loud as a *mf* on the modern piano. This explains why Mozart marked the orchestral accompaniment piano even in passages whose character is clearly that of a forte. Although one should try to avoid tampering with Mozart's expression marks, in these cases there is not the slightest objection to letting the orchestra play the forte demanded by the music; there is no longer any danger of drowning the solo instrument. One must obviously think very hard about any alteration of this kind, i.e. one may only turn a piano into a forte when this is really in keeping with the character of the music. This is the case in the first movement of the festal C major Concerto (K.503); the full orchestral entry in bar 9 clearly demands a forte, and this is what Mozart writes. But at the corresponding points in bars 120 and 298 the orchestra have a *p*, because the piano is playing at the time; if this is taken literally, the powerful chords of the modern piano make the orchestra sound rather feeble. There are also a number of passages of this type in the first movement of the D minor Concerto (bars 110–11, 169–71, 283–4), also in the first movement of the E flat Concerto (K.482) (bar 346), or the first movement of the B flat Concerto (K.595) (bars 218–28). Here again the orchestra should play the climax of the melody at least *mf*, as against the *p* prescribed (which is a relic of the concerto style of Vivaldi's time where at the beginning of the solo the orchestra automatically had to play *p*.)

Bar 218 onward (contrapuntal variant of the first subject).

Very occasionally, though extremely rarely, it is in order to make slight alterations in the scoring. Although Mozart's instrumentation is for the most part masterly, he sometimes asks too much of certain instruments, particularly the flute and bassoon; moreover, our modern orchestra has got so much louder that there are passages in which solo wind instruments cannot penetrate. In bars 362–4 (plus upbeat) of the first movement of K.482 the flute has to play an important counter-melody against the entire orchestra, and in modern performances one can never hear it properly. The best solution to the problem is to double the flutes at this point. But since most orchestral managers will be unable to afford this, one may try another possible way out and let the first clarinet play the part instead of the flute. The modern clarinet has a much more powerful tone than the flute; this solution has been tried and found satisfactory.

There is a similar problem in the A major Concerto (K.488). In the first movement, bars 19–20, 83, 214 and 310, the flute can never be heard properly, but here no change of instrument is possible, except in bar 310.[164]

A good conductor should above all prevent the orchestra from accompanying the soloist with a monotonous *piano* devoid of nuances—for this means the end of all effective partnership.

Chapter Eleven

CADENZAS AND LEAD-INS

THE art of free improvisation flourished in the eighteenth century, to an extent only possible in centuries of great musical creativity. It was an indispensable part of every virtuoso's equipment, if he hoped to be able to satisfy his listeners' artistic standards. But improvisation was not only a duty; it was also a right which he would occasionally exercise even in performing other composers' works. Thus in the instrumental concertos of this period there are places where, in accordance with an old tradition, the orchestra stops playing and the soloist is given the opportunity to show off his abilities and indulge his fantasy.

These places, which were an integral part of the concerto form of that time, also occur in Mozart's concertos, and are a challenge to the performer to improvise a cadenza or a lead-in. They are always marked by a fermata. If the fermata (in Mozart) is over a $^6_4$ chord, the soloist is to play a cadenza; if it is over a half-close of the dominant, he has merely to provide a lead-in to the next part of the work. Cadenzas are usually longer than lead-ins and almost always develop themes and motives from the concerto movement in which they occur. Lead-ins, on the other hand, are usually non-thematic, unrelated to the motives of the concerto movement. They vary in length, and often consist of only a single scale. Whereas lead-ins are as a rule based on one single harmony, cadenzas are usually marked by a wide harmonic range.[165]

In many cases Mozart, rather against the prevailing custom at the time, wrote down these cadenzas and lead-ins.

> Herewith I send my sister the three cadenzas for the concerto in D and the two short cadenzas for the one in E flat.

as he wrote to Salzburg on 15th February 1783.[166] In many cases more than one cadenza by Mozart for one and the same concerto has survived,[167] so we have excellent material on which to base views on how he treated the cadenza. However, it appears that in playing his own cadenzas he sometimes followed the inspiration of the moment;

> I shall send the cadenzas and introductions to my dear sister at the first

> opportunity. I have not yet altered the introductions in the rondo, for when-
> ever I play this concerto, I always play whatever occurs to me at the moment.

as he wrote in another letter to his father.[168] But it is probable that in his longer cadenzas he did not improvise, or seldom did so. This is suggested by the balance and careful working out of many of the surviving cadenzas, which make them unlikely to be improvisations. The cadenza for the A major Concerto (K.488) is even written into the score, 'composed' in full, like the cadenzas for Beethoven's 'Emperor' Concerto or Schumann's Piano Concerto. Yet Mozart must indeed have been a most extraordinarily gifted improviser. This is shown, for instance, by Abbé Stadler's description of his brilliant extempore playing which he told to Novello.[169]

As we know, Mozart did not write out cadenzas for all his concertos. For most of the great concertos from his years in Vienna, such as the two in minor keys and the great Concertos K.482 and 503, there are unfortunately no surviving original cadenzas. Since the classical concerto form would be upset by their omission, we are faced by the difficult task of preparing our own cadenzas for these works, or of looking (usually in vain) for good cadenzas by someone else.

Let us say, first, that the stylistic characteristics of any particular concerto will also determine the character of its cadenza. It is quite impossible to make up anything that can stand comparison with Mozart's own music in any style. But cadenzas in a wholly un-Mozartean style are still a good deal more disturbing than those which, for all their paleness as compared to his own wonderful cadenzas, do at least keep within the limits of his style. A cadenza in a later style (romantic, impressionist, etc.) cannot help offending the spirit of the work. The soloist must throw new light on the themes occurring in the piece; in the cadenza he must further extend the range of what has already been said, give his own personal view of it, but he must go no further, for this will endanger the external and internal unity of the concerto. Mozart gave the cadenza only a fairly subsidiary place in his concertos. Its function is to delay the final robust tutti, and at the same time to enhance its effect. Thus the cadenza must always have a linking character, and should not run to seed—inappropriate (unstylish) cadenzas often suggest a tumour in an organism that is otherwise perfect and healthy.[170]

We shall now try to make some suggestions as to how one can prepare cadenzas for the concertos where none survive from Mozart's pen, and how to ensure that they are as faithful as possible to his style. In this respect his own cadenzas are naturally the ideal models. As one might be expected, they are very varied in form. For purposes of analysis the most useful ones are those for first movements, since Mozart was usually rather freer in laying out the cadenzas for his other movements; moreover, in his mature concertos he usually only wants a cadenza in the first movement.

In almost all Mozart's major cadenzas one can make out a clear division into three; an 'opening' (I), which begins either with one of the themes of the concerto or with virtuoso passage-work, some of it new and some of it already used; in either case, the opening passes over into a middle section (II), which is almost always a sequential development of some important theme or motive from the concerto movement, usually leading to a sustained chord or a long note in the lower register. This is the starting point for a number of virtuoso runs, arpeggios, etc., which lead to the closing section (III) of the cadenza, usually ending on a trill.

I. OPENINGS OF CADENZAS

Let us first look at the two possible ways of opening a cadenza:

(a) *A Thematic Opening.* If a Mozart cadenza begins in this way, it tends to use the first subject of the movement (e.g. the first movement of the Two-piano Concerto (K.365), the Concerto in G (K.453), and most of the cadenzas in rondo movements), but it can also use the motive heard in the orchestra immediately before the fermata (as in the cadenzas for the first movement of the E flat Concerto (K.271), the Concert Rondo (K.382), the first movements of K.415 in C, K.449 in E flat, K.450 in B flat and K.456 in B flat). In this case it can often happen that the piano takes up for the first time a motive previously heard only in the orchestra; this way of revealing new strata of the work's material is very effective. It is distinctly rare for Mozart to use a theme from the middle of a movement at the opening of a cadenza (he does this in the first cadenza for the first movement of the A major Concerto (K.414), and in that for the Finale of the F major Concerto (K.459)). Lastly, in slow movements he often will introduce a quite new theme (e.g. the first cadenza for the slow movement of the G major Concerto (K.453), and the recently discovered cadenza for the slow movement of the B flat Concerto (K.238)); this is a liberty which only he could be allowed to take in one of his works.

These thematic openings almost all give way to passage-work. This virtuoso continuation is again often taken from the movement concerned. Thus in the cadenza for the first movement of K.450 the first eight (thematic) bars are followed by a chain of runs taken from bars 119 et seq., although in a different harmonic context:

bars 119 et seq. of the movement:

bars 9 et seq. of the cadenza:

In this cadenza the continuation passes directly into the second subject, the middle section of the cadenza. But there are many cases in which this virtuoso continuation of the opening reaches a brief point of rest (mostly on a dominant seventh chord), from which there arises further free passage-work as a transition to the middle section.

Cadenza for the first movement of the B flat Concerto (K.595), bars 9–12:

(cf. also bars 12–16 of the cadenza for the first movement of K.271.)

An exception which proves the rule is the first cadenza for the B flat Concerto (K.456), in which the middle section is preceded by not one but two points of rest:

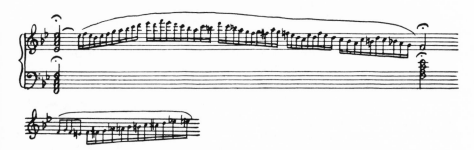

To compensate, the middle and closing sections of this cadenza are kept unusually short.

(b) *Virtuoso Opening.* This, too, is taken, more or less clearly, from the preceding movement, as in the cadenzas for the first movements of the concertos K.459 in F, K.488 in A, K.595 in B flat; only rarely is it cast in a completely free mould, as in the second cadenza for the first movement of the B flat Concerto (K.456).

From the harmonic point of view, both types of opening, thematic and virtuoso, have the task of making the transition from the $^6_4$ chord at the fermata to a motive or theme that is in the tonic, and this transition has to be as interesting as possible. Thus all openings of cadenzas are 'written-out' dominants.

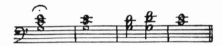

It is remarkable that the themes quoted in Mozart's cadenzas are always in the tonic; when the opening is thematic the theme is usually over the second inversion of the tonic chord, but when the theme does not appear until the middle section it will have its original harmonization.

Two apparent exceptions to this rule are the cadenzas for the third movement of the B flat Concerto (K.450) and the first movement of the A major Concerto (K.488). In the Finale of K.450 the first subject seems to be in E flat when it enters in bar 20 of the cadenza. But this is merely an opening in the subdominant, as is shown by the occurrence of the note A (not A flat) in the succeeding bar. In K.488, the subsidiary figure of the cadenza enters surprisingly in B minor, but here again A minor is reached after two bars (variant of the tonic A major):

Harmonic scheme of the first fourteen bars of the cadenza:

This B minor has a subdominant function akin to that of the chords (apparently in F major) at the opening of Beethoven's First Symphony.

In his cadenzas Mozart wanted to confirm the key of the movement, not to call it in question, as is done, for example, by the very widely ranging modulations in Beethoven's cadenzas. It is a pity that most interpreters who write cadenzas for Mozart's concertos ignore this principle.

Harmonically, Mozart usually makes a link with the final chord of the tutti. First-movement themes are rarely quoted in their original harmonization (on the tonic), but mostly over an implied $^6_4$ chord, usually without any bass in the first two bars, so that for the moment the harmony is only latent. This is the case in K.453, first movement (free continuation with a new motive):

K.450, first movement (new motive, related to the motives of bars 27 or 217):

The regular eight-bar period that begins this cadenza is a rare exception. Cadenzas usually contain no periods, i.e. periodic themes are never quoted in full, but continued sequentially before they have reached the end.

One of Mozart's favourite harmonic successions at the opening of the cadenza is built on a descending bass line: E flat Concerto (K.449), first movement:

The openings of the cadenzas for the first movement of K.271 and the second movement of K.414 (second cadenza) are built to the same harmonic scheme. Many cadenzas also begin with a pedal point, e.g. those for the first movements of K.413 and K.459, and the Concert Rondo (K.382).

The cadenza for the first movement of K.365 starts on the tonic, after a rising run leading from the $\frac{6}{4}$ chord, and there is a surprising interrupted cadence in the fifth bar:

The harmonic scheme in the cadenza for the first movement of the B flat Concerto (K.595) is also very interesting (motive from the movement):

(The falling bass line first descends four times through a third, and then, as a harmonic accelerando, three times through a fifth; the upper part moves in contrary motion, three times through a fourth, taking in the intermediate chromatic steps.)

One of the finest cadenza openings is that in the first movement of the F major Concerto (K.459); first, passage-work, starting in bar 373, over a pedal point (with chromatic intermediate steps in bars 3 and 4), then the first subject is introduced with a harmonization unusual for Mozart—the third inversion of the dominant seventh, at the start of a descending bass progression:

It is also rare for Mozart to introduce the second theme of the cadenza over a $^6_4$ chord, as he does in K.459.

The harmonic progression at the outset of the cadenza in the third movement of the Piano Sonata in B flat (K.333), is also interesting, in that the tonic minor is introduced in the third bar:

Openings of cadenzas vary greatly in length, but are rarely shorter than six bars or longer than twelve.

II. MIDDLE SECTIONS OF CADENZAS

As we have said, the opening of the cadenza always culminates with a theme in the tonic. Here Mozart prefers cantabile second subjects, as in the first movements of the Concertos K.271, 415, 450, 453, 456, 459 and 595. In the second cadenza for K.414, however, the opening of the cadenza is followed for once by the first subject, which Mozart has refrained from using in the introductory passage. In the Finale of the Concerto K.450 the first subject in fact appears twice in the course of the same cadenza; at the beginning in the upper part, and in the second section in the bass, apparently in the subdominant, as we have said. The motivic technique in the third movement of the B flat Concerto (K.595) is particularly taking. The first section of this large-scale cadenza develops only the opening bars of the first subject in two 'waves' (bars 1–10 and 11–27); the second section then uses bars 5–6 of the first subject, as a kind of new theme (bars 31–9). The themes of the E flat Concerto (K.449) are interestingly treated in its cadenza. In the exposition of this movement, Mozart follows the trill by a striking motive (bars 169–76). At the close of the movement he does not give this motive to the orchestra, so that it will be effective when it appears as the second theme in the cadenza. The cadenza for the Concerto in A (K.488) is a special case, since here Mozart introduces a completely new motive at an important point, a thing he otherwise only does in cadenzas for slow movements (K.238, 453).

In quoting themes in the middle sections of cadenzas, Mozart generally follows a scheme. Whereas in the body of the movement these themes are rounded off to form a self-contained whole by means of a cadence in the final bars, in the cadenza Mozart uses a technique that is best described as 'continuous development';[171] before there is a cadence, some motive from the theme is unexpectedly treated in sequence, often in rhythmic diminution; this is done in such a way that the motive almost always ends with a sustained chord or note. Often this section leads on to the dominant (of the tonic), e.g. in the cadenzas for the G major Concerto (K.453), but most often on to the dominant of the dominant, whence it passes back to the dominant or on to the second inversion of the tonic, as in the cadenzas for the Concertos K.449, 456, 459 and 595 (first movement in each case). We quote four examples of this cadenced flow of Mozart's middle sections, and in each case we quote the theme as it appears in the body of the movement and as it is used in the cadenza.

1. E flat Concerto (K.271), first movement, bars 225–32:

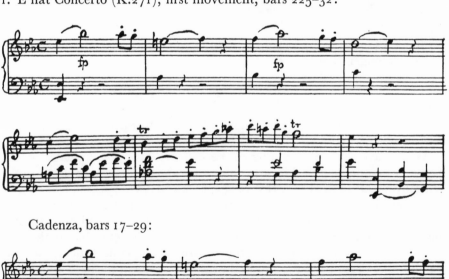

Cadenza, bars 17–29:

2. E flat Concerto (K.449), first movement, bars 63–70:

Cadenza, bars 15–25:

3. G major Concerto (K.453), first movement, bars 290–7:

First Cadenza, bars 19–26:

(The bold harmonies are a result of a succession of first and third inversions, plus accented passing notes, over a chromatically descending bass. This theme is originally over a diatonically descending bass line, with each entry of the motive a fifth lower than the preceding one. In the cadenza the bass line's diatonic motion is held up when it reaches the submediant; it remains stationary for a while, and then surprisingly continues downward chromatically.)

4. B flat Concerto (K.456), first movement, bars 299–302:

Cadenza, bars 14–17:

Another interesting cadenza occurs in the first movement of the B flat Concerto (K.595), where the sequential treatment culminates not in a sustained note, but in a 'G.P.' (twenty-first bar). In this way Mozart makes a clear distinction between the way he uses themes in the body of the movement and in the cadenza. In the concerto itself the themes are linked in a very fluid way, interwoven with no apparent seams, whereas in his cadenzas he was obviously anxious to show that this network, for all its apparent firmness, could be pulled apart again without difficulty. In this respect Beethoven had a quite different technique for building up his cadenzas. They are self-contained, rounded musical essays, which for dramatic quality can compete with the main body of the movement, or even surpass it; one should examine a cadenza such as that in the B flat Concerto, op. 19, which opens with a fugato in the style of the 'Hammerklavier' Sonata.

III. FINAL SECTIONS OF CADENZAS

It is in shaping final sections of his cadenzas that Mozart allows his fantasy freest play, without tying himself to any scheme. All the same, one can say that as a rule the final section of a cadenza contains a number of virtuoso runs, some of which are written in small notes. These runs occur frequently, not only in the cadenzas of his piano concertos, but also in cadenza-like passages in other piano works, such as the finale of the B flat Piano Sonata (K.333), the Rondo K.494 and, above all, his sets of variations. In these works the cadenzas are usually nonthematic, for the obvious reason that the theme has already been quite sufficiently developed and varied. There is a great deal to be learned from these nonthematic cadenzas, just because they have this 'neutral' character, as a result of which one can incorporate considerable parts of them in one's own cadenzas for the concertos.

Whereas in the 'Salzburg' Concertos (e.g. K.271) the closing sections of the cadenzas are distinctly short, Mozart later extended this section and enriched it with thematic material. In those cases where the continuation of the middle section led to the dominant, the final section almost always leads, after a scale-passage, to a new motivic quotation in the tonic, then to the $^6_4$ chord again, usually with the aid of the sharpened fourth (dominant of the dominant), as in the first cadenza of the G major Concerto (K.453), from the 26th bar onward:

The motive marked 'NB' comes from bars 275 et seq. of the movement.

Another possible harmonic turn is toward the subdominant, in order to delay the end of the cadenza:

(cf. also the cadenza for the first movement of the B flat Concerto (K.595), bars 27–31).

In the final section of the second cadenza for the Concerto K.456 we find motives from bars 95 and 136 of the movement. In the B flat Concerto (K.595) we first hear the 'call' motive, interestingly harmonized, and later, after some runs and arpeggios, a slightly varied form of the first subject of the movement, treated in canon:

It is a harmonic characteristic of these closing sections that Mozart often introduces the supertonic or subdominant, possibly using interdominants, to ensure a more definite feeling that the cadenza is reaching its final cadence.

The final trill is usually very simple:

Double (or even treble) trills very rarely occur, and only in the concertos for two and three pianos. However, since Mozart did sometimes write these trills it is clear that he considered them possible and musically admissible, avoiding them only on grounds of technical difficulty. Modern pianists trained on Beethoven and Chopin should find them less difficult, so there is no objection to the use of a double trill in one's own cadenza.

One of Mozart's most original cadenzas was written for the third movement of the F major Concerto (K.459). At the end of this cadenza Mozart interchanges the two opening motives from the principal subject, thus deriving new material:

There is a pleasantly Beethovenian effect when Mozart uses the main motive of this movement in the left hand, as a 'counterpoint' to an eight-bar long trill, before he finally rounds off the cadenza:

The cadenzas' texture is mainly homophonic. There are, however, a few short passages of quite masterly polyphony. The way in which Mozart alters his themes, most of them not very suitable for polyphonic treatment, is extraordinarily interesting. By a great stroke of good fortune, the original cadenzas for the E flat Concerto (K.365) have been rediscovered.[172] The cadenza for the third movement is a good example of this kind:

Mozart added an extra twenty-seven bars to the Rondo K.494, and these have very much the character of a cadenza. The interval of a third, so characteristic of the principal theme, is simply altered to a fourth or a fifth, so as to facilitate imitation. Mozart ties the first quaver of the second bar to the preceding note.

becomes:

There are other themes which are suited to polyphonic development without any alteration. In the third movement of the A major Concerto (K.414) the motive of bar 8 reappears in the cadenza in two-part canon:

In the twenty-second bar of the cadenza for the third movement of the D major Concerto (K.451), Mozart uses the (unaltered) second subject as the basis of a delightful fugato, which starts off with a stretto:

The cadenza for the first movement of this concerto also starts polyphonically, with a canon at the fifth, but this has already occurred in the course of the movement and is therefore not felt to be new when it occurs in the cadenza. The most interesting passage in this connection is the 'Cadenza in tempo' in the Quintet for piano and wind (K.452), opening as it does with a four-part fugato.

To write stylistically correct cadenzas one must be absolutely familiar with the harmonic and modulatory scheme of the concerto concerned. Mozart's diatonicism is much easier to imitate than his often very complicated chromatic progressions and enharmonic changes. To imitate the latter, while remaining in style, is particularly difficult, because even in his boldest chromaticisms Mozart kept strictly within certain limits which are difficult to define. (One element of a personal style is the voluntary recognition or imposition of certain limits, within which one's fantasy is entirely free. Without such limits, fantasy would lose its sense of direction.) Mozart rarely uses complicated harmonic alterations. We have already seen that in his cadenzas he never strays very far from the tonic. Even when a cadenza modulates strikingly, it always returns after a few bars to the tonic or a related key; after a short pause, the play of sequences and exploratory harmonies will then start anew. Even Mozart's boldest turns of harmony are achieved with the aid only of major and minor triads, major and minor seventh chords, the dominant seventh, the diminished triad and the various inversions of the diminished seventh. Augmented triads and ninth chords hardly ever occur in their own right, but only as passing harmonies or suspensions. Mozart's harmonic boldness lies mostly in the surprising juxtaposition of chords which are only indirectly related, i.e. it is horizontal (arising from the flow of the music) and not vertical. In bars 11 et seq. of the C minor Fantasia (K.475), Mozart uses a succession of ordinary dominant sevenths and minor first inversions over a chromatically descending bass, and achieves an absolutely breathtaking effect without making a single chromatic alteration.

There is only one alteration that Mozart does use frequently—the augmented sixth, usually in the form of an augmented sixth chord plus fifth. In his later works he often makes an enharmonic change in this chord, making it into a dominant seventh, before he finally resolves it:

But the frequent occurrence of the augmented sixth in Mozart is matched by his equally decided avoidance of its inversion, the diminished third. Here he adopts a view which survived into many twentieth-century harmony books—that this dissonance is 'displeasing' and therefore 'forbidden'. He usually replaces it by the minor third if it would be produced by an inversion:

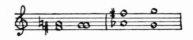

It follows that in making up one's own cadenzas one should if possible avoid harmonies such as that marked +, if one wants to keep in style:

For Mozart the diminished seventh chord was still a very acute dissonance, whereas in Beethoven's time it had already lost some of its pungent effect. It is the basis of many of Mozart's chromatic harmonies. There is a typical example in the C major Fantasia (K.394), bar 46. This succession of six diminished-seventh chords was unprecedentedly bold in Mozart's day.

Mozart had the great composer's ability to exploit passing notes, suspensions, pedal points and stationary parts in order to create harmonic tension. We quote bars 31 et seq. of the B minor Adagio (K.540), to illustrate a special effect that Mozart achieved by the use of accented passing notes against dominant sevenths and diminished sevenths:

Harmonic scheme:

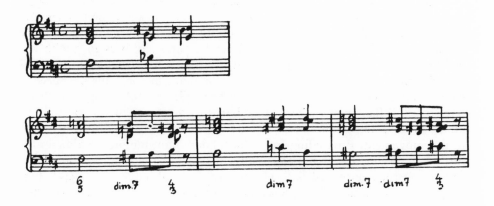

So much for analysis. Now, to illustrate the practical application of these ideas, perhaps we may briefly describe how we composed a cadenza for the first movement of the E flat Concerto (K.482). (Cadenzas for this concerto were published by Doblinger, Vienna, in 1956, also a cadenza for the C minor Concerto (K.491), and the C major Concerto (K.503).)

In laying out the opening of the cadenza, we were guided by the fact that a motive in bars 188 et seq. is very like the motive used by Mozart to introduce his own cadenza for the first movement of the B flat Concerto (K.595); we therefore took the opening of the latter cadenza as our model. As in K.595, the motive from bar 188 was first developed, ascending steadily in a sequence based on the notes of the ascending tonic chord (the implied harmony is a different inversion from that originally used). Mozart's cadenza descends from this climax over three bars, the harmony falling a third each time. The motive from bar 182 of our movement was very well suited to this descent by thirds. The next bars (8–10) of our cadenza are a literal transposition of bars 7–8 of the Mozart cadenza mentioned. A point of rest having been reached on the dominant seventh, there should now be a run leading to a theme in the tonic. Here we could have taken as model either the run in bars 26 et seq. of the first cadenza of the G major Concerto (K.453), or a run from the first cadenza of the B flat Concerto (K.456); we decided on the latter and adopted it, with slight alterations.

We used the second subject (bars 51 et seq.) for the middle section. Useful additional material was provided by the clarinet counterpoint from bar 53, which never occurs in the piano part during the movement. Naturally, the second subject was not rounded off with a cadence, but had to be continuously developed. Its consequent (bar 55) is treated in sequence, leading to the dominant of the dominant (bar 17 of the cadenza), and from there, by a run (developed out of the accented-passing-note figures in the preceding bars, first and third beats) to the dominant in bar 19 (B flat in the bass). Four bars of transition to the end of the cadence are based on the $\frac{6}{4}$ chord, and here the motive from bars 13–14 of the movement is used in free imitation.

We need hardly go deeply into the way the closing section of the cadenza took shape. We would only mention that one often has to be rather ingenious if a non-modulating cadenza is to avoid harmonic monotony. Even though Mozart's own cadenzas do not modulate to distant keys, their harmonic content is astonishingly varied. To avoid any effect of harmonic monotony or flatness, we did not immediately follow the $\frac{6}{4}$ chord of bars 20–3 with the obvious dominant seventh (run + trill), but tried to add extra interest by introducing the first inversion of the subdominant minor. This produced a convincing chromatic movement in the bass (G, bar 15–A flat, bar 16–A, bars 17/18–B flat, bars 19–23–C flat, bar 24); moreover, it was possible to allude to the B flat minor theme in bars 128 et seq., which occurs only once in this movement. Proceeding from the subdominant minor, we aimed at a further variation, E flat minor, finally to reach the closing section of the cadenza at the augmented-sixth chord (plus fifth) of bar 34: bars 34–7, first subject in diminution, bars 38–41 in its original form + trill, bars 42–3 final run, exceeding the limits of Mozart's keyboard. We have recently composed an alternative ending for this cadenza, keeping within strictly Mozartean limits.

Finally, we would say that Mozart's concerto movements can usually be classed in one of a small number of categories: thus there are cantabile and 'festal' allegro movements, grazioso allegretto finales or elegant $\frac{6}{8}$ final rondos. For almost all of these types there exist appropriate original cadenzas, which one can take as models in writing one's own. In composing cadenzas, it is useful to begin by selecting from the movement all the motives and passages that may be suited to development of the kind customary in a cadenza; these should be written out. This makes it much easier to see new ways of combining them. We see no objection to incorporating into one's cadenza whole passages from those by Mozart (transposed if necessary). Thus bars 23–30 of the cadenza for the third movement of the Concerto K.595 can be used without more ado in a cadenza for the Finale of K.482, because they are nonthematic and 'neutral'. On more than one occasion Mozart copied himself literally in his cadenzas (cf. bars 23–4 of the second cadenza for K.414 with the cadenza for K.488, or the final run in the cadenza for K.449 with that in K.453 at the corresponding point). The first twelve bars of the long (second) cadenza for the first movement of K.414 could thus be used, for example, to open a cadenza for the first movement of the 'Coronation' Concerto, the only alterations being transpositions to D major and a slight change in the spacing of the arpeggios.

Nearly all the cadenzas added to Mozart's concertos by other composers are too long. But the worst offenders in this respect are the intolerable cadenzas usually played by violinists—excessively long, completely lacking in musical originality and stylistically inept.*

As early as D. G. Türk's *Clavierschule* we find an express warning against excessively long cadenzas:

> I should be saying nothing new, but repeating a complaint that has already been made many times, if I were to speak out against the very great misuse of decorated cadenzas. For it not seldom seems that a concerto, etc., is played merely for the sake of the cadenzas. In them, the performer goes astray not merely in respect of the length that is fitting, but also introduces all kinds of passage work, etc., which have not the slightest connection with the work that has preceded, so that the impression made by the work upon the hearer is to a great extent effaced.[173]

Mozart's longest cadenza for a $\frac{4}{4}$ movement is thirty-nine bars long (for K.453), for a $\frac{6}{8}$ movement forty bars (K.595), and for a finale in $\frac{2}{4}$ fifty-four bars (K.459). The longest cadenza in a $\frac{3}{4}$ movement is that for the first movement of K.413 (thirty-two bars). All his other cadenzas are shorter, some considerably so. Thus the cadenza for the first movement of K.246 is a mere five bars long,† and the recently discovered cadenza for the first movement of K.238 also consists merely of a few runs and a final trill. If only we could always hear such short cadenzas, which do not jeopardize the unity of the movement—in the violin concertos, for instance!

Finally, we should mention two things which Mozart avoids in his cadenzas:

1. He avoids introducing one motive or theme after another, without any clear division, as in a pot-pourri.

2. Nor does he ever make the ending of the cadenza identical with the ending of the final solo. In particular, the left hand must have a sustained chord at the end of the cadenza (and not an Alberti bass, such as that proposed by Soulima Stravinsky in an otherwise good cadenza for K.503).

IV. LEAD-INS

We have already mentioned that lead-ins, unlike cadenzas, rarely show any motivic connection with the main body of the movement (K.415 and 450

---

*Ernst Hess has written an excellent cadenza for the A major Violin Concerto (K.219), and this is printed in the new complete edition (N.M.A.). We ourselves have tried to devise a cadenza for the G major Violin Concerto (K.216) (see p. 296) and also for the Violin Concertos K.218 and K.219 in A and in D, which were published by Doblinger, Vienna. We should also mention the cadenzas by the Dutch composer Marius Flothuis, which are good both musically and stylistically. We particularly recommend his cadenza for the D major Concerto (K.218).

†Two long original cadenzas for this concerto have been recently discovered and are reproduced for the first time in this book, pp. 299–302.

are exceptions), but consist of scales, leaps, various kinds of passage work and ornaments. They are mostly found at points where two successive but clearly distinct sections of a movement are to be linked by a short solo. Despite this transitional character, they are best regarded as 'lead-ins', since the preceding section is never reflected in them. In the piano concertos they are always on the dominant of the succeeding section, and should naturally be kept shorter than cadenzas. In other groups of works, e.g. in the G major Violin Concerto, there are also imperfect cadences on the dominant of the relative minor. In these cases the lead-in must contain two different harmonies:

Vln. Concerto, (K.216), third movement, bar 217:

But usually they linger on one harmony, as in the sixteen-bar lead-in found in the Finale of the Concerto K.450. The following variants are, however, possible:

(*a*) Transitional harmonies (see the lead-in in the third movement of K.271). Harmonic scheme as written:

Played (basic scheme):

or:

(*b*) Detour to the dominant of the dominant: (scheme)

(cf. the lead-in in the third movement of the Piano Concerto K.595).

Here again there is an implicit progression G–F sharp–F, but it is to some extent obscured by the treatment of the bass and the way the notes of the progression are distributed among the different parts.

One should naturally avoid anticipating the tonic triad in the course of a lead-in. In example (*a*), above, it would be a mistake to play the following bass (the upper parts remaining the same):

A good example of a lead-in by Mozart is found in the third movement of the Concerto K.271, and others in the Concertos K.415, 450 and 595. (For lead-ins in slow movements, see the two in the A major Concerto (K.414).*)

But the most instructive examples were written for the Variations K.613 (on 'Ein Weib ist das herlichste Ding'), in which each variation contains a different version of the original lead-in contained in the theme. This is a *locus classicus* and is immensely informative.

The transitional run found in the theme becomes (in Variation I) an even quaver movement for the right hand; in Variation II the lead-in is given to the bass, in Variations III triplet movement is used, in Variation V the movement is in semiquavers throughout, in Variation VII the lead-in is a particularly fine and complex adagio passage, and, finally, in Variation VIII there is a very extended lead-in to the Allegro Finale.

*Facing p. 291 of this book there is a hitherto unpublished lead-in by Mozart, designed for this concerto.

Theme, bar 32:

Variation I:

Variation II:

Variation V:

Variation VII, Adagio:

Variation VIII, Allegro:

On pp. 253 and on p. 281 the reader can see how we put into practice these suggestions for writing lead-ins. Perhaps we may quote one more lead-in of our own, from the third movement of the F major Concerto (K.459):*

Allegro assai

*In 1959 Mozart's hitherto unknown lead-in for this movement was discovered by Hellmut Federhofer. It bears a certain resemblance to our own, written in 1956. It also proves that at such fermatas as this one Mozart wanted a lead-in to be played. Cf. Supplement, plate 10.

We have still to discuss the possibilities of introducing lead-ins. Whereas cadenzas have a clearly marked place in concerto movements, it is sometimes hard to decide where a lead-in should be added.

As a rule, the place for a lead-in is where two successive sections of a movement are to be joined by a brief transition, and where there is a fermata, so that a short interlude is the natural way of making the join. Thus the presence of a fermata is the *sine qua non* for adding a lead-in. However, not every fermata in Mozart's works is to be embellished in this way! The principal function of the fermata, even in eighteenth-century works, is to indicate 'tenuto', i.e. that one is to linger, to pause for a moment.[174] Unfortunately, the theory books of Mozart's day never say just which fermatas are to be embellished and which not. But, for example, Sulzer is clearly referring only to fermatas that should not be embellished, when he writes (in his *Theory of the Fine Arts*):[175]

> The fermata helps to express powerful emotions at points where they reach their climax, also to enhance the expression of amazement, like an outcry. They interrupt the melody, just as a man strongly moved may hesitate slightly after an outburst, and then go on still more violently.

On the other hand, there are cases in which we should say that fermatas *must* be embellished, i.e. that stylistically correct interpretation demands a short lead-in as a transition to the next section. In Mozart's instrumental music this type of fermata occurs almost exclusively in concerto movements.[176]

Of course, in theory one could still consider embellishing a fermata in one or other of the solo piano works. But this is only rarely practical, since Mozart wrote out his solo piano works with scrupulous care unusual for his time (especially when he could have them printed), and put down most of the lead-ins himself. Mozart often did not add a lead-in at a fermata, as at the end of the slow introduction to the Fantasia K.475 (bar 41), and such fermatas frequently rule out the addition of a lead-in, which would only weaken their musical effect. Here they really do serve the purpose mentioned by Sulzer: in the C minor Fantasia, as part of a surprise effect, produced by the ensuing forte outburst with its tremolo broken chords. Again, the many fermatas in a movement such as the Finale of the C minor Sonata (K.457) can only match Sulzer's descripton, and should therefore not be embellished. Here there could be no question of lead-ins, since the fermatas do not precede the opening of a new section. It is obvious that the question, when a fermata may or may not be embellished, has not yet been definitely settled, as we see from the most recent publications of the new complete edition of Mozart. There is no direct proof that lead-ins should (with a few exceptions) only be added in the concertos. But it is striking that whereas Mozart left numerous lead-ins for the concertos, written down on odd sheets of paper, there is not a single lead-in for a solo piano work on a separate sheet. This is food for thought, since as a teacher Mozart used his piano sonatas even more often than his concertos, and if he had thought a lead-in necessary at any point he would surely have helped his pupils (who had small talent for composition) by writing one out for them. In Mozart's chamber works, too, it is rarely possible or necessary to embellish fermatas and add lead-ins. We, at least, know very few passages in these works where we should welcome the addition of a lead-in: perhaps the fermata in the third movement of the Piano Trio K.496, immediately after the Adagio Variation, before the tempo primo; between bars 108 and 109 in the third movement of the F major Violin Sonata, in bars 69 and 203 of the Piano Duet Sonata in C (K.521), and in bar 135 of the third movement of the Piano Quartet K.478; at all these points a lead-in should be added.

For caution demands that we make it our principle only to add a lead-in when we can justify it by pointing to another, written out by Mozart himself, at some point in his works that corresponds formally and architecturally. We find it wrong to introduce lead-ins if there is no parallel passage with an original lead-in to show we are right. Research has now shown, for instance, that Mozart never embellished fermatas at the end of the slow introductions to his allegro movements. Moreover, it would be unsatisfactory on musical grounds to anticipate (for example) the effect of the Allegro in the 'Prague' Symphony by adding a virtuoso run on the flute at the end of the short Adagio introduction. The same applies to the fermata at the end of the introduction to the 'Linz' Symphony (K.425), or the Wind Serenade K.361. But if we feel embellishment is out of place at these fermatas, then, to be consistent, we must also leave unembellished all the other fermatas at formally similar points. Thus lead-ins are wrong at the end of the slow introductions to the Piano Duet Sonata (K.497), the Quintet K.452,[177] or the Violin Sonata K.454.

Türk was one of the theorists who formulated rules for constructing cadenzas and lead-ins.[178] These are also wholly valid for Mozart's cadenzas, and we therefore end this chapter by quoting them:

1. If I am not mistaken, the cadenza's main effect should be not only to sustain the effect made by the piece, but also to reinforce it as much as possible. This can be most surely done if it presents the main ideas with extreme terseness, or at least recalls them by similar phrases. It must therefore have the most exact connections with the piece that has been played, or rather it should take its material from the latter, on the basis of what is most important.

And in a note:

If this is correct, it follows that much talent, insight, judgment, etc., is necessary to construct a cadenza which will satisfy the demands mentioned.

2. The cadenza, like all embellishments introduced at will, should consist not so much of carefully introduced difficulties as of phrases which are appropriate to the general character of the piece.

3. Cadenzas should not be too long, particularly in pieces whose character is sad, etc.
Monstrously long cadenzas lasting several minutes are on no account to be excused.

4. One must on no account stray into musical country where the composer has not been in the course of the piece. This rule has its basis, I think, in the law of the unity of a work of art.

And later:

9. Moreover any cadenza, including one that has been sketched and written down beforehand or learned from memory, must be played as if it were a fantasy which has only just been thought of in the course of playing.

Chapter Twelve

REMARKS ON SOME OF THE PIANO CONCERTOS

No interpretation of a great work can claim more than a certain limited degree of objective validity; we have constantly tried to emphasize this. There are, of course, many other problems for which one must discover and pass on an objectively 'correct' solution—this has been the principal aim of the present book. On the other hand, to be really thorough and treat every question in detail, as an analysis demands, often involves decisions that can only be subjective; but as these can be based on careful study, it is of general interest to investigate them thoroughly.

In the ensuing analyses there is much that is subjective, even the choice of particular works and the extent of the treatment accorded them.

Though we have chosen Mozart's three best-known concertos for interpretative analysis, we would emphasize very strongly that we believe the less well-known concertos to be quite unjustly neglected. Some of them are fully comparable with their better-known companions. We would mention the enchanting Concerto in D (K.175), with the Concert Rondo K.382 as its last movement; even in his mature years Mozart still played this concerto with great success. He wrote proudly to his father after a performance:

> . . . but the audience would not stop clapping and so I had to repeat the rondo; upon which there was a regular torrent of applause.[179]

Other concertos which should be given much more attention are the fine work in E flat K.449, with a slow movement of Schubertian intimacy and a graceful contrapuntal finale; the brilliant B flat Concerto (K.450); above all, the tender and reflective G major Concerto (K.453), full of romantically bold turns of harmony, the wonderful F major Concerto (K.459) and the grandiose, noble work in C, K.503, whose first movement has a dramatic power comparable with that of Beethoven's 'Emperor' Concerto. The superb Concertos K.271, 414, 451, 456 and 467 also bear limitless repetition. Indeed, if one wishes to select particular works it is better to look for the 'weaker' concertos—but there is hardly a single one, apart from the four youthful ones which he modelled on works by other composers.

Mozart followed an old tradition in marking the solo part of his concertos

'Cembalo': the only exception is the 'Coronation' Concerto. But there is not the slightest doubt that his concertos, like all his keyboard works with the possible exception of some compositions written during his childhood, were composed for the forte-piano.

This is indirectly proved by the fact that in his correspondence only forte-pianos and clavire (= clavichords) are mentioned, never harpsichords.[180]

The ensuing interpretative analyses are intended to provide suggestions for studying the works. The reader should take them 'with a pinch of salt' if he wishes to avoid mistakes, since the subtle musical nuances of tempo, dynamics or touch can never be described more than approximately in words.

CONCERTO IN D MINOR (K.466)

Best editions: Kurt Soldan and Edwin Fischer, Edition Peters; Friedrich Blume, Eulenburg; Franz Kullak, Steingräber (out of print), reprinted in the U.S.A. by Schirmer, New York.

Cadenzas: No original cadenzas survive. The best cadenzas, though not by Mozart, are those by Beethoven, published separately by Doblinger, Vienna, and also reprinted in the Kullak edition (Steingräber, Schirmer); they are also contained in the complete edition of Beethoven, Series IX, No. 70A. Cadenzas by Alfred Brendel and Paul Badura-Skoda are also published by Doblinger.

Suggested basic tempi: First movement, Allegro $\mathbf{C}$ ♩ = *c.* 138–44
Second movement, Romanze $\mathbf{\mathbb{C}}$ ♩ = *c.* 84–8,*
middle section in G minor, somewhat quicker,
♩ = *c.* 96.
Third movement (Presto) $\mathbf{\mathbb{C}}$ ♩ = *c.* 144

Mozart's works in minor keys always contain his most personal expression; they show him coming to terms with the suffering which was not spared him from the earliest days of his youth. One is deeply moved, following him on the bitter path from his nervous collapse at 22, having experienced within a year the utter failure of his concert tour to Paris, the death of his mother and the permanent wound left by his rejection by Aloysia Weber (' . . . it has been impossible for me to write to you . . . today I can only weep.')[181] to the inconceivable self-abasement of his begging letters to Puchberg in the last years of his life, and his tears on his death-bed as he realized that he would be unable to finish the Requiem. His works in minor keys all explore

---

*In view of the alla-breve time signature, ♩ = 42–4 would be more correct, but it is our experience that almost all metronomes are inaccurate and uneven when beating as slowly as this.

the wide territory between passionate revolt and resignation, exhaustion. He was finally inclined to let resignation have the last word. In his last works his smile returns; but it is often a heart-breaking smile—melancholy, stemming from the conquest of his despair, from a region of the mind where neither joy nor sorrow seem to exist any longer[182] but only a composure that resembles a 'weightless state'; the only desire left is for ultimate rest, release from everything mortal.[183]

But in the D minor Concerto Mozart is still a long way from this divine resignation. The very first bars open up a sombre, tragic abyss:

So let us try to offer solutions for all the detailed problems that arise in performing this concerto!

It is very difficult to catch the mood of the first movement from the outset. The syncopations are often too strongly accented, and thus sound like a hammering rhythm, instead of creating an atmosphere of a sustained and yet excited D minor harmony. The syncopated chords should be separated as little as possible. This is best done by allowing each of the syncopations to materialize 'from nowhere' and accenting them quite evenly. On no account should one make the sort of overstrong accent usually associated with 'syncopation'. The piano marking at the beginning is also often overlooked. If the opening is played at a thick mezzo-piano, any trace of a sombre atmosphere disappears.

The rising phrases in the bass have something mysterious and disturbing about them. They must not be played too quickly, and should not make a crescendo up to the final note—rather the reverse, so that the triplets are made clear.

Not until the third bar should the violin line take on a more expressively melodic quality, still within the limits of a sombre piano. From the ninth bar onward a note of anxiety creeps in, then the music dies down again before the forte outburst.

In this ensuing forte the horns have upbeat A's which should be played with the utmost emphasis. The high notes of the first violins in bars 18 and 20 are usually played too short and with too much hard attack, whereas the three lower crotchets are insufficiently accented; the dominant cadence in bar 32 is often too abruptly broken off. It does no harm to prolong the rest in this bar a little, for the F major entry in the succeeding bar should enter as if from another world, quite softly, the wind instruments 'speaking' without any audible ictus. The renewed outburst (forte) in bar 44 should leave room for a further crescendo. It is best to start the second note of this bar *mf* and let the dynamic level follow the pitch:

The strings should make a deliberate diminuendo just before the bar-line; otherwise, together with the sforzati of the wind on the first beat, they will unduly emphasize the barring and obscure the overall line. The same applies to the identical figures of the 'celli and basses from bars 58 onward. In bars 66–7 the orchestra must on no account get softer. Bar 68 must then have a completely different feeling and be played very reflectively. An excess of outward expressiveness would also be wrong in the two succeeding bars. In the codetta only the minims on the violins (and violas) should be given a slight expressive accent:

This passage tells of spiritual collapse after passionate protest. Unfortunately, it is often played too loudly and superficially.

Whereas in most of his concertos Mozart begins the first solo entry with a free 'intrada', a 'lead-in' (as in K.450, 467, 482, 503), or immediately gives the piano the first subject (K.449, 453, 456, 488, 595), in the two concertos in minor keys he gives the piano its own introductory subject which by its pronounced subjectivity contrasts with the impersonal, fatalistic first subject. This contrast is further underlined by the fact that in the course of the movement the solo theme is never given to the orchestra, and the first four bars of the orchestral first subject are never given to the solo instrument.

The expressive solo subject has a recitative-like character, and it may well be played a little slower than the basic tempo ($\flat$ = 132). It should have a directness that tugs at the heart-strings, but this is incredibly difficult to achieve and can hardly be taught. The melody should 'sing'—too soft a 'piano' would thus be inappropriate. In the first full bar the right hand should make a slight diminuendo while the left—which should play in an expressive *pp*— makes a slight crescendo; the minim should be hardly separated from the preceding quaver, and given as little accent as possible.

In the last four bars before the entry of the first subject (bar 91) one should unobtrusively return to the basic tempo of the movement (not making a sudden change). This is made a good deal easier by the changing figurations and the unusual instrumentation (bass part given to trumpets and kettledrums!) in bars 88–90. Here the semiquavers should not sound like passage-work, but should be played as if they were a melody, continuing the previous cantilena.

In the next solo entry a long crescendo should be built up after bar 99; first in two two-bar sections (99–100 and 101–2, with their upbeats), then continuously until the forte at bar 108. This crescendo is also 'orchestrated'— the basses are added at bar 104 and the accompanying string parts 'condense' from broken-up quavers to slurred crotchets. Obviously the entire passage should be played non-legato. The following fingering is recommended for those with small or medium-size hands:

In bar 110 the wind should play at least *mf*, to match the incomparably greater power of the modern piano. In bar 121 the strings are usually too loud, one reason being that most orchestras play the passage legato instead of in a gentle, melodious non-legato (as Mozart wanted). Again, in bars 124–7, and in the Scotch-snap figures in bars 129–35, the string accompaniment is often too heavy. One must ensure that the final crotchets in bars 131 and 135 are not accented. Naturally, the semiquavers of the second subject should be duly brought out:

without dragging them. (In bars 148–9 the only edition that reproduces Mozart's own phrasing marks is by Peters, but there are no musical objections to the readings found in the two other editions recommended earlier.) After bar 153 the musical texture should become ever denser, and one should make sure that the musical line is not interrupted before the tutti at bar 174. The tremolos from bars 153 and 159 onward must sound very excited and be given a good deal of dynamic nuance. In bars 162–4 the contrast of *f* and *p* must not be obscured (no diminuendo in the first half of the bar!).

The three entries of the solo subject after the F major tutti should be moulded so as to differ as much as possible in character. The F major entry can be played a little more gently than at the start of the movement, and the one in G minor rather more dramatically. In bars 213–14 one should make a crescendo, in bar 215 a diminuendo; on the other hand, the crescendo in bars 227–8 should culminate in a forte at bar 229. The development section, which now follows, can be moulded as a triple wave; E flat major (with the very low E flat added in bar 230), at a dynamic level around *mp* (subito), F minor *mf* or *f*, G minor *f* or *ff*. The orchestra should also observe these three dynamic gradations, within certain limits (perhaps between *p* and *mf*). In bars 234 and 238 we recommend a modern fingering: 1 2 3, 5 2 1 2, 3 1 2, etc. The climax of the development is reached in bar 242 (arrival on the dominant). From about bar 249 onward there should be a slight diminuendo to about *mf* in bar 252 (first crotchet)—the bass tremoli, bars 250–1, suggest thunder rumbling in the background, and in the two ensuing transitional bars the quaver rests should be unobtrusively prolonged in order to underline the contrast of *p* and *f*.

There should be something uncanny about the next octave tremoli (bar 261 onward); here there should be no crescendo to act as a transition to the tutti (in contrast to the exposition). Bars 278–80 should be played non-legato, so as not to obscure the orchestra's play of motives; bar 281 should be played *f* subito.

The way Mozart alters the second theme of the second subject group in the recapitulation is interesting (bar 302 onward). In the fifth bar there is a complete surprise—an upward leap of an octave (instead of the sixth that is expected). This effect is the stronger since the harmony (Neapolitan sixth) is also unexpected. The theme should start very quietly and then give a noticeable accent to this high B flat; the change much enhances its expressive quality in the recapitulation.

The left hand's accompanying quavers from bar 323 onward should be played non-legato. Here it is important that the wind chords in bars 327–8 should be played tenuto; if possible, each chord should be played with a slight crescendo. Bars 333–5 should be played staccato, with a very slight accent on the second and tenth semiquavers. The final crescendo should be as dramatic as possible. The last crotchet of bar 343, despite its *piano* marking should be emphasized a little because of the change of harmony; the string and wind chords should be clearly accented *fp* (and tenuto). There must be room for a further crescendo from these bars to the climax in bar 348. The low bass octaves, G–G sharp, should have a full sound!

Now we arrive at the cadenza. Although Beethoven's cadenza for this movement is beautiful and poetic, there is much about it that is un-Mozartean—for example, its modulation to a key as distant as B major, and the martellato repeated notes after B major has been reached, its use of sequences,

and the way the bass motive is angrily tossed about toward the end of the cadenza. The triplet accompaniment of the piano's main theme, and the ending (in itself a stroke of genius) are purest Beethoven. But this cadenza has the great virtue of dramatic conciseness, and this makes it well suited to the movement, despite the faults mentioned.

The orchestral postlude is wonderfully beautiful. There is no need to say that the closing bars should be played without any trace of a ritardando. 'The pianissimo conclusion of the movement is as if the furies had simply become tired out and had lain down to rest, still grumbling, and ready at any instant to take up the fight again', as Einstein writes in his book on Mozart.[184]

The second movement, the superb Romanze, is not in the relative major (F major) as is usual, but in the 'darker' key of B flat.

The theme has a warm, intimate quality and a light, graceful touch, and it is very difficult to mould correctly. But the listener must not be aware of the difficulties. This is why the movement (expressly marked ¢ in the manuscript, as we were able to verify for ourselves) should on no account be played too slowly; to do so destroys its hovering quality, its ecstatically spanned melodic curves.

Every note is important. For example, the five B flats in the bass are decidedly reminiscent of a horn, and should be separated as little as possible; this can be ensured by keeping the key depressed after each attack, and only allowing it to rise half way before it is again gently pressed down.

The last three quavers before the tutti should naturally be played crescendo (octave grace-notes which prepare the way for the octaves in the tutti). But in making this crescendo one must take care not to give an unintentional accent to the preceding chord, which resolves the dissonance occurring on the first beat.

The main problem in the second half of the theme (bar 17 onward) is to let the semiquaver triplets 'unroll' lightly and evenly, without blurring them:

By analogy with the ensuing tutti, bars 18–19 could be played più piano; but here it is perhaps better not to conform with the orchestra, because of the danger that the theme may become monotonous in the course of its numerous repetitions. The last three high F's in bar 20 must be an expressive lead-back to the opening motive, whether played diminuendo or (as is perhaps better) with a slight crescendo. It is as well to pedal them so that the individual notes merge into one another to some extent.

In the ensuing cantabile passage, bar 40 onward, Mozart shows that the piano can be a wonderful melodic instrument. Here one must sing from the heart. 'Open wide the shutters of your heart', as Edwin Fischer once remarked to his lady pupils about a similar passage. This expressive cantilena can also be played a shade quicker than the basic tempo. This eases the pianist's (and the listener's) task of grouping the bars four at a time to produce extended phrases. Bars 56 et seq. should be rather more dramatic (*mf* or *f*), but calm, long-drawn phrasing should return at bar 60 (with its upbeat). There should be nothing feeble or toneless in a song such as this. (The long notes should be played like bell notes, the arm being held loose. After each attack the hand should instantly leave the key and let the pedal prolong the note. Conductors should not overlook the fine subsidiary part for the violas from bar 60 onward.

The written-out lead-in bar 67 must, of course, be played with some degree of freedom; we recommend a *sf* on the high E flat, then a diminuendo and poco ritenuto.

When the main theme now returns it may certainly be slightly varied. There is good reason to believe that in the later appearances of this theme Mozart added embellishments, perhaps in the fourth and sixth bars; one should compare the thematic recurrences in the second movement of the C minor Sonata (K.457). Leopold Mozart's report to Nannerl is evidence that Mozart only finished writing out this concerto at the very last moment before the performance—in his haste he must surely have omitted to write out the various variations. We feel that the following slight alteration is quite justifiable:

The tutti in bars 76–83 is more richly orchestrated than on its first appearance. The horn solo must be allowed to make its full effect!

In the G minor section the first movement's excitement flares up again (see the syncopations in bar 87). The right hand's semiquaver triplets should be played legato when they contain a melodic element (bars 84–5), but staccato when they are merely a means of maintaining the excitement (bar 86 to first half of bar 90). In bar 92 the chord written on the upper stave can be played with the left hand, to avoid a tiresome leap. In bars 93 and 94 the G flats should be slightly accented (within the prevailing piano).

In the next few bars one should modify one's touch to minimize the thickening of tone that occurs as the lowest register of the piano is approached:

Throughout this middle section the flute must maintain its espressivo, particularly in bar 99; on the other hand, the sustained wind chords in bars 86, 93–8 and 102 should not sound too thick.

Bars 111–14 are a dynamic climax. Mozart certainly marked the strings and wind here *p* only because the piano of his time had a weak tone. These chords must of course be softer than the forte chords in the preceding bars, but a reasonable *mf* is best. In bars 113–14 the pedal should be kept down, and the succeeding bars should be played diminuendo with changes of pedal. In the last bar before the recapitulation a ritardando is quite in place. Mozart has moulded this 'return home' very convincingly and organically.

The ensuing return of the theme should be played very simply and at a very gentle pianissimo, after the preceding storm: there should be a joyful sense of release. The effect of this calm is enhanced by the fact that the piano no longer alternates with the tutti, as in the exposition, and that Mozart writes in only a single embellishment. When the orchestra re-enters at bar 135, it should not break in on the 'romantic' mood, but should continue it. In view of the increased size and volume of tone of the modern orchestra, Mozart's intentions will probably be better served by a careful *mf* and (a bar and a half later) *pp* than by taking his *f* and *p* too literally. In bars 142–4 the Breitkopf & Härtel parts contain a 'cresc.-forte' which is not Mozart's and should certainly be ignored. The mood here is still more dreamy and abstract than at the beginning, and an orchestral crescendo would oblige the pianist to force the tenderly hovering arpeggios in these bars quite unnecessarily. Nor should one overlook the subtlety of articulation in bar 145, where Mozart omits to write a slur over the first half of the bar: this is surely deliberate.

The coda must be played intimately and intensely, particularly in bars 148 and 152, the latter even with a ritardando. One should be careful with the pedal in bars 154–7, so as not to blur the staccato. In the penultimate bar not more than a 'pochissimo rit.' should be made, in order to safeguard the subtle effects of the syncopations with which this movement reaches its weightless end. In the second movement of the D minor Concerto the horns must at all costs be in B flat alto, not B flat basso. Some conductors do not know this.

The MS. contains no tempo marking for the Finale. Different editors mark it allegro assai, presto or even prestissimo, but, whichever of them one follows, this movement is one of the stormiest, most elemental that Mozart ever wrote —a movement matched perhaps only by the Finale of the G minor Symphony.

The first five quavers are a problem both for the soloist and for every member of the orchestra. Although it is usually a good idea to make things easier, here one should not distribute the figure between the two hands, since this would make the upbeat phrase all too easy, all too comfortable. Only by playing these quavers with one hand can one underline their unique momentum, using the arm and the entire body in sympathetic movement with the motive. We find that Edwin Fischer's suggested fingering is the best of many possibilities:

Within this extended up-beat, the first note must certainly be felt and played as an 'up-beat to the up-beat', if the listener is not to be misled into hearing a group of quintuplets. Another vital thing here is great rhythmic discipline.

An important difference between the piano and the stringed instruments must be compensated by adaptation of touch and attack when the theme passes from one to the other: the keyboard instrument has a 'built-in' diminuendo toward the upper register, where the strings are shorter and the sounding-board smaller. The very opposite is true of the violin, i.e. the lower strings are always a little weak in comparison with the sparkling E string. If a violinist were to play a crescendo such as is necessary on the piano, the first three notes would inevitably be too soft and be 'swallowed'. This also applies to the flute and most of the other orchestral instruments. The violins must therefore play this theme in an 'unnatural' way, if it is to be clearly heard:

Even so, the listener will hear a crescendo, but will at the same time be able clearly to make out the lower notes.

In the Eulenburg edition and *A.M.A.*, bars 4 and 171, the accidental is missing before the G sharp in the left hand (second note; it is in the MS.), but at the corresponding points elsewhere (bars 77, 210, 350) this augmented sixth is correctly given, as in the MS.

This theme should be played molto energicamente, the accompanying harmonies espressivo and legato, except for the hammered crotchets in bars 2 and 6. In bars 9 and 12 the slur

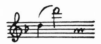

must be emphasized by an energetic accent on the upper note, and in bar 10 the articulation must be clearly audible:

The tutti should be stormy throughout; in bars 31 and 41 there should be on no account a drop in intensity. In bars 53, 55 and 57 it is the low notes of the strings that should be accented (the higher ones will penetrate in any case), and here again it is the last quaver that needs special accentuation in order to be heard clearly:

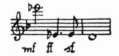

The solo from bar 64 onward should be played with great excitement, so as not to be an anti-climax after this tutti. The thematic relationship of this theme with the solo subject of the first movement has often been mentioned. Whereas the latter theme was lyrically expressive, this one is a pugnacious, energetic transformation of it. The rests in this theme are rarely given exactly their right length, nor is bar 70 often played rhythmically. Special care must be taken with the very short upbeat notes. The triplets in bar 66 must be played very quickly, but clearly. In the passage-work from bar 80 onward, all the quavers must be played separately (non-legato or staccato).

Even with the entry of the second subject (F minor, bars 93 onward) there is no relaxation. Ever since the music of the Netherlands school there has been a specially expressive poignance about figures that juxtapose the fifth and the minor sixth (in this case D flat); unfortunately, this passage is usually played in a gentle melancholy, or even lachrymose, way—surely the wrong treatment for a figure which, beside being intrinsically eloquent, is doubled in octaves with an energetic, drum-like accompanying rhythm.

Obviously the semibreves should be slurred, and the D flat should be louder than the C. From bar 99 onward the flute must play very expressively. In the figure

the E is likely to be inaudible unless it is given a slight accent. The change from minor to major must be deeply felt by the pianist and should bring with it a noticeable lightening of the gloom. After bar 112 the accompanying string parts should be played 'détaché', but not staccato. Not until bar 124 does Mozart split up these accompanying parts into alternate staccato and legato. In bars 131 et seq. the flute's forte must be loud and clear so that it is not drowned by the piano's flood of tone (con pedale!).

The codetta-theme, bar 140 onward, is very 'light' and dance-like, but does not endanger the unity of this dramatic movement. On each of its appearances it has a different significance. Here, at its first entry, it is like a slender silver lining behind the clouds. Its 'bright' F major dies away, and in three bold modulatory strides Mozart is back in D minor.

The build-up of tension on the dominant in bar 167 definitely needs some form of release, such as can be provided by a short 'lead-in'. An immediate entry of the theme in the tonic would be a much too abrupt resolution of this dominant harmony that has been reached so dramatically. Note, too, how long Mozart stays on the dominant before the next D minor entry (bars 272 onward). The one and a half bars of rests and the two fermatas are further evidence that a lead-in is necessary here. If a 'general pause' were all that were intended, a single fermata would have been quite enough.

The following lead-in can be played at this point; it is inspired in part by a run occurring at a similar point and fulfilling the same function—release of dominant tension—in the D minor Fantasia (K.397):

Another possibility here is to take over the second lead-in from the D minor Fantasia (bar 44): it need hardly be altered at all, and has simply to be rounded off with the final E of this bar.

The ensuing entry of the rondo theme leads to a development section that is unusually long for Mozart. A ghostly play with the main motive begins in bar 211. From bar 212 onward Mozart adds a slur over the last three crotchets of the theme—this is a 'softer' variant which lets the motivic play of the piano, flute and bassoon emerge more clearly. (This slur is missing in the Eulenburg score.) When the solo subject reappears in bar 231, it must not burst in energetically as it did on its first appearance, but be played quietly and sadly. This seems to fit the character of the development section, which deliberately avoids anything passionate or stormy. If all the instruments play strictly in time, the redoubtable passage from bar 247 onward is not so very difficult to play, provided that the upbeat quavers are not taken too slowly. The quaver movement should flow from one instrument to another as in a perpetuum mobile.

In the recapitulation Mozart does not use the main theme and is content to recall it by twice quoting its initial soaring upbeat phrase (bars 269 onward). A little earlier (bars 258 onward) one should make a slight crescendo, to smooth over the change in atmosphere.

The codetta theme occurs rather sooner than in the exposition, partly in order to separate it more from its later appearance in the coda, but mainly because Mozart needed more room to manage the transition from this theme's 'light' mood to the stormy atmosphere of the opening. In the recapitulation of this theme Mozart's switches from major to minor harmony and vice versa are a stroke of genius. The minor third F is replaced in the very next bar by F sharp, and the next bar introduces the major sixth, B. In this way the work's major close is already hinted at. What a contrast to the despairing second subject in the recapitulation of the first movement, where the collapse that occurs in the coda is already beginning to break through; but what a contrast, too, to the second subjects of most of Beethoven's movements in minor keys, which keep the same bright character unaltered in the recapitulation! This world of iridescence and subtle gradations is Mozart's most personal world; the only other composer who set foot in it was Schubert.

The lead-back to the tutti in the bars from 330 onward is one of the finest passages of its kind. The enormous leaps in bars 334–5 should not be divided between the two hands, for the same reasons that applied in the opening bar. In a violin concerto there would be no question of playing such a passage on two violins instead of one. 'Better an enthusiastic near miss than lifeless accuracy!'

After the tutti Mozart indicates a cadenza. Beethoven's cadenza for this movement is certainly not one of his best ideas. It rather lacks terseness. Perhaps it indulges in rather too many new 'moods' and 'illuminations', and thus has a retarding effect at a point where an enormous pile-up of tension makes a fierce, concentrated release indispensable. For example, what is the point of the switch to F major as early as the third bar—to a key which in this movement has long since been exhausted, finished with? One can take it as almost certain that in his own cadenza for this movement, which unfortunately has not survived, Mozart did not quit the key of D minor, and that here, at the culmination of the movement, he had no time to spare for virtuoso effects and chains of trills. So near the end, there is only one question—major or minor?—and Mozart probably confirmed the feeling of a minor key in a short dramatic cadenza, so that the ensuing major would emerge all the more gloriously.

We have made an attempt to compose a cadenza that perhaps might correspond to what Mozart wanted. The result is printed in the supplement to this book.

We are firmly convinced that in bar 354 there should be a long 'general pause'. Mozart did not write a fermata over the rest, perhaps because, according to contemporary practice, this would have implied that a lead-in was to be played. But it is quite out of the question to plunge straight into the D major coda after thus breaking off the theme on a diminished seventh chord, which at this point has all the shattering effect of a natural cataclysm. A long silence is absolutely necessary here, an 'eloquent' silence, during which the pendulum can swing from minor to major—the turning-point before the final apotheosis.

The major tonality does not burst straight in 'with trumpets and drums', as in a work such as Beethoven's Fifth Symphony—it appears almost hesitantly, in the oboe, after its way has been prepared by the 'neutral' dominant (bar 355). This wind entry should sound as gentle as possible; the whole mood is destroyed if there is any trace of abruptness. But the theme rapidly gains confidence, and in bar 359 it has already become almost exultant. (In the MS. the last crotchet has a thick staccato stroke!) The piano takes over the theme, and in bar 371 the entire tutti bursts jubilantly in with a phrase which, though related to the 'stormy' motive from bars 31 et seq., sounds completely new in the major.

Here the piano practically ceases to be a solo instrument. It is part of the general rejoicing, and it should play even in the bars where many editions contain rests instead of 'col basso' (cf. pp. 197 et seq.). In the tutti from bars 371 onward and 383 onward, where the texture aims at a complete blend of all the various tone colours, the main melodic line can well be doubled by the piano (not too loud, of course)—in particular, the oboes' up-beat quavers can be given support, since otherwise they will never be heard:

In bars 373, 375, 385 and 387 the violins' high D should be deliberately accented, since it is the climax of the upper part. In bars 380 and 392 the flute and bassoon can take over the melody from the oboe and horn, and make an expressive continuation of it. From bar 402 onward a completely new motive is added, a wind ostinato which from bar 410 onward is very artistically interwoven with the remainder of the texture, so effortlessly that one does not notice the artistry with which it is done. The string chords in bars 414–15 and 417–18 can well be supported by the piano.

This whole coda should be played with a sense of quiet urgency, particularly from bar 395 onward, as a major-key stretto that brings release; but the mood should not be exaggerated. The canonic stretto of the ostinato figure from bar 418 onward should not be drowned by the piano. The piano's figurations should be played in a translucent non-legato, with almost no crescendo, so that the violins' final run can be felt as a last triumphant enrichment of the texture.

CONCERTO IN A MAJOR (K.488)

Best editions: Edwin Fischer and Kurt Soldan (Peters); Hermann Beck (*N.M.A.*), Friedrich Blume (Eulenburg).

Cadenza: Mozart's original cadenza is reprinted in all the editions recommended.

Suggested tempi: First movement, Allegro **C** $\downarrow$ = *c.* 132–8
Second movement, Adagio $\frac{6}{8}$ $\downarrow$ = *c.* 100–8
Third movement, Allegro assai **¢** $\downarrow$ = *c.* 138–44

This concerto is famous for its wealth of themes and musical ideas. It is also more subtly, introspectively intimate than almost any other concerto, so its interpretation will depend to an unusual degree on the performer's personality.

The performer should avoid any trace of harshness or hardness in the first movement, which is the most cantabile of all cantabile Allegro movements. The orchestral forte must be full and noble, never forced. A good way of judging the quality of the orchestra is to listen for the flute part in bars 19–20: it is a counterpoint to the violins and ought to be clearly audible. In bars 50, 57, 59 and 60 the first and second violins should accent the D[3] and detach the following B.[185]

On pp. 160–161 we have already discussed the way one of Mozart's themes creates a varying flow of tension by playing off metric against melodic accents, and both the first and second subjects of this concerto show similar features.

Here the right hand must aim, above all, at a cantabile, which is best achieved by strong pressure. The left-hand accompaniment must be played very softly.

Second subject:

The semiquavers in bars 1, 3 and 5 should be clearly audible. Here the natural melodic 'accents' are in bars 2, 4 and 8, also in the middle of bars 5 and 6. Of course our suggestions for slight crescendi and diminuendi, for the sake of tension, should on no account be exaggerated.

This latter theme contains a free motivic diminution which is extremely attractive; bars 5 and 6 correspond exactly to bars 1–4. Whereas in bars 1–4 the tension runs in periods of a bar at a time, in 5 and 6 it runs in half-bars; this can also be seen from the phrasing. The decrease in the number of notes is compensated by the greater melodic tension (sixth instead of fourth). Bars 7 and 8 return to the whole-bar scheme, and round off the theme, which is a miracle of musical creativeness, all the more since the harmonic tension also overlaps to some degree with the melodic tension:

(greatest degree of harmonic tension: dominant of the dominant, bar 3).

Mozart's passage-work never completely lacks an expressive purpose, but in this work it is more than ever necessary to treat semiquaver passages so that their melodic content emerges clearly.

Bars 87–8 should be played in some such way as this:

(As we have already said a number of times, non-legato is by no means in-compatible with markedly melodic interpretation, and here we would again point out that in Mozart's passage-work non-legato should be the principle type of touch.)

Bars 93–4 should probably be played *p* and leggiero, bars 95–6 (left-hand octaves) at a powerful forte, so that the woodwind must play at least *mf* in order to be heard. The piano's off-beat groups of semiquavers should not be rushed; this can best be avoided by giving the second of each group a slight accent.

Mozart's slurs are not always clear, but in the second subject at bars 100 and 102 Peters' reading is certainly preferable, with the slurs beginning on the first quaver.* The leaps of a fourth in the bass of the piano, bars 103–4, must be clearly separated, whereas the middle part should be played legato. This passage is more exactly notated on its previous appearance, tutti, bars 35–6, with crotchets and rests for the basses. The contrast of major and minor, in bars 114 et seq. and 117, should be underlined by nuances of *p* and *f*, as in the introductory tutti. In bar 120 it is advisable for the orchestra to play *pp* subito, by analogy with the subtle dynamic gradations in bars 50 and 52. In the next few bars a motive suggesting entreaty is repeated three times, and this passage must be handled very expressively by the soloist (but piano, and with the accent not on the A but on the succeeding G-sharp, to avoid giving the impression of a triplet).

It is rare to find a third subject introduced, as happens in bar 143. It is true that in his earlier works Mozart often replaced a real 'development' by a play of virtuoso passage-work around a new motive, and in this way he achieved a very personal synthesis of sonata form and three-part *Lied* form (A–B–A), but even he rarely succeeded in making a wholly new theme arise so organically out of what had gone before; it is such a natural necessity that it hardly seems new at all. This theme has a particular significance of its own, as compared with the motives that are its counterparts in earlier works, since in this movement it returns at the end (in canon between the piano and clarinet). (The only parallel instance we know occurs in the first movement of the E flat Violin Sonata (K.481).) Here the preceding 'general pause' does not have any separative effect—it is a link, and more effective than any transition.

*In the MS. the slurs clearly start over the first note of bars 100 and 102, but at the corresponding points later (230 and 232) they begin over the second note. (Cf. the slurs in the orchestra, bars 31, 33, 40, 42, 108, 110, etc.)

When the piano takes up a variant of this new theme in bar 149, we reach one of the climaxes of this concerto. Only by relaxing completely can one play this passage adequately; the semiquavers must seem to flow of their own accord (but not to run away!), and the long notes must be slightly accented. But one must not appear to be trying to play the passage 'effectively' or 'correctly'.

The development that now follows tends towards the minor keys, and is of elegiac character throughout. All Mozart's works of his Viennese period are intermittently clouded by minor keys. These minor passages symbolize the inner distress that comes to disturb all enjoyment and all gaiety. The phrasing given in the Peters edition seems the best:[186] when the upbeat to the phrase rises, it is played 'separated' and the rest of the phrase legato; when it descends (the fifths in bars 164–9) there should be a legato, and accordingly, in the next bar, the semiquaver should be separated from the preceding quaver:

In the bars after 170 the piano should maintain a crystalline, vital feeling in the decorative lines it spins round the theme, and the bass octaves must be played firmly enough to support the whole polyphonic texture. Figures such as these should always be grouped as follows:

bars 170 et seq.:

In this way, with every second and tenth note slightly accented, and the first and ninth unaccented, the bar line can be prevented from becoming depressingly audible, as is too often the case.

There should be a crescendo toward the end of the development. In bars 198–9 the scoring is full, and in addition there is the interval F–D sharp, with its sharpened leading-note, and in this context the piano should certainly play loudly (ff). The ensuing lead-in is long and should have a degree of pathos. The dominant has finally been attained after the disturbances of the development, and this gives a certain feeling of strength; the tension does not ebb until bar 197, with the return to the basic mood of gentleness associated with the opening. (According to the MS., this last bar should be played legato.)

The next solo entry can, of course, be rather more bright and forceful than at the opening of the movement. The ensuing recapitulation brings nothing new until bar 259, where the piano takes over the violins' motive. The rest at bar 261 must be an 'open' one, an effect to be achieved by playing bar 260 crescendo right up to the last note, so that the next bar seems to be deliberately thrown away. The bar may be prolonged if its inner tension demands. The chord on the third beat (of bar 261) must at all events sound completely calm and relaxed, coming from another world.[187] But it goes without saying that here the phrasing of the theme must be exactly the same as on its first appearance on the strings (bars 143 onward).

In the cadenza (by Mozart himself) the opening motive, which comes from the development and uses a kind of tremolando, should not be played too forcefully; as it descends sequentially, one should aim to make the tone 'darker'. Only Mozart would have dared to introduce into a movement so rich in themes yet another motive, peculiar to the cadenza, and of an anxiously questioning character; its existence is justified, so to speak, by its rhythmic connection with the closing idea of the tutti (bars 63 onward).* These questioning phrases are answered by a clap of thunder in the bass, which sounds especially effective on a Mozart piano. Mozart surely used his pedal board for this passage when he could, and added the lowest octave; the same can very well be done on the modern piano, with its greater compass:

The passage between the high D and the beginning of the trill, two bars later, only makes sense if the pedal is kept down—then the effect is magical.

The close of the ensuing tutti is full of problems, since the flute usually sounds too weak in bar 310, and one always has the impression that the forte only begins in the second half of the bar. We recommend doubling the first A on the second clarinet, which is not otherwise occupied, or else re-scoring this passage so that the flute plays a middle part and a clarinet has the melody. A third solution, perhaps the most plausible, is to exploit the greater compass of the modern flute and rewrite the parts to correspond with the succeeding bar:

The piano passage in the penultimate bar of the movement is very fully

*There is a trill written very illegibly over the first semiquaver of the thirteenth and fifteenth bars of the cadenza; this has been overlooked by most editors, and only appears in the Peters edition, so far as we know.

scored, so the entire orchestra must take care to play softly if the movement is not to end at a dull, 'lukewarm' mezzo-forte.

The slow movement is of indescribable sadness; it is marked 'Adagio' in the MS., but 'Andante' in most later editions. Mozart must have chosen the 'Adagio' marking in order to ensure that the movement was not played too lightly and flowingly, as if it were a Siciliano. If he had known that later generations would tend to let his slow movements drag sentimentally, he would certainly have agreed to an 'Andante' marking.

Whereas at the opening of the solo, above all in bar 2, each of the six quavers counts for something, most of the movement is based on a rhythm that runs in half-bars, with two beats to the bar. For this reason a slightly more flowing tempo may be adopted as from the first tutti (Andante $\flat = c$. 108–14), inadvisable though perceptible changes of tempo usually are in Mozart. This will make the transition from six in a bar to a very peaceful two in a bar easier. If one were to insist on adhering exactly to the tempo of the opening ($\flat = c$. 100–8), the 'innocent ear' would hear a decrease in tempo, since in the tutti the quavers have far less 'expressive density' than in the solo.

Note that the first three notes of the first subject are not slurred. Played in this way, it sounds far more sad and hesitant than when slurred as if it were *bel canto*. The low E sharp in the second bar is not merely a bass note—here the melody seems to sink into the underworld:

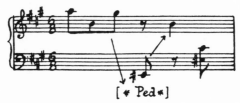

[✠ Ped ✠]

(If Mozart had felt this passage differently, he would surely have written this low E sharp as a crotchet, like the other bass notes that come on the beat.) The quaver rests must on no account be obscured by over-pedalling. The third and fourth quavers of bar 4 must be the merest breaths—no easy matter.

This movement is in every way such a personal document that its interpretation depends on intuition to an unusual extent. How can one find words to describe the deepening emotion of bar 7, the pallid dreariness of the Neapolitan sixths in bar 9, or the expressive quavers in bar 10 (which should be very gently separated, and conjure up a vision of slowly falling tears?)

The second solo, beginning at bar 20, has to make three attempts before it can get beyond the beginning of its song. The first brief comfort comes with the A major theme from bar 35 onward. The triplet accompaniment in bars 39–40 must suggest woodwind tone (cf. the second clarinet in bars 37–8), and should be played without pedal, non-legato and not too softly, since it is accompanying not merely the right hand of the piano, but the entire wind section of the orchestra.

Bars 51–2 are in two ways a brief lead-back to the opening mood; a modulation from A major to F sharp minor, and a transition from two in a bar to six (through the introduction of upbeat demisemiquavers in the flutes, and the way the clarinet parts are written in bar 52). As the individual quavers thus take on added weight, a slight ritardando will occur almost automatically, as will a corresponding slight decrescendo.

The Neapolitan sixth chords are made more of in the reprise of the first solo than at the beginning. Bar 61 should be played absolutely *pp*, with a crescendo in bar 63 leading to the interrupted cadence in bar 64, which should be clearly accented. The wind instruments should also play a slight *fp* at this point, to emphasize the unexpected harmony. In the next two bars the melody takes on almost a painfully grotesque character. The low G in the right hand automatically suggests the open G string of the violin, and the ensuing isolated high D is like a despairing cry of pain. Pay special attention to the length of the notes in this bar (66). It is best to let the left hand take over the G (silently), and hold it a fraction too long, so that the melodic continuity is made clear. The bass chord must, however, stop exactly on the third quaver, and should not be prolonged, even with the pedal. We are also opposed to the idea of filling in this wide melodic leap with a broken chord; this will only weaken the effect of the passage. In the last bar of the solo the tension finally relaxes, and the leap of a third in the melody (instead of the enormous leap that occurred before) gives the impression of complete exhaustion after extreme excitement.

When the orchestra now takes up the sad tale, it should do so very gently. In bar 76 the piano takes over the superb tune which has previously only appeared in the orchestra. The little slurs in bar 77 should not break up the line, i.e. the second notes of these slurs are not to be cut off but joined to the following note legato, as follows:

(The little slurs can be quite adequately expressed by slightly under-accenting the first, third and fifth notes, etc.)

We have already said that from bars 80 onward some embellishment is necessary.[188] In these bars the left hand should alternate (non-legato) with the first bassoon, as if this were chamber music. From bar 84 onward, only the *N.M.A.* edition gives the correct reading: first and second violins should play 'arco' and not 'pizzicato'. Mozart's autograph has the 'pizzicato' markings only for Viola, 'Cello and Bass, but not for the first and second Violins. The Manuscript is quite clear on this point. The close, bar 92 onward, brings a final dying glow of the plaintive orchestral theme, three times and each time with more intense instrumentation and harmony; here the solo adds a part whose childlike simplicity is most moving.

After this movement, the entry of the sparkling finale is like a change of scene in an opera, as if one were set down in the middle of some exciting celebration, and there is no doubt that this movement was influenced by *The Marriage of Figaro*, the opera which was in Mozart's mind night and day at the time. The leap to high A in the second bar tells of confident strength. The next bar should be articulated as in the succeeding tutti:

(Mozart indicates this articulation by a slur over the first two quavers in bar 3, and two small slurs in bar 7. Thus the only element missing, as compared with the tutti, is the second slur in bar 3.) The accompaniment in these first bars must also take part in the rejoicing, and must 'tingle'.

We feel that the solo subject should be ever more effervescent with each repetition. This view is suggested by the last bar of the solo, which is more energetic each time it reappears.

In bars 16–20 and 24–8 there is something about the string parts that suggests a swaying dance; this should be underlined by slightly accenting the upbeat slurred crotchets. The interrupted cadence on to F sharp minor in bar 52 is naturally a reference back to the F sharp minor Adagio, and at the same time an energetic repudiation of the mood of the slow movement.

In the next solo (bar 62 onward) the E sharp must be slightly accented, so that the listener feels it is a link to the next bar. In bar 74 the high E should be given a cheeky accent, and the remaining quavers played staccato. In bars 98 et seq., and later in bars 129 et seq. and 150 et seq., the short upbeat notes should be sharply accented. This can best be done by 'scattering' these notes elastically with the forearm.

With the second subject, in E minor, the mood darkens slightly. The centre of gravity is, of course, the third bar (108). The semiquaver figure in this bar, and the triplets later on, from bar 158 onward, show that Mozart did not want this movement played too quickly, since they are unplayable at the 'presto' given in many editions of this movement. (In bar 113 a legato slur should be added, by analogy with the slurs in the MS. at bar 337 during the recapitulation.) The high pathos of the modulation to C major at bar 121 recalls an *opera seria* aria, and can be emphasized by appropriate dynamics. The passage that follows (from bar 129 onward) seems to gloat over the E major that has at last been reached, with festive harmonies over a confidently descending bass. The strings and wind should realize from bar 151 onward that they are part of a play of powerful harmonies; above all, the wind should not play too softly here, particularly when they have the secondary parts from bar 157 onward. In bars 135 and 157 the soloist should play piano subito, not only to let the woodwind come slightly into the foreground, but to leave room for a further crescendo. In bass figures such as occur in these bars the weaker beats should always be accented:

In the figures from bar 163 onward the second of each pair of slurred notes should be similarly emphasized, so that the feeling of playful energy is further enhanced:

But the rejoicing reaches its bubbling climax in the codetta theme, which is introduced in canon between the piano and wind. Mozart, unlike many of his editors, did not provide a single slur'for this theme[189] and this makes it sound much more fiery and full of life:

(played approximately)   non legato throughout

It is as well to make a slight diminuendo from bar 189 onward, or else to play piano subito in bar 196, so that there is room for a crescendo as the piano surges up to the re-entry of the first subject.

Now there is a powerful crescendo by the orchestra (whose modulations can be supported by a few chords on the piano), and the music moves to a very energetic, almost wild F sharp minor (bar 230 onward),* with occasional plaintive interjections from the woodwind. In bars 230 and 246 Mozart wrote a four-part chord for the right hand (including A), a fact which has been overlooked by every editor in the last 175 years. Then he introduces yet another theme (in D major) into this movement that is so uniquely rich in melody.

In bars 254–5 the left hand should play legato, like the orchestral basses, whose phrasing should also obviously be adopted by the pianist in bars 267–8 and 429–30. The half-bar slurs in bar 288 and the slurs over each crotchet in bar 291 should be carefully observed. The surge up to the high C in bar 298, being a distant reference to the first subject, should be as powerful as possible.

As so often in Mozart's rondos, the recapitulation does not begin with the first subject, but goes straight into the solo subject, saving up for the coda the triumphal re-entry of the first subject. Making allowances for a different plan of modulation, the recapitulation follows a course similar to that of the

---

*According to the manuscript, at this point (and also sixteen bars later) the right hand should play not the three-part chord wrongly printed in all editions, but a four-part chord: C sharp–F sharp–A–C sharp.

exposition, though with a few important deviations. Thus the second subject surprisingly enters in the major (bar 330) and is not used in the minor until taken over by the piano eight bars later. The modulation from A minor through F major to A major is extended as compared to the corresponding passage in the exposition: this is a stroke of genius, suddenly opening up terrifying depths of emotion unexpected in a concerto that is supposed to be 'social' music.

We suggest playing the passage as follows:

After the codetta a superb crescendo (bars 437 and 444) leads to the return of the first subject. The 'swaying' motive from the opening (bars 17 et seq.) now returns for the first time, and this time the piano also takes part. Here the upbeat notes should be a little louder than the ensuing longer ones. In bars 468–71 the left hand amusingly imitates the bassoon solo from bar 28 onward, and the humour can be underlined by playing staccato, to suggest a bassoon. The final crescendo is now due, but by a brilliant manipulation of the form it is further postponed—as if Mozart wanted to play a practical joke on his audience, who were already on the verge of applauding; instead of the expected cadence, the cheerful third subject returns once more. But at the same time the progression to the subdominant (D major) makes it clear that this will only be a short delay and that the concerto is nearly over. And in fact the long-delayed final cadence, all the more eagerly awaited, now appears with virtuoso piano figurations woven round it. It is hardly likely that Mozart meant the soloist to have done with the concerto five bars earlier than the orchestra, and his notation of the bass (continuo) also supports such a view, so during the two closing tutti passages the pianist should play powerful chords, and the last three notes in unison with the strings.

C MINOR CONCERTO (K.491)

Best editions: Edwin Fischer and Kurt Soldan (Peters); Hermann Beck (*N.M.A.*), Friedrich Blume (Eulenburg); Hans Redlich (Boosey & Hawkes); Hans Bischoff (Steingräber, out of print—reprinted by Schirmer, New York).

Cadenzas: No surviving original cadenzas or lead-ins. The cadenzas by Saint-Saëns and Brahms are too foreign in style to be recommended. Relatively the best cadenza is still that by J. N. Hummel, Mozart's favourite pupil. It was reprinted in the Steingräber (Schirmer) edition. A cadenza by the present authors has been printed by Doblinger, Vienna (1956).

Suggested tempi: First movement, Allegro $\frac{3}{4}$ ♩ = *c.* 144 (*c.* 152–60 in solo passages such as bars 165–99 and the excited passage in bars 330–61).
Second movement, Larghetto, ₵ ♩ = *c.* 52–6.
Third movement, Allegretto ₵ ♩ = *c.* 80, intermittently a little slower (76).

It is natural to compare Mozart's two concertos in minor keys. Although only thirteen and a half months separate them, they are worlds apart. In the D minor Concerto Mozart still faces suffering firmly; he is ready to fight, and the works's triumphant D major close is a quite Beethovenian victory over tragedy. The C minor concerto is quite different. Although the work contains episodes of passionate rebellion and of gentle consolation, its ending is not triumphant—it is a macabre dance of death and despair. No wonder that to this day the C minor Concerto has not attained the same popularity as the D minor. It is too complicated, too oppressive to appeal to the average listener, who prefers a 'happy' end in music, as in the cinema.

The difference between the two works is evident even in their smallest details. The D minor concerto's self-possession is apparent in its clearly diatonic harmony; its principal themes, for all their tragic quality, are based on the cadential progression between tonic and dominant. This gives them a certain inner firmness. There is little trace of this in the C minor Concerto. The opening theme has a tendency to sink towards bottomless depths, after its brief initial upsurge, and this effect is intensified by boldly chromatic harmony:[190]

The concerto is not wholly lacking in assertive, energetic figures that pull in the opposite direction, and these constantly recur, but the music is definitely dominated, particularly toward the end of the development and at the end of the first movement, by the dark, sombre forces in it.

Whereas the first movement of the D minor Concerto was in a march-like $\frac{4}{4}$, with frequent rests for the whole orchestra, the present work is in a flowing $\frac{3}{4}$ time that tends to bind everything together. Whereas the first solo subject of the D minor Concerto settles firmly on the tonic in the very first bar and the subdominant in the third, here the solo subject 'slips' from the tonic to the seventh in its fourth bar. Hearing a sequence, one expects that the tonic will at least be confirmed in bar 8:

Instead, the second phrase runs down still lower than the first. The tonic is only reached in the ensuing four bars, then immediately afterwards the theme lingers indecisively on a 'labile' chord, an inversion of the supertonic seventh. After these four bars lingering on D, the final cadence of the theme seems like a powerful effort to pull oneself together. Of the two slow movements, that of the D minor Concerto is again the more forceful. The intimate Larghetto theme of the C minor work is more melancholy than the Romanze, and instead of a stormy middle section there are two wonderful lyrical episodes, a plaintive oboe melody in C minor and a blissfully ecstatic A flat section dominated by the clarinets. But the distinction is clearest in the two Finales: instead of the D minor Concerto's pyrotechnic rondo theme, we find an apathetically drooping melody that is the basis of a set of variations:

The chromatic descent found in the first movement reappears here, in bars 10–12.

In its form, the first movement of this concerto is one of the greatest masterpieces in all music. The dominating power of the first subject is immediately apparent. Not only does it return in the codetta of the orchestral and solo expositions, but its constituent motives appear in the most varied forms, in sequences now of two bars, now of one, and they pervade the movement to such a degree that all the subsidiary themes seem like brief, moving interludes, never able to break the spell of this fateful principal theme. Its importance can be gauged by the fact that whereas the typical Mozart theme confines itself to one particular register, this one appears everywhere—now in the bass, now in the topmost register of the melodic instruments; it is all-pervading, like some uncanny supernatural force or a premonition of death, lying in wait even in the few passages where there seem to be motives not dominated by the main theme.

The technique of composition displayed by Mozart in this movement is astonishingly reminiscent of J. S. Bach's handling of concerto form in such a work as the D minor Cembalo Concerto, where the principal theme returns in various keys in the course of the movement, like the ritornello of a rondo; it may return complete, or only its opening, and the accompanying parts are formed by sequences built from its constituent motives: this is symphonic thought of a kind quite unknown to most of Bach's contemporaries. The construction of Mozart's theme also recalls Bach; it is not symmetrical like most classical themes, but is of the 'continuous development' type, with a distinct, clearly shaped opening and sequential continuation. These relationships are all the more striking since in all probability Mozart did not know Bach's concertos and thus seems to have created this form, unique for him, on his own.

Starting from his first subject, which, despite its apparent simplicity and self-containedness, has an unprecedentedly complex structure, Mozart derives a wealth of rhythmic and melodic figures on which the entire movement is built:

Mozart often uses the two halves of motive (*b*) separately during the movement; (*c*) is an augmentation of the second half of (*a*); (*d*) is an inversion and diminution of (*c*); (*f*) is related melodically to the first half of (*b*).

Later on Mozart freely alters these constituent motives' melodic steps and leaps, and also their phrasing, but it is always clear that they are derived from the first subject. Its opening often appears forte, with the notes separated, and not slurred, and motive b_1 often appears later non-legato or staccato.[191]

Formal analysis cannot teach one how to perceive this entire movement of 523 bars as a single unit; this can only be achieved intuitively. For us this movement is a permanent wonder, before which we can only stand in awe.

As already remarked, this movement contains a tense inner conflict between solo and tutti. The first tutti theme seems to symbolize an impersonal destiny which man, the soloist, must face—suffering, complaining, now in angry revolt and then exhausted, resigned. Thus it seems quite natural that the first four crucial bars of the first subject are never given to the solo piano,* just as the solo subject (bars 100 onward), with its personal quality, is reserved for the piano throughout the movement.

But a further division is discernible throughout this concerto, within the orchestra; there is often a contrast between the strings, which have many players to a part and are therefore in a sense 'impersonal', and the 'subjective', solo wind instruments; the latter thus occupy a middle position between the solo and tutti. Particularly in the second and third movements, the woodwind become so independent that one could speak of a 'concertino', a second competitive group, as in concerto grosso form.

The opening of the concerto should conjure up a fatalistic, gloomy mood. Here it would be a mistake to play with 'warmth'. The first three bars should be played very legato, and the change of bow between bars 2 and 3 should be as little perceptible as possible. It may be advisable to divide the strings and make half of them change bows after the first bar:

Dynamic nuances should be kept to a minimum, to ensure an 'impersonal' quality, e.g. the two crotchets in bar 4 should be played quite indifferently, with a slight diminuendo to compensate for the string instruments' natural crescendo (and brightening of tone) toward their higher register. There should be a slight crescendo up to the third bar, to emphasize the legato. The third crotchet G in bar 3 should not sound too short; many interpreters take the first twelve bars of this movement a shade slower than the basic tempo (but with great regard for rhythm in the phrases with short upbeats, and with great inner tension), at ♩ = c. 138 (or even slower); this enhances the uncanny feeling of 'calm before the storm' that pervades the opening.[192] The passionate outburst at bar 13 is then all the more powerful.

In bar 27 the trumpets should play marcato. The original articulation of the string parts in the ensuing bars (23–33) should be scrupulously observed. In bar 34 the three horn notes are still forte. In the ensuing tender piano passage the upbeats must not be played as quavers! In bar 40 the flute must play at least *mf*, since this is a continuation of the oboe part and there must not be the feeling of a diminuendo. In bars 59 et seq. it is as well for the flute and bassoon to make a slight crescendo up to the third crotchet of each bar. From bar 74 onward the first violins should play very expressively and cantabile (within the limits of *piano* dynamics, of course), and the important passing quavers E and F sharp (second violins, bars 77 and 79) must be clearly accented. In bars 89 the first violins' semiquavers should be played

*Except where the piano plays continuo, as an orchestral instrument.

very clearly and rhythmically. Figures such as these (like those of the second violins, bars 271 onward), and thematic figures such as the first theme of the second subject group (bar 147 onward) show why we recommend a rather moderate Allegro tempo for this movement. The *p* in bar 98 must be clearly marked off from the preceding *f*.

The first solo subject* should be played strictly in time. All too often the first note is not held long enough, and the quavers in the second bar played unevenly and too quickly. In a movement such as this, sentimental variations of tempo are to be avoided at all costs. Even the eloquent subjective solo subject must fit into the general scheme. Although this is a long movement, there is scarcely a single place where one need alter the tempo. The form can only be properly brought out by some degree of rhythmic severity.

In bars 123 et seq., as throughout the movement, the upbeat semiquavers should be incisive and staccato. The three slurred crotchets, on the other hand, should sound very expressive, the leaps separated (i.e. without pedal) but with no shortening of the upper notes. The second violins' counterpoint in bar 134 should be slightly emphasized (espressivo), as should the viola part in the next bars. The piano's runs in bars 135 et seq. must have a markedly melodic effect (while played non-legato), and here the dynamics must exactly follow the rise and fall of the line. The new theme in bars 146–7 arises organically out of the preceding flow, in the way so characteristic of Mozart. Here one can make a slight unforced ritardando, and take the ensuing second subject a little slower than the basic tempo. (This exception should be regarded as merely proving the rule that this movement is to be played strictly in time.) It is typical of Mozart (and a fact whose importance is not yet sufficiently appreciated) that in such passages, which 'flow into' a new theme, he writes legato slurs in the last bar, and only there (cf. K.488, first movement, bar 197 (Peters edition), K.491, first movement, bar 38; K.482, first movement, bar 246). Obviously this use of legato loses its point if one also plays the preceding music legato. The quavers in bars 143–5 should therefore be separated, if possible with pedal vibrato, i.e. from three to six changes of pedal in each bar.

The string accompaniment of the ensuing second subject cannot be played too softly; only the crotchets in bars 149 and 151 can perhaps be played slightly espressivo. The soloist must realize that the first bar of the melody should be felt as an upbeat, so that he should make a slight crescendo up to the high B flat. The B in bar 153 should probably be slurred over to the next bar. A slight echo effect can be made in bar 154, with a return to a louder dynamic level at the cadence in the next bar. In the next solo, which is to be played at the basic tempo, the first bassoon has a very fine subsidiary part, which is unfortunately never audible (the minor ninth as an accented passing-note in bars 165 and 167), because the piano's figurations steal the limelight. This bassoon part should be played forte, and doubled if necessary. In bar 170 there are again difficulties, this time for the flute and oboe, who alternate with a singing line that should not be played too softly. Bars 175–7 should be

*cf. p. 160.

played forte, and then piano in the next bar, so that there is room to make a suitable crescendo in the two ensuing sequences. The strings' counterpoint should be clearly articulated:

The stretto between the piano and the double-basses (bars 190 et seq.), with its octave motive, must be well brought out:

Bass of the piano:

Orchestral basses:

In the bar 201 the second theme of the second subject group enters, distributed among the various woodwind instruments. Although this consolatory theme seems to fall (literally) prey to the dominating pull of the lower regions, there is a counterpoint on the oboe and horn which soars upwards and provides one of the few rays of light in this gloomy movement:

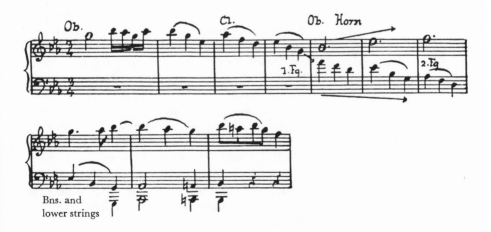

The theme is taken up by the strings, with accompanying figurations on the piano. As in so many of Mozart's cantabile themes, the first bar should be felt as an upbeat to the second (although from the point of view of construction it is a 'strong' bar). This is made admirably clear by the rhythmic scheme

of this passage, and the position occupied within it by the beginning of the
theme:

The interpolation at '*' means that two strong bars follow each other, but the
listener does not notice this till later. The piano's melodic figurations are best
given life by a slight crescendo up to the third beat of each bar.

At this point the mildness of E flat major is broken by a recurrence of the
demonic first subject, in the key of E flat minor (tonic minor of the relative
major of C minor). It is very unusual for Mozart to choose such a distant key.
But he goes farther: in the middle of this thematic entry he surprisingly comes
to rest for four bars on F sharp (G flat) major, using the first inversion of the
F sharp major triad. Bars 220–38 make up one unit, in that the bass gradually
descends an entire octave from bass-clef E flat to the E flat below the stave.
The octave is divided naturally into two by emphasis on the fifth, B flat (A
sharp). One can hardly speak of a modulation to F sharp major here, since
the harmony is transitional and the result of part-writing; there is no cadence
to confirm the key, nor would one be appropriate, since it would break up
the gradual descent through the octave. The F sharp (G flat) chord is in first
inversion—this is indispensable if the overall structure is not to be disturbed,
for a root position chord would be out of place here. (This is the kind of point
overlooked in textbooks of academic harmony, and also in Riemann's
functional harmony.) To make clear the division of the octave into a fourth
(E flat–B flat) and a fifth (B flat–E flat), both of them filled in stepwise,
Mozart not only dwells on B flat (A sharp) in bars 228–32, but also elects to
make the change of octave necessitated by the compass of his instruments just
after this B flat. (The fourth in bars 220–2 is filled in using every chromatic
step; the fifth, bars 232–8, omits one semitone, A natural, but is filled by
conjunct motion.) This clear division is also furthered by the piano's figurations, which remain unaltered till the end of the bass octave, and only change
from bar 239 onward, as Mozart finally reaches a cadence (in E flat major).[193]

The score gives no dynamic indication for this entry of the first subject (bar
220 onward). Since the piano texture is fairly full here, the flute must play
forte and expressively, while the excited string chords should be *mp*. From bar
228 onward the first bassoon must stand out slightly. The piano's two F sharp
major scales can be played with slight differences between them (alternating
legato with staccato, or an echo effect, or a combination of the two). The
series of string and wind chords from bar 232 onward has a definitely
thematic character and should not be played too softly, despite the marking

p. Not until bar 239 is there a cadence in E flat major, after which the relative major is free to unfold with no further hindrance. The horn solo in bars 261–2 should sound triumphant, as should the tutti starting at bar 265; here the low notes of the first violins are a problem that can only be solved if the wind play their sustained notes rather softer than their crotchets. There can well be a slight broadening at the last two crotchets and the dramatic rest before the piano in bar 280. (This also applies to bars 96 and 506.)

With the ensuing solo entry there is an abrupt change of mood. E flat major, which in the preceding tutti had a triumphant quality, takes on a regretful, melancholy character in this solo—which is not to say that this theme should be played otherwise than cantabile. Melancholy is not the same as lachrymose. In particular, the first note of the melody must sound full and firm. It is not easy to play the three chords in bar 289 quite evenly, with a slight break between each pair, as if on the woodwind. The simple melodic step from C flat to B flat is extremely expressive—the previous feeling of a definite major key disappears at one stroke. The woodwind interpolations (bars 291–2) should be expressive and not hurried. The right hand's 'counterpoint' in bars 295 and 299 must sound as independent of the theme in the left hand as possible: the right hand legato with a slight crescendo, the left slightly staccato (without pedal) and diminuendo. In bar 300 the E natural in the middle part should be more accented than the C in the top part, otherwise the latter note will sound like the start of the ensuing melody. This bar has to be practised very thoroughly. There is an apparently innocuous new motive:

which is the nucleus of the stormiest outburst in any of Mozart's piano concertos—the passionate and powerful bars from 330 onward. In bar 300 this motive should therefore be played as if it had some hidden significance, and articulated as it appears later on the strings:

The first subject appears forte at the beginning of the development, and then continues sequentially, *p* and legato, with a counterpoint that seems wholly new but in fact originates in bars 59–62 of the opening tutti. There follows a ghostly play of various motivic figures; these at times combine to produce acrid false relations—for instance, it is hard to find any other passage like the 'Brahmsian sixth' of bars 319–20, where the part-writing produces quite extraordinary clashes.

Throughout this section (302–29) the piano simply weaves a web of passage-work, which should be expressively but not obtrusively played. The play of motives dies away in the orchestra, and after five bars' solo, which should probably be played crescendo, there follows the stormy outburst already mentioned. The pianist who does not instinctively make a slight accelerando in this passionate section is rare indeed. This is only natural, for it has always been customary to express intense emotion in music by an accelerando (though only a slight one!) that corresponds to the quickening of the pulse when one's emotions are aroused. Naturally, if one makes an accelerando here the tempo must not become excessively quick—not more than $\bold{J} = 160$. A feeling for the right degree of agogics is indeed something that cannot be taught. Although the whole sound builds up in this passage, the pianist should not force his tone. The piano's figures must not be played as if they were Brahms' heaviest outbursts—this would make them sound convulsive instead of powerful. (The arpeggios in this passage must obviously be played with pedal. Bars 337, 341 and 345 are slightly easier if one plays the top note with the left hand.)

The excitement of this passage leaves its mark on the ensuing bars (from 346), and takes some time to die away completely. The way Mozart notated the piano part in bars 346–53 very much suggests a forte. In these bars the left-hand phrases which are a free diminution of the first subject:

b. 346

derived from:

should be articulated like the bassoon part (bars 346–7 legato, 348–9 staccato, etc.).

The motivic interplay of the woodwind over a pedal point in bars 354–61 should have biting clarity; the upbeat semiquavers, in particular, need the utmost plasticity. In the MS. Mozart's notation of the piano's scales at this point is not entirely clear, but we find the reading in the Eulenburg and Peters editions the most convincing. In bar 355 Mozart could equally have wanted A natural, since the natural-sign is also missing before the fourth semiquaver. In bar 360 the only possible reading is the one given in the two editions mentioned:

The two outer notes of the scale from A flat to B natural both function as leading notes to C minor. If the top note were A natural not only would there be an ugly tritone (A–E flat) within the scale, but the outer notes would give a quite impossible interval:

Thus the piano's A flat, like the orchestra's A natural (part of the rising fourth G–A–B–C) is a logical result of part-writing. We cannot accept the reading suggested by the editor of the Boosey & Hawkes edition, since he pays too little respect to the melodic independence of these scales in relation to the harmonic scheme. (For instance, he questions the F sharp in bar 354, which is completely authentic.) This use of notes foreign to the harmony, in order to avoid melodic tritones, is something Mozart learned from Haydn and frequently used in other works, e.g. the first movement of the Concerto K.449, bar 181:

In this passage the pedal note should, of course, be played with a gradual diminuendo. (And *no* crescendo in the last bar before the tutti!) In bar 362 the first subject should break in at a sudden forte and summarily dispel the haze that has accumulated during the bars leading in to it.

In bar 390 one can underline the feeling of transition by a slight ritardando. The tempo should broaden noticeably at the third crotchet of bar 400. This bar is all the weightier since it contains two main harmonies, whereas throughout the remainder of the movement there is only one harmony to a bar. The violins must make a real *p* in bar 401, since otherwise the piano will not penetrate. The other main theme of the second subject group follows immediately. Mozart rejected all three 'possible' versions:

in favour of a fourth:

which clearly brings out the feeling of a minor key and also exploits the contraction of the octave-leap to a sixth, to suit the oppressive character of the recapitulation; instead of the consolation brought by this theme in the exposition, all has turned to heartrending lamentation. Even the cheerful triplet accompaniment of the clarinet (bars 156–60) here turns into earnest legato quavers on the first bassoon. Because of its expressive content this passage (from bar 410 onward) should be played still more softly than on its first appearance. In playing the final bars of this theme the effect should be the opposite of that in the exposition; bar 417 not softer but louder, though the final bar should fall back as if exhausted.

The unexpected diminished seventh in bar 428 has something sharp and cutting about it; the lamentation of the preceding bars is brusquely cut off by the return of the first subject. If the second subject has been played a little slower, then it is best to return to the basic tempo at this point. Here again the wind syncopations are thematic and should therefore be slightly accented. The circle is now closed by the return of other thematic figures heard in the exposition. This time, of course, the triumphant horn-call is missing before the final trill—not simply because of the limitations of the natural horn, for Mozart could quite well have given the figure to the bassoons, as in so many other of his works. Instead, in the immediately preceding bars (463–8), the oboes and flute have yet another new complaining figure.* This runs inevitably into the first subject, which breaks off dramatically on the $\frac{6}{4}$ chord customary before a cadenza. (The horn solo in bars 480–6 should emerge clearly, and the $\frac{6}{4}$ should be prepared by a crescendo and ritardando.)

It is small wonder that nobody has been able to write a satisfactory cadenza for this movement, which is unique even in Mozart's works. What possible form could it take? Every theme, every mood, has already been exploited to the utmost, and to recapitulate moods and emotions already experienced would only weaken the effect. This makes it not improbable that when Mozart played this concerto he introduced a wholly new theme and developed it dramatically (as in many of his earlier concertos). A further argument in favour of this idea is provided by the first three bars of the ensuing tutti, which are new and have no relation to any motive from the rest of the movement. Perhaps they are linked to some motive from Mozart's

*We have already said that the piano's figurations must be maintained through bars 467–8. cf. pp. 193–5.

own cadenza. But who else would dare to invent a new theme for this movement? One can, however, take two things for granted:

1. That Mozart did not modulate to the sharp keys in his cadenza. This follows from the fact that in the entire concerto he does not quit the flat keys a single time. (The F sharp major of bars 228 et seq. must be regarded as an enharmonic notation of G flat major, in view of the surrounding tonality—E flat minor, bar 221, D flat major, bar 233.) Mozart's feeling for the 'gravitational field' of his basic tonality would certainly have prevented his overstepping the bounds of the 'dark' minor keys anywhere in this work, even in the cadenza.

2. That the cadenza must have been highly dramatic, but not too long. Too extended a cadenza would only disturb the balance of the movement, which for all its spaciousness is very concentrated.

Hummel's cadenza satisfies both these conditions. The first bars, for instance, are good; so is the increase in excitement in the middle, where his rising sequential treatment of one of the motives from the first subject throws new light on it, and the later diminution of the first subject:

The sequence from bar 18 onward, and the long chain of trills in the middle of the cadenza are less satisfying; the trills make a rather superficial effect. They are better omitted, as can easily be done if the preceding bar is altered:

Another slightly disturbing feature is the way that towards its end the cadenza lingers in the topmost register of the modern piano (a register that did not exist in Mozart's day)—this reduces the effect of the highest melodic notes in the rest of the concerto, without adding anything of its own to the composition. Here we would recommend playing the right-hand an octave lower than written (while keeping the left-hand as it is), also shortening the chain of trills by two bars.

Edwin Fischer used to play the coda after the cadenza (bars 509 onward) softly, 'glassily', without pedal; this made the passage sound very uncanny. He also played the left-hand an octave lower than written (*pp*, of course), like a very soft, low note on the organ. There would certainly be no objection to this, were it not for the fact that the closing three bars of passage-work oblige one to leave this low note. Mozart was more fortunate, since he had a pedal board. He could play the end as follows:

and probably did. It is an illuminating fact that this 'organ pedal' never appears in his notation, except in the already-mentioned example from the first movement of the D minor Concerto: the pedal board was a 'special attachment' that nobody else owned, so there would have been no point in habitually writing down a part for it.

The lonely, lamenting flute that hovers above the gloomy waves of this coda should certainly be treated as a solo part. The end dies away in a resigned *pp*. It must be played strictly in time, with no trace of a ritardando—as if the music moved on inaudibly to infinity, beyond the final cadence. For all its gloom, it is an inconceivably beautiful ending.

To talk of 'errors' on Mozart's part may seem an act of great boldness; but he must have made a mistake when he marked the Larghetto of this concerto 'alla-breve' ₵. More than once in this book we have insisted that his alla-breve markings in slow movements should be observed and acted on. But just by comparing this movement with the other, 'genuine' alla-breve movements in the Concertos K.466, 537 and 595, we had to conclude that this Larghetto should be felt and played in $\frac{4}{4}$.

There are various reasons for thinking this. The smallest unit of movement in this Larghetto is the demisemiquaver. No such figuration as that in bars 24–5:

ever occurs in the concertos mentioned, nor can one imagine them with a ₵ time signature. The note values in this movement correspond to notes twice as long in alla-breve movements, as can be seen if one compares these two identical syncopated rhythms:

C minor concerto, second move-   Larghetto of the B flat Concerto
ment, bar 48:   (K.595), bar 71:

For this same reason, the opening solo is only four bars long, not eight as in the second movement of the 'Coronation' Concerto. Finally, in no alla-breve movement would one find a harmonic rhythm like that in the second (and even more the sixth) bar, where each quaver takes on importance because of the change of harmony; this is in fact not found elsewhere in Mozart.

It is easy to see how Mozart made this mistake. A composer who left behind such an enormous body of music certainly had little time for subtle distinctions when writing out his music. The surprising thing is rather that he so seldom went wrong in his markings for tempo and time signature.[194]

Mozart probably marked the movement 'alla-breve' because of bars 9–12, which do in fact only contain two strong beats in each bar, and also because of the numerous repeated notes in the main theme. Although it is not practical to play the movement 'alla-breve', one can 'feel' it in this way, so that the intimate opening motive, built out of four single-bar cells, does not disintegrate. (This single-bar cellular structure would in fact be impossible in a true 'alla-breve'.)

In the utterly simple but eloquent theme of this movement, every note must 'speak'. The semiquavers after the dotted quavers must not be made too short.

All five notes in the fourth bar should be played quite evenly and calmly, without any crescendo or diminuendo.

If played from the heart, this simple theme can move the listener to tears. And what trouble Mozart took in handling it! Every repetition shows some harmonic and rhythmic variation: this taxes the interpreter's memory quite severely. In the second part of the melody particular care must be devoted to the quavers in each bar: they must not be hammered out, but played with an even, sustained tone; on them depends the whole expressiveness of this passage. The bar before the pause should be begun a little softer than those preceding it, with a fairly considerable crescendo up to the pause (the clarinet and bassoon should, of course, join in the crescendo). The pause should be held by the strings only, not by the wind instruments; this is often overlooked. After the pause there should obviously be a short lead-in: it would be grossly out of style to leave the melody 'hanging' on the dominant seventh (as unfortunately sometimes occurs). Here we can recommend Hummel's very tasteful lead-in:

Or perhaps it is still better simply to use the lead-in from a similar passage in the D minor Concerto, second movement, bar 67, in a suitable transposition:

or possibly one from the 'Coronation' Concerto, second movement, bar 17:

On the other hand, for the corresponding passage in bar 73 we are decidedly against Hummel's lead-in, whose virtuoso character is quite out of keeping with the movement's lyrical nature. There are so many possible ways to effect the simple melodic transition back to the theme, for example:

Edwin Fischer once played the following, as a continuation of the bassoon part:

Mozart's choice of a five-section *Lied*-form (ABA'CA + coda) for this movement shows once again his unique feeling for the importance of moods. A single middle section in C minor would have over-emphasized the dark side of the movement, so that there would have been too little contrast with the outer two. A single middle section in a major key, on the other hand, would have made it too 'innocuous', so that it lacked weight to balance the first movement.

The woodwind phrases in bars 20–3 must be played with great expression. The demisemiquaver figures for flute and bassoon are usually too disturbed, too heavy and insufficiently even in their rhythm. It helps if one can persuade the players not to be nervous about these exposed solo phrases. We recommend playing bar 20 as follows:

The marked D flat (x) should be very expressive, since it marks the inversion of the oboe's motive.

In bar 23 the piano should 'grow' out of the tutti in a slight crescendo. In bars 24 et seq. the strings should play expressively but softly, avoiding too full a tone. Here again it is better to use only two or three desks, piano and with vibrato.[195] If the string parts are played by sixteen first violins and fourteen seconds (as often happens), these can only avoid drowning the piano by playing so softly as to preclude almost all expressiveness. It goes without saying that here the piano must 'sing', even through the phrases in very short note values. The rising arpeggio up to A flat in bar 24 should be played very expressively. In bar 25 of the MS. the turn is written as follows:

not as given in the *A.M.A.* and many other editions:

Again, in this theme every single note matters. For example, how difficult it is to give the right weight to the upbeat semiquavers before bar 26, and to make the demisemiquavers in this bar light and delicate without robbing them of their effect as part of the melody! The F sharp in the next bar must be slightly separated from the preceding D.

In the second part of this solo (bar 32 onward) the accompanying G on the first violins is higher by a third than the beginning of the piano part, so it must be played quite softly, but should still sing.

There is now a brief lead-back to the first reprise of the main theme. The demisemiquavers in bar 37 must again be particularly even and cantabile. It is important to feel the rest at the beginning of this bar correctly. The first A flat must be played as an upbeat to the high C, without an accent, otherwise the listener is given a confused impression of the entire bar. The first half of bar 38 should be played non-legato, with a slight crescendo up to the middle of the bar, after which the remaining notes can build up a little tension, with a slight ritardando as they flow into the main theme. Only four bars of the latter are quoted at this point. (We have already mentioned Mozart's obvious oversight in writing two simultaneous harmonizations of the theme.[196])

The second (A flat) episode follows immediately. Mozart rarely uses this key; when he does so, it always carries a feeling of some secret ecstasy.* The first bassoon progression F–F flat–E flat in bar 43 should not be overlooked. The mellow sound of the clarinets contrasts wonderfully with the rough, pastoral quality of the oboe tone in the preceding episode. The two clarinets interweave in bar 45, and in the next bar all the instruments blend in a warm glow of sound.

At the solo entry in bar 46 the strings' accompaniment should be the merest breath. Two bars later, however, when the first and second violins alternate as the clarinets did a few bars earlier, they should take over the melody from the piano. The syncopations are more effective if they are played all with the same finger, using the pedal, since this obliges one to make use of the arm, thus achieving a quite unusual bell-like tone.

This time it is the turn of the wind instruments to lead back to the theme. In bar 59 the lower strings should feel that their motive from the episode-theme is a melodic line, but should not make too much of a break between the pairs of slurred notes:

(In many editions of the orchestral parts the flat is missing before the double-bass C.) In bar 62 all the players must make a marked diminuendo down to *pp*, together with a slight ritardando to ease the transition to the main theme.

Edwin Fischer used to play the ensuing solo even more quietly and simply than at the opening of the movement, probably because he realized that the version occurring here is the simplest of all: no dotted rhythm on the second beat of bars 1 and 3, no woodwind added in bars 2 and 4. He played the semiquavers in bar 64 particularly peacefully, and also began the second half of the melody very quietly and reflectively. Not until just before the pause would there be a crescendo leading to a forte. The last 'refrain', where the woodwind join in approvingly, does indeed require a full, round tone from the pianist.

The coda stays throughout in a blissful E flat major. The scales on piano and flute must of course be non-legato. It is not a bad idea if everybody plays the entire repetition of the first four bars softer, i.e. as an echo effect. It is not easy to achieve a sufficiently transparent sound in the closing bars (from bar 85 onward); the best way is to treat the passage as a duet between the piano and the first bassoon, accompanied by the remaining instruments. There is

---

*cf. the slow movement of the E flat String Quartet (K. 428).

an unusually bold harmonic clash in bars 86–7, between the piano and the clarinets:

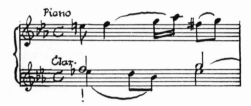

This movement, like the first, 'dies away' rather than ending (so a ritardando at the end would be out of place)—only this time with a dreamlike feeling of light and contentment.

With the third movement we are back in the C minor mood of the work's opening. But the harmonic colour is richer, because for the first time in this concerto Mozart makes use of the Neapolitan sixth (D flat in C minor, A flat in the dominant, G minor); he seems to have kept the chord in reserve for this movement, and he uses it not in its usual form (first inversion):

but in the even more poignant second inversion:

This gives a specially sombre quality to the entire movement. The choice of variation form for the last movement of a concerto is also unusual. Unlike most of Mozart's variations, these have nothing playful about them; the movement is caught up in an inexorable march-rhythm. Each variation is linked to the next without a break, and the customary Adagio variation is missing. The relentless succession of eight-bar periods gives the impression of hopeless movement in a never-ending circle.

To catch the basic rhythm that binds these variations together, despite their great differences in character, is a very tricky problem. It will be impossible without perceptible and disturbing changes of tempo unless one captures exactly the right tempo in the very first bar.

The whole movement seems overlaid with a veil that only parts twice—in the forte variation, starting at bar 73, and in the last three bars. It is therefore not a good idea to play the theme too expressively at the outset. The motive in bars 5–8, repeated time after time during the movement, is like a melancholy refrain, suggesting the similar mood in Schubert's song, 'Der Leiermann'. It would be a mistake to play this theme with the crescendi and other expressive devices appropriate in a romantic sonata. The only place where a slight accentuation is needed is at the chromatic harmonies in bar 11—the upbeat note should be emphasized; but the remainder of the theme can be played almost without conscious expression, though every articulation marking must be most exactly followed. The wind and timpani must establish an iron march rhythm in the first two bars, and must make the crotchets not a fraction of a second too short or too long. The repeats in the first two variations may be played more softly, but this is not essential.

Even nowadays many editions place a mysterious turn over the first note of the piano in bar 16—this has no business to be there, and is the result of a misreading of the text.[197] This bar's way of circling chromatically round G is another reminder of the first subject of the first movement. There is a hovering, weightless quality about this first variation, and one can understand why it is often played noticeably faster than the theme. But Mozart's intentions are probably better served if the movement contains no audible alterations of tempo. (If the change is limited to one, or at most two degrees of the metronomic scale, $\downarrow = c.$ 80–4, this can certainly be regarded as an 'imperceptible quickening', and there could be no possible objection.) The fine subsidiary part for the first violins at bar 22 deserves attention, as does the rhythm

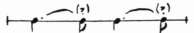

of the violas (bar 21). The piano's scale up to top D in bar 26 should ripple, and 'rippling' is also the word to describe the way the next piano variation (starting at bar 41) should be played—this is dovetailed with one for woodwind, i.e. No. 2 is a double variation. But these runs must not be inexpressive, and here it is important to ensure that the rise and fall of the piano's figurations is matched by the scheme of dynamics. In bar 59 the middle part (G–F sharp–F, played with the thumb) should be slightly emphasized, as should the top part in the next bar (E–E flat). Variation III (starting at bar 65) must be played subito forte, and with the utmost energy. It is important to play the semiquavers after the dotted quavers marcato, particularly in bars 70 and 71. The last five notes in bar 72 are best taken by the right hand, so that they sound with greater power. The ensuing orchestral entry must also be very energetic—it is a truly demonic outburst—but the second violins' scales, like tongues of flame, must not be obscured. After this tutti outburst, the piano's entry at bar 80 must be suitably powerful. In bar 84 there should be considerable dynamic gradation during the left-hand figures. The last crotchet of this bar should be meno forte, so that one can make another big crescendo up to the end of the variation.

The next variation (IV), in A flat, starting at bar 97, should follow straight on at the same tempo. In the bars with an accented minim it is important to cut off the final note and to let the piano's rhythm emerge clearly.

There is a mistake in the Breitkopf & Härtel orchestral parts at bar 125: the first note of second violin and bass parts should be D flat, not D. In the course of this variation, which is scored for exactly the same instruments as the A flat major section of the Larghetto, one can gradually get a little slower. But this must seem to happen quite unintentionally, and must not be noticed by the listener. This gradual slowing-down is in order, because it is hardly possible to play the expressive polyphonic variation (V, beginning at bar 129) in the same tempo as the stormy one ($\quad = c.$ 78–82). This variation's delicate network of parts and its frequent chromatic melismata will sound clear and beautiful only at a slightly slower tempo.

However, on no account should one go down below $\quad = c.$ 72–6! There should still be the feeling of a prevailing basic tempo. One could draw a comparison with a group of people who walk along deeply engrossed in a conversation. If the discussion gets livelier, they automatically start to walk a little faster, and vice versa, but without being aware of it.

This variation must be very carefully practised, and the first thing is to choose the best fingering. Here are some suggestions for fingering and for other points of performance:

This is another double variation. Whereas the first (polyphonic) section must definitely be played piano (and cantabile), it is difficult to decide exactly what are the right dynamics for the second section (bars 137–46, 155–64). This kind of energetic rhythm, and the scales in the bass, usually denote forte in Mozart's music. But on the other hand, the section's very similarity to the variation beginning at bar 65 should make one stop and think; Mozart can scarcely have meant to repeat this forte outburst with less powerful resources, for this would only weaken the formal structure of the movement. Moreover, as far as we know Mozart never accompanies his forte passages with sustained chords on the strings, as he does here; on the other hand, this is just the kind of accompaniment one constantly finds in typical soft passages (cf. the first movement, bar 147 onward). So we feel it is not unreasonable to regard this section as a sombre reminiscence of the previous passionate outburst. The introductory bars (136, 154) also support the case for a *p*: they grow out of what has preceded, without contrast. If, instead of writing a phrase so analogous to bar 128—

Mozart had written an insistent upbeat:

then the case for a forte would be much stronger. As it is, we recommend that this variation should be played in a ghostly, rhythmic mezza voce, with a slight crescendo in the last four bars. It is interesting that the second half-period of this section is extended from four bars to six.

And now we come to the last, and brightest, ray of light in this concerto—the wonderful C major variation. (C major for the first and only time in the work: this is economy raised to the level of genius.) We shall not try to settle the question whether this is a very free variation or a new episode. One could perhaps call this section an 'anti-variation', for although the modulatory scheme is the same as that of the theme, everything else is different—and this is in itself enough to link them very closely. Instead of the drooping first motive of the theme, there is a wonderful phrase that rises through more than an octave:

this is related to the very similar melodic phrase at bar 205 of the first movement:

perhaps there is more than coincidence here. Instead of the march-like crotchet rhythm of the theme, here we find a filigree quaver and semiquaver figuration; the close of each half (bars 8, 16) becomes a feminine ending, the chromaticism in bar 11 is replaced by diatonicism, etc.

If this variation is played at the right speed (not too slowly, and most definitely not slower than $\downarrow = 74$), there is something ethereal, unreal about it. The entire variation must be therefore played with great 'sensibility'. The first crotchet of bar 171 should not be staccato, but sustained. In bars 173–6 the strings should be very soft, but from bar 176 onward they come to the fore. The pianist must also play the theme gently and expressively, with a switch to glittering passage-work in bars 176–9. The last four bars are repeated, the string parts being replaced and intensified (transposition an octave higher) by the wind, and the piano can also stand out a little more here.

At this point C minor makes its sombre reappearance, in a variation which has such close relations with the theme that it sounds like a recapitulation. (If the C major variation has been played a shade slower than the basic tempo, this must, of course, return here, but there should be no feeling of an abrupt change of tempo. It is probably better to make a very slight accelerando in the first four bars than to quicken up suddenly at bar 201.) There are no particular interpretative problems in this variation.

After a short build-up of four bars, there is at last a moment of rest, on the poignant augmented-sixth chord (bar 219). In these bars the woodwind have multiple leading notes that create some acute dissonances, such as the clash of B flat, B and C in bar 217, or the 'Brahmsian' harmony in bar 128, which must have been an enormously bold stroke in Mozart's day.

The fermatas in bars 219 and 220 indicate lead-ins. Hummel's lead-in for bar 219 is excellent, but there is no reason to begin on the topmost E flat of the modern piano (an octave higher than Mozart's top note); we would recommend simply omitting the top octave of Hummel's lead-in:

Hummel's rather empty passage-work in bar 220 is less satisfactory. After the complex run in bar 219, a simple arpeggio would probably be better:

The player must use his judgment as to whether he goes straight into the closing section after this, or plays another short lead-in in bar 220.

The ensuing final section, whose mood is unusually sombre, begins with a $\frac{6}{8}$ variation of the theme, in which the Neapolitan $\frac{6}{4}$ is further enriched by an enharmonic alteration.*

*The phrasing of bars 228–33 is correct in the *N.M.A.* and Peters editions, wrong in Eulenburg's.

As we have said, the piano can only resort to an accent on the F sharp as a substitute for the difference in intonation between G flat and F sharp, which on a stringed instrument is not inconsiderable.

From the second half of bar 236 onward, it is as well to make an echo-effect. The whole of this closing Allegro (for it is an Allegro, though Mozart has not left any tempo-indication for it) must be played extremely rhythmically; particular care must be taken over the figure

The first note must be held long enough, and the short semiquaver played very clearly staccato, otherwise it will be swallowed up.

The coda (bar 241 onward) is marked by a mood of sombre chromaticism. Whereas the first subject of the first movement moved chromatically round the dominant, here there is chromatic movement round the tonic. It is very difficult to decide whether this coda should be played forte or piano.[198] Piano seems more in keeping with its macabre, dance-of-death quality, but one could also find convincing reasons for playing it forte: the searing upward scale in bar 240, the left-hand tremoli, and the wide arpeggio in bar 250. Whether one decides on piano or forte, the chromatic melody from bar 241 onward must at all events be played with the maximum expressiveness and excitement.

Toward the end of the coda it begins to look as if the music is going to settle on the Neapolitan sixth for good (bars 253–5, 270–6). The bass octaves (A flat) should be louder each time this harmony reappears! The passage-work at the end (bar 278 onward) should certainly be played without any crescendo—a final descent into the depths, with a final gesture of dismissal from the full orchestra, a clap of thunder that brings to an end this uniquely tragic masterpiece.

4. Facsimile of a page from a contemporary copy of the Piano Concerto in C, K.246, with material added in Mozart's hand. The sheet contains the end of the first movement, a cadenza for the movement (four bars only!) in Mozart's hand, and the opening of the second movement. It is very interesting to see that when the piano plays with the tutti, Mozart wrote out a continuo for it. (*Salzburg Mozarteum.*)

5. Facsimile of the manuscript (hitherto lost) of Variations VIII and XI from the piano Variations on 'La belle Françoise', K. 353 (now in a private collection in England).

6. A hitherto unknown Mozart cadenza to Piano Concerto K.246, first movement.
(*Autograph Conservatorio Giuseppe Verdi, Milan.*)

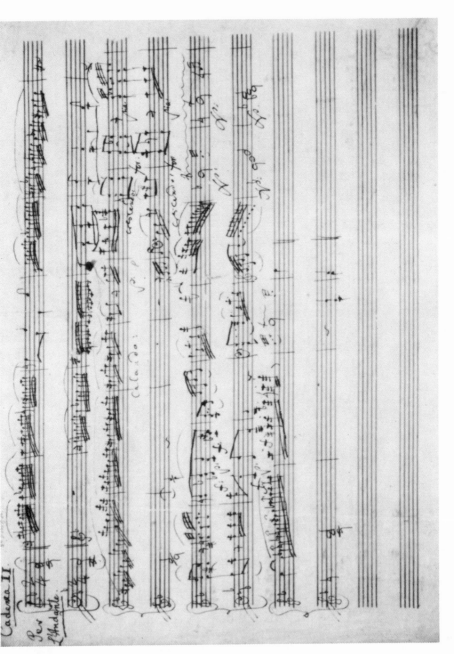

7. Cadenza to K.246, second movement. (*Autograph Conservatorio Guiseppe Verdi, Milan.*)

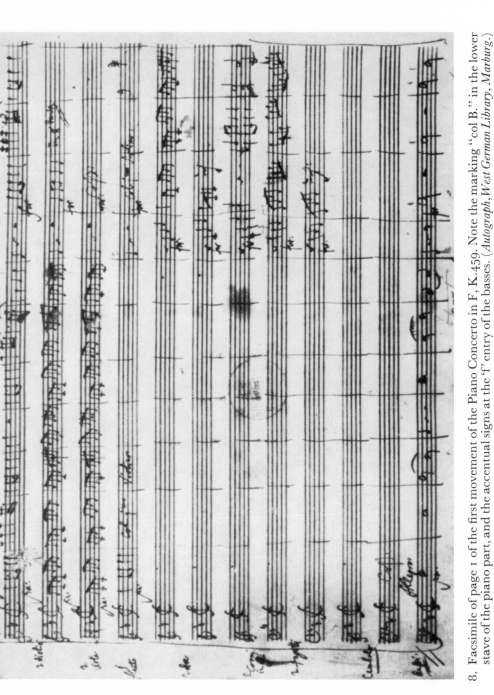

8. Facsimile of page 1 of the first movement of the Piano Concerto in F, K.459. Note the marking "col B." in the lower stave of the piano part, and the accentual signs at the 'f' entry of the basses. (*Autograph, West German Library, Marburg.*)

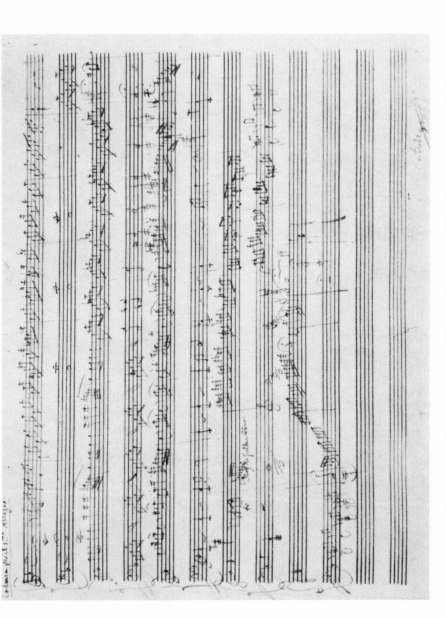

9. Mozart's Cadenza to first movement of K.459. (*Autograph, West German Library, Marburg.*)

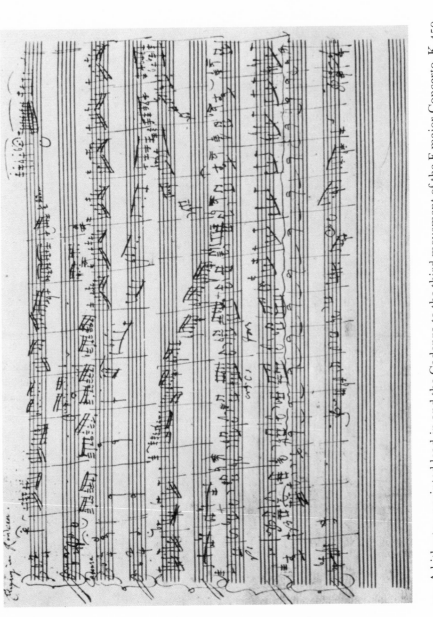

10. A hitherto unprinted lead-in and the Cadenza to the third movement of the F major Concerto, K. 459 in Mozart's handwriting. (*Autograph collection, Federhofer, Graz.*)

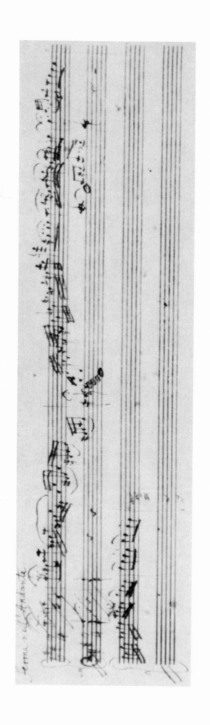

11. Facsimile of the manuscript of a hitherto unknown lead-in for the second movement of the Piano Concerto in A, K.414 (386a). (*West German Library, Marburg.*)

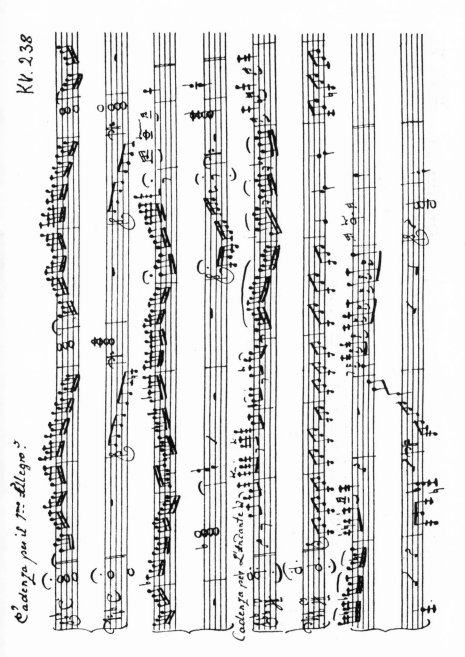

12. Contemporary copies of the original cadenzas for the three movements of the Piano Concerto in B Flat, K.238 (they were only discovered in 1955). In bar 10 of the cadenza for the third movement there is a copyist's mistake: the eighth note in the upper stave should be 'd'. (*Salzburg Museum.*)

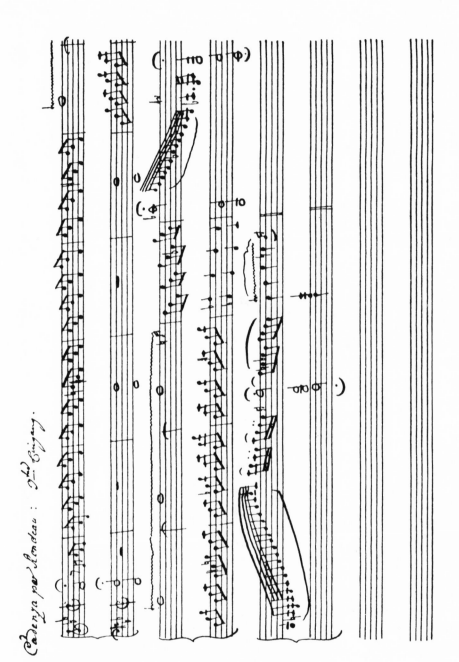

13. (*Continued*) Cadenzas for three movements of the Piano Concerto in B Flat (K.238)

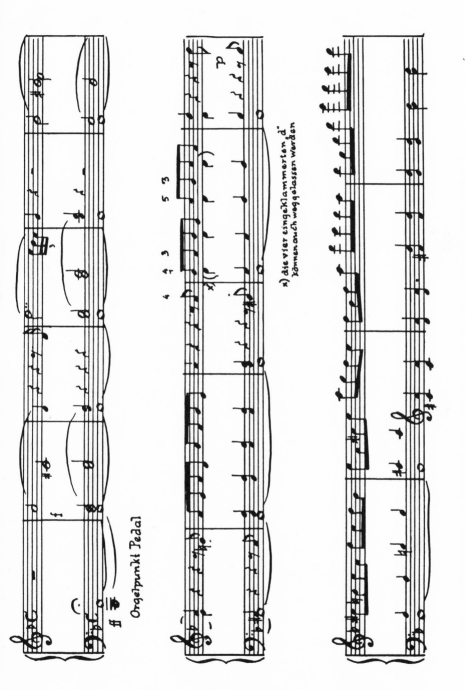

14. Cadenza by Paul Badura-Skoda for the third movement of the Piano Concerto in D minor, K.466.

294

16. (*Continued*) Cadenza for the third movement of the Piano Concerto in D minor, K.466.

17. Cadenzas to Violin Concerto, K.216, by Paul Badura-Skoda.

18. (*Continued*) Cadenzas to Violin Concerto, K.216.

19. (*Continued*) Cadenzas to Violin Concerto, K.216.

CADENZA I   Per L'Allegro

20. Original cadenzas to Piano Concerto, K.246 (cf. plates 6 and 7).

21. (*Continued*) Original cadenzas to Piano Concerto, K.246.

CADENZA II   Per L'Andante

22. (*Continued*) Original cadenzas to Piano Concerto, K.246.

23. (*Continued*) Original cadenzas to Piano Concerto, K.246.

REFERENCES
BIBLIOGRAPHY
INDEX TO WORKS DISCUSSED

REFERENCES

1. C. P. E. Bach, *Essay* (see Bibliography), I, III, 13. Leopold Mozart writes to the same effect in his *Violinschule*: 'Finally, in practising every care must be taken to find and to render the effect which the composer wished to have brought out; and as sadness often alternates with joy, each must be carefully depicted according to its kind. In a word, all must be so played that the player himself be moved thereby' (English translation by Editha Knocker: see Bibliography), XII, 7.

2. F. Busoni, *Entwurf* (see Bibliography), p. 21.

3. cf. *Entwurf*, p. 26, cf. also the ensuing pages.

4. J. Huneker, *Franz Liszt* (see Bibliography).

5. Lecture given at the opening of the 1953 Summer Course, Lucerne Conservatoire.

6. cf. H. Matzke, *Unser technisches Wissen von der Musik*, Vienna, p. 417, 1949. There are good descriptions of the Mozart piano in R. Steglich, *Studien an Mozarts Hammerflügel* and *Der Mozart-Klang* (see Bibliography). Cf. also A. Hyatt King, 'Mozart in Retrospect', pp. 242 onwards, also Luithlen's study in the 1954 *Mozart-Jahrbuch*.

7. The first forte-piano may have been the one made in Florence in 1709 by Christofori. But the instrument did not become generally known for another half-century. Cf. Matzke, op. cit., p. 411.

8. Letter of 28th December 1777.

9. cf. Einstein, *Mozart* (see Bibliography), pp. 237 onward. .

10. Taken from Mueller von Asow, *Briefe W. A. Mozarts*, 1942, vol. II, p. 259.

11. cf. the chapter on *Some Technical Problems*. . . .

12. The work referred to is K.284.

13. Walter Gieseking, 'Mozart mit oder ohne Pedal'; cf. also his article, 'Mozarts Klavier-Werk' (see Bibliography).

14. cf. Hugo Worch, *Piano-makers of the Evolutionary Period*, New York, 1907.

15. Letter of 12th March 1785.

16. cf. Abert, *W. A. Mozart*, note to p. 1,007.

17. The symphony was probably K.338, which is particularly festive in character.

18. cf. Einstein, *Mozart*, Chapter 13. The following works contain tables giving details of the constitution of orchestras in various European cities in Mozart's lifetime: R. Haas, *Aufführungspraxis*, Potsdam, 1931, pp. 217 onward, and F. Dorian, *The History of Music in Performance*, New York, 1942, pp. 174 onward.

19. Letter of 4th November 1777.

20. J. J. Quantz, *Versuch einer Anweisung* (see Bibliography), XVII, VII, §30 (p. 254).

21. cf. *Versuch*, XVII–VII, §26 (p. 253).

22. cf. H. Kroyer's Foreword to the Eulenburg miniature score of this symphony.

23. Letter to his father, 14th November 1777.

24. Letter of 26th September 1781.

25. I/2, §7 (p. 33).

26. Letter from Mozart to his father, 17th January 1778.

27. Letter to his father, 4th February 1778.

28. Letter to his father, 26th November 1777.

29. Letter from Leopold to his son, 29th January 1778.

30. *Allgemeine Musikalische Zeitung*, Leipzig, 5th May 1813.

31. Letter of 9th June 1784.

32. Letter of 20th April 1782.

33. cf. Einstein, *Mozart*, p. 312.

34. cf. Steglich, 'Über den Mozart-Klang', *Mozart-Jahrbuch*, 1950, p. 69.

35. R. Strauss, *Recollections and Reflections* (see Bibliography).

36. *Violinschule*, I, II, §1 (p. 30).

37. Letter from Mozart to his father, Augsburg, 24th October 1777.

38. *Violinschule*, IV, §38 (p. 87). This paragraph continues: 'Such an evil must therefore be avoided and such pieces be played at first slowly . . . not pressing forward but holding back, and in particular, not shortening the last two of four equal notes.' This has lost none of its validity; in passage-work, particular attention should be paid to the notes at the end of a group.

39. Liszt, Preface to his symphonic poems. Quoted by Wilhelm Furtwängler in *Ton und Wort*, Wiesbaden, 1955, p. 262.

40. We would describe as 'unnoticeable' those adjustments of tempo which amount to not more than one degree of the metronomic scale (e.g. from $\downarrow = 132$ to $\downarrow = 138$).

41. op. cit., XII, §20 (p. 223-4).

42. One has only to think of Mozart's adagio variations, or the final allegro variations in his andante movements in variation form, e.g. the second movement of the F major Violin Sonata (K.377); here Variation IV should also doubtless be played più mosso e energico, though there is no indication of a tempo-change at this point.

43. Letter of 23rd October 1777.

44. cf. Tosi, *Opinioni de cantori antichi e moderni*, Bologna, 1723; cf. also L. Kamienski: 'Zum "Tempo Rubato" ' (see Bibliography).

45. *Violinschule*, XII, §20 (p. 224; also footnote 1).

46. The Breitkopf & Härtel Urtext Edition (and that of Edwin F. Kalmus) reproduces the version given in the first printed edition, Vienna, Artaria, 1784.

47. *Violinschule*, XII, §20 (p. 224, footnote).

48. idem. I, iii, §11 (p. 41); cf. also the musical examples in IX, §4, and IX §20.

49. idem I, iii, §11 (p. 42).

50. cf. pp. 100 ff. for a discussion of the normally valid way of resolving this kind of figure containing a turn.

51. Schubert, too, obviously intended such rhythms to be 'ironed out' at times; for instance, in the MS. of the song 'Wasserflut' (from the *Winterreise*) his notation suggests this, since in bar 3 (and similar places, e.g. bar 17) he writes the semiquaver of the dotted figure exactly under the third of the triplets. This can hardly be an accident, since Schubert was very precise in his notation. Even in Chopin there are still passages of this kind—cf. the commentary in Paderewski's edition of the B minor Sonata, op. 58, first movement, bar 73.

52. On this point, cf., also K. Ph. Bernet-Kempers, *Hemiolenbildungen bei Mozart*, *Festschrift Orthoff*, Kassel, 1961.

53. cf. also the bass parts in bars 25-8 of this movement.

54. cf. Hermann Keller, *Die musikalische Artikulation, insbesondere bei J. S. Bach*, Stuttgart, 1925, and the same author's *Phrasierung und Artikulation*, Kassel, 1955.

55. The use of phrasing-marks is often defended on the grounds that 'A piano pupil needs help in order to make out how motives and phrases are laid out'; the answer to this is that any pupil who cannot see for himself how music hangs together must be completely unmusical. Moreover, an intelligent teacher can help a child by adding any necessary phrasing-slurs himself; cf. also an article by Heinrich Schenker, 'Weg mit den Phrasierungs-bogen', in *Das Meisterwerk der Musik, Yearbook* 1, 1925, pp. 41-6.

56. VII, §10, p. 76.

57. Marpurg, *Anleitung zum Klavierspielen*, Berlin, 1755, p. 29.

58. Türk, VIII/III, §442, p. 400.

59. On this point cf. R. Steglich's essays, particularly *Über Mozarts Adagio-Takt*, pp. 110 onward (see Bibliography).

60. Taken from p. 110 of R. Steglich's article mentioned in note 59.

61. cf. Einstein's Foreword to *The 10 Celebrated String Quartets by Mozart, First Authentic Edition*, Novello, London, 1945, p. viii.

62. cf. *Die Bedeutung der Zeichen Keil, Strich und Punkt bei Mozart. Fünf Lösungen einer Preisfrage*, Kassel, 1957; also E. Zimmermann, 'Das Mozart-Preisausschreiben der Gesellschaft für Musikforschung', in *Festschrift Schmidt-Görg*, Bonn, 1957, and Paul Mies, 'Die Artikulationszeichen Strich und Punkt bei Mozart' (see Bibliography), pp. 428 onward.

63. *Essay*, III, §17.

64. On pp. 429 et seq. of the article mentioned above, Paul Mies asserts that Mozart's accentual signs also originally shortened the notes, but his arguments are not very convincing.

65. Thayer-Deiters I¹, pp. 197 onward.

66. Carl Czerny, 'Vollständige theoretisch-praktische Pianoforte-Schule', (see Bibliography), p. 72.

67. op. cit., XII, §11, p. 220.

68. C. P. E. Bach, *Essay*, I, II, General, 1, p. 79.

69. cf. pp. 76 and 88.

70. We are grateful to the owner of this MS., Mr. Rudolf Nydahl of Stockholm, for his kind permission to examine it.

71. cf. pp. 80–1.

72. cf. C. P. E. Bach, *Essay*, II/2, §12, and L. Mozart, *Violinschule*, IX, §5.

73. Taken from R. Haas, op. cit., p. 246, Ex. 198.

74. A. Beyschlag, *Ornamentik*, p. 168.

75. B. Paumgartner, *Von der sogenannten Appoggiatura*; also H. J. Moser, 'Mozart-Interpretation in den jüngsten vier Jahrzehnten' (see Bibliography).

76. This fine example is taken from Moser's *Musiklexikon*, third edition, Hamburg, 1951, p. 1,271.

77. See p. 83.

78. XI, §8 (p. 206).

79. At this point in the MS. it is impossible to tell clearly whether Mozart wrote the turn over or after the first note.

80. On this point cf. Schenker, 'Ein Beitrag zur Ornamentik'.

81. On this point cf. Beyschlag, op. cit., p. 145.

82. The MS. of this piano tutor is in the library of the Gesellschaft der Musikfreunde, Vienna. Albrechtsberger lived in Vienna as an organist and composer; he was a friend of both Haydn and Mozart, and in 1791 succeeded Mozart as Kapellmeister at the Cathedral of St. Stephen in Vienna.

83. As in an edition of the Concert Rondo (K.386), published by the Universal Edition, bars 43 and 51. In this connection, the opening of the theme of the variation movement in the A major Violin Sonata (K. 305) is also interesting. In all the old editions there is an appoggiatura D before the trill, both here and in Variation I. But the MS. has a C sharp in both cases.

84. cf. Türk, op. cit., §310, p. 293; also C. P. E. Bach, *Essay*.

85. The editor's ignorance of Mozart's notation can be seen simply from the fact that he refers to the legato marking which Mozart often used when he wrote extended runs. But as far as we know the written word 'legato' almost never appears in Mozart's manuscripts. It is remarkable that this fact also seems to have escaped the notice of the author of the article on 'Artikulation' (Hermann Keller) in the encyclopaedia *Die Musik in Geschichte und Gegenwart*.

86. The indispensable source of information on the whereabouts of manuscripts is the Third Edition of Köchel (see Bibliography), supplemented by the following recent publications mentioned in the bibliography: Albrecht, *A Census of Autograph Music Manuscripts of European Composers in American Libraries*, Mueller von Asow, *Mozartiana*, Hyatt King, *A Census of Mozart Musical Autographs in England*, and Virneisel, *Mozartiana*.

87. The editor of the *N.M.A.* edition has done a service by also mentioning the need for lead-ins. But we have our doubts about his suggestion that there should be a lead-in at the

end of the slow introduction to the first movement of the F major Piano-duet Sonata (K.497). We do not know of a single passage in which Mozart embellishes sustained chords at the end of the slow introduction to a movement laid out on symphonic lines. The editor is certainly right in all his other suggestions for the introduction of lead-ins, but we are not enthusiastic about the actual lead-ins he suggests.

88. The first edition (Boyer) of K.175 was reprinted by Schott, Mainz, but has been out of print for a long time.

89. There are numerous mistakes in all the editions of this concerto, since they all follow the *A.M.A.* The present authors are revising the text according to the MS. for the *N.M.A.*

90. We do not believe that the ambiguous passage in bar 298 of the first movement of the D minor Concerto (K.466), which Blume, as editor, corrected in the text and mentioned in his Foreword as an error, represents a mistake on Mozart's part. The last quaver must certainly be a B, and not, as Blume suggests, a D. The D would produce an ugly doubling of the seventh, whereas the B is a welcome enrichment of the harmony (adding the third above the bass).

91. On this point, cf. P. Badura-Skoda, 'Missing Bars and corrupted Passages in Classical Masterpieces', *Music Review*, May, 1961; in *Neue Zeitschrift für Musik*, vol. II, 1958).

92. cf. p. x of the Foreword to *The Celebrated 10 String Quartets*. . . . This foreword also contains the following passage: 'On the other hand, Mozart's peculiarity of dividing his quaver and semiquaver figures into groups instead of stringing them together indiscriminately on a single line or set of lines—a refinement with which even the first editions play havoc—has been respected. It is true that even in this point Mozart is not quite consistent, but it is better to ponder over an inconsistency of Mozart's than deliberately to efface it.' Other editors please imitate!

93. cf. Einstein, *Mozart*, pp. 142–3, and his *Mozart's Handwriting* . . ., pp. 145 onward. It is easy to see that Mozart used this two-stage method of writing, from the different coloured inks.

94. We are grateful to the conductor George Szell for pointing out this copying mistake on Mozart's part.

95. This mistake has since been mentioned in an essay by W. Gerstenberg, 'Zum Autograph des Klavierkonzertes K.503', in *Mozart-Jahrbuch, 1953*.

96. Niemetschek, *Mozart*, p. 71; cf. *Köchel-Einstein*, p. 874.

97. cf. *Mozart-Jahrbuch*, I, 1923, p. 18.

98. Letter from Mozart to his father, 7th June 1783.

99. Mozart's letter of 17th October 1777.

100. Letter of 24th October 1777.

101. The long bass strings of the concert grand are richer in overtones than those of small grands and upright pianos, so that chords of this kind sound a good deal better on a concert grand than on a smaller instrument. The tone of a concert grand is in all respects not merely more powerful, but also noticeably more distinguished than that of a short grand, which is why it is to be preferred even in a small room.

102. We are grateful to Herr E. Thomas, of Frankfurt-on-Main, for pointing this out.

103. For instance, in the opening theme of the C minor Sonata (K. 457), the staccato of the crotchets, which are energetic and at the same time elastic, must on no account be blurred by the pedal.

104. Chr. Fr. D. Schubart, *Ideen zu einer Ästhetik der Tonkunst*, Vienna, 1806, p. 373.

105. Letter from Mozart to his father, 28th April 1784.

106. Mozart's letter of 24th April 1784.

107. Letter from Mozart to his father, 13th November 1777.

108. Letter from Mozart to his father, 7th June 1783.

109. Letter from Mozart to his father, 16th January 1782.

110. cf. Mueller von Asow, op. cit. vol. II, p. 152.

111. Karl von Dittersdorf, *Autobiography*, translated by A. D. Coleridge, Bentley, London, 1896, p. 251.

112. *Versuch*, reprint, p. 226.

113. *Violinschule*, XII, §9 (p. 219).

114. *Violinschule*, XII, §13 (p. 221).

115. *Hommage à Dinu Lipatti*, Geneva, 1950.

116. On this problem, cf. the excellent studies by W. Fischer, 'Zur Entwicklungs-geschichte des Wiener klassischen Stils', and G. Becking, *Der musikalische Rhythmus als Erkenntnisquelle* (see Bibliography).

117. We are grateful to the conductor George Szell for pointing out that enharmonic alterations can be emphasized in this way by the performer.

118. Letter to Aloysia Weber, written in Italian, Paris, 30th July, 1778.

119. Letter to his father, Vienna, 26th September 1781.

120. cf. the letters from Munich to his father, September 1780–January 1781, and from Vienna, 19th, 26th September, 13th October 1781, 21st June 1783; to Jacquin, 16th October 1787, and others; all these make it clear that for Mozart opera stood at the centre of his creative life.

121. On this point, cf. E. Schenk, 'Zur Tonsymbolik in Mozarts *Figaro*' (see Biblio-graphy).

122. cf. W. Fischer, 'Der, welcher wandelt diese Strasse voll Beschwerden' (see Biblio-graphy).

123. Letter from Mozart to his father, 3rd July 1778.

124. cf. Dittersdorf, *Autobiography*, pp. 251–2.

125. *Allgemeine Musikalische Zeitung*, Leipzig, 7th November 1798.

126. cf. Otto Zoff, *Die grossen Komponisten, gesehen von ihren Zeitgenossen*, Berne, 1952, p. 112.

127. Letter to his father, 22nd November 1777.

128. Letter of 28th December 1782.

129. ibid.

130. Letter to his father, 24th October 1777.

131. Letter from Mozart to his father, 12th June 1778.

132. ibid.

133. *Violinschule*, V, §14 (pp. 101–2).

134. Letter to his father, 7th February 1778.

135. Mozart to the singer, Michael Kelly; cf. Zoff, op. cit., p. 21.

136. Edwin Fischer, *Reflections on Music*, Williams and Norgate, London, 1951: originally published as *Musikalische Betrachtungen*, Leipzig, 1949.

137. *Ideen zu einer Ästhetik der Tonkunst*, p. 295.

138. cf. C. P. E. Bach, *Essay*, I, 2, i, §6 (p. 80).

139. K. Marguerre (Darmstadt) was the first to cast doubts (not without reason) on the authenticity of these variants.

140. cf. H. P. Schmitz, Foreword to *Die Kunst der Verzierung im 18. Jahrhundert*.

141. Türk, *Klavierschule*.

142. *Violinschule*, XII, §2 (pp. 215–16).

143. See, for example, his suggested embellishments for the A major Concerto (K.488); the MS. is in the Westdeutsche Bibliothek, Marburg.

144. *Violinschule*, I, §iii, footnote (p. 27).

145. *Autobiography*, p. 44.

146. *Essay*, I, II, General, 1 (p. 79).

147. Although our discussion is here confined to Mozart's piano music, we should mention in this connection the aria, 'Non so d' onde viene' (K.294), for which embellish-ments in Mozart's handwriting have recently been discovered; cf. *Acta Mozartiana*, fourth year, 1957, pp. 66ff.

148. Leopold Mozart's *Violinschule* also contains hints about embellishments. Some of his examples make a wholly 'Mozartean' effect; cf. Chapter XI, §19, third and fourth examples, §20, third to sixth and ninth to tenth examples (pp. 211–13).

149. cf. bars 58–74 of the second movement of the piano concerto K.467, reproduced in facsimile in Hyatt King's *Mozart in Retrospect*, p. 80. For Hummel, cf. pp. 97, 98, 100, 103,

140, 153, 157, 159, etc., of the Litolff edition of Mozart's concertos, arranged by J. N. Hummel (Plate No. 2,842).

150. Reproduced in facsimile in Schünemann, *Musikerhandschriften von J. S. Bach bis Schumann*, Plate 42; cf. also Gerstenberg, *Zum Autograph des Klavierkonzerts C-Dur KV 503*, pp. 38 onward.

151. In his book on Mozart, Einstein says: 'Now, we do not know exactly how he played any of his concertos. Only four were published during his lifetime, and while in his autographs he wrote out the orchestral parts with complete care, he did not do the same with the solo parts; indeed it would have been in his interest not to write them out at all, so as not to lead unscrupulous copyists into temptation. For he knew perfectly well what he had to play. The solo parts in the form in which they survive are always only a suggestion of the actual performance, and a constant invitation to read the breath of life into them' (p. 313).

152. The Finale of the Concerto K.595 also provides hints for completing—as is certainly necessary—the turns, as in the opening bars of this movement.

153. The already-mentioned copy of the A major Concerto (K.488) by A. Fuchs is one proof among many that in the early nineteenth century the embellishment practised in Mozart's time was still familiar. On the other hand, the embellishments he proposes are, as already remarked, not to be recommended.

154. In the Boosey & Hawkes edition of this concerto H. F. Redlich puts forward the wholly incomprehensible view that the text found in the manuscript is to be followed blindly, and that the notation of this passage is not an abbreviation on Mozart's part. It would be quite out of the question for Mozart, with no apparent reason, suddenly to break off continuous semiquaver movement—in a variation, what is more. One could explain it if he did so to coincide with the entry of the new motive in the upper part (bar 141). But it is incredible that he should have wanted to slow down the semiquaver movement to a quarter the speed in the second bar of a motivic chain (bar 142). Redlich says that the 'logical thematic diminution' of bar 145 proves Mozart's desire for crotchet movement in the preceding bars, but this is false reasoning, for bar 145 is a cadential figure, in which the right hand drops the phrase it has maintained throughout the previous four bars; moreover, the rhythm of the orchestral parts also alters.

155. cf. Mozart's letter to his father, 11th September 1778: 'I can assure you that this journey has not been unprofitable to me, I mean, from the point of view of composition, for, as for the clavier, I play it as well as I ever shall. But there is one thing more I must settle about Salzburg and that is that I shall not be kept to the violin, as I used to be. I will no longer be a fiddler. *I want to conduct at the clavier* and accompany arias.'

156. p. 175; taken from R. Haas, *Aufführungspraxis*, p. 220.

157. cf. pp. 13 ff.

158. cf. the quotation from a letter in the Foreword to the A major Concerto (K.414), Eulenburg edition, and the letter of 15th May, 1784.

159. *Essay*, II, 6, 'Some refinements of accompaniment' (pp. 386–7).

160. cf. H. C. Robbins Landon, *The Symphonies of Joseph Haydn*, Rockliff, and Universal Edition, 1955, p. 125.

161. cf. Blume's Foreword to the Eulenburg score of this concerto. The first edition, however, also marks the bass part 'solo'.

162. Letter of 26th April 1783, reprinted in the Foreword to the Eulenburg score of the Concerto K.414.

163. cf. Foreword to the Eulenburg score of the Concerto K.449.

164. cf. pp. 260 ff.

165. cf. H. Knödt, 'Zur Entwicklung der Kadenzen im Instrumentalkonzert', p. 375 (see Bibliography).

166. The concertos concerned were K.175 in D and K.271 in E flat.

167. e.g. for the concertos K.246, 414, 453 and 456.

168. Letter of 22nd January 1783.

169. cf. A. Hyatt King, op. cit., p. 251.

170. A quotation from Schubart will show that Mozart's contemporaries had a strongly

developed sense of stylistic unity: 'If I am to perform a Sonata by Bach, I must sink myself so completely in the spirit of this great man that my identity disappears and becomes Bach's idiom' (from *Ideen* . . ., p. 295).

171. The extraordinarily relevant and important concept of *Fortspinnung* (here translated as 'continuous development') was developed by W. Fischer in *Zur Entwicklungsgeschichte des Wiener klassischen Stils*; cf. also F. Blume, 'Fortspinnung und Entwicklung', in the *Peters Jahrbuch*, XXXVI, 1930, pp. 51 onward.

172. cf. Mandyczewsky's Foreword to the facsimile edition of newly discovered cadenzas, issued by the Mozarteum, Salzburg, in 1921.

173. cf. Türk, *Klavierschule*, p. 387.

174. cf. L. Mozart, *Violinschule*, I, iii, §19, and J. S. Petri, *Anweisung zur praktischen Musik*, Leipzig, 1782.

175. J. G. Sulzer, *Theorie der Schönen Künste*, chapter on fermatas.

176. On the other hand, Mozart's vocal music contains far more places where lead-ins should be added, e.g. before the da capo of a da capo aria (as in *The Marriage of Figaro*, in the Countess's aria, 'Dove Sono').

177. We are obliged to mention this, since unfortunately the new complete edition makes suggestions for embellishments at these points in the Piano-duet Sonata and the Quintet. The editors of the volumes concerned were following instructions from the general editors, but have since become convinced that lead-ins are out of place at these points.

178. Türk, *Clavierschule*, pp. 387ff.

179. Letter of 12th March 1783.

180. cf. also p. 9.

181. Letter from Mozart to his father, 29th December 1778.

182. Letter from Mozart to his wife, 30th September 1790. See also Einstein, *Mozart*, pp. 80–1.

183. cf. Mozart's letter of 7th July, 1791.

184. p. 306.

185. In the MS. the slur clearly ends on the B.

186. The slurs at this point in the MS. are inconsistent, and so do not indicate clearly what Mozart wanted. But, as in bar 157, first bassoon, there is a slur over the second crotchet, and as the slur also starts at the second crotchet in the second clarinet, the Peters version is probably preferable to that of Eulenburg.

187. In the Peters edition a tie is missing in the bass at bars 262–3.

188. cf. p. 190. In bar 84 the first note in the right hand is, naturally, F sharp. The D in the Eulenburg edition is a printer's error.

189. The Eulenburg edition wrongly allows a legato slur to remain in bar 177.

190. There is an obvious kinship with the first subject of the C minor Fantasia (K.475). There, too, there is a chromatic movement around the fifth (F sharp–G–A flat), and descending sequences with very bold chromaticisms.

191. There are very good formal analyses in C. M. Girdlestone's book, *Mozart and His Piano Concertos*, Cassell, London, 1948.

192. cf. p. 160 for a discussion of the dynamic course of the first solo subject.

193. We are grateful to Professor H. Federhofer for pointing out this passage and for a harmonic analysis along the lines of Schenker.

194. The opposite case is found in the Finale of the 'Haffner' Symphony, a $\frac{4}{4}$ presto which must certainly be taken alla-breve, like, for instance, the Overture to *Figaro*, whose rhythmic structure is exactly similar. Mozart also referred to this in a letter of 7th August 1782: 'the last [Allegro] [must be played] as fast as possible'. Perfectionists who insist at all costs that Mozart was 'infallible' should note that Mozart marked the first version of the first movement of this symphony ₵, and the second, more fully instrumented version ₵.

195. cf. p. 209ff.

196. cf. p. 142.

197. cf. the commentary to Bischoff's edition.

198. cf. p. 22.

BIBLIOGRAPHY

Among the vast literature on Mozart there are two books to which every Mozart scholar of our generation owes a debt of gratitude. Alfred Einstein's revision of Köchel's Catalogue, extending the range of works, adding many new details and revising their chronology, is the foundation-stone of present-day Mozart research; and although there have been important additions to the literature since Hermann Abert's two-volume biography, this book is still the standard work and the basis of any musician's study of the subject, because it is unique in its understanding, thorough description of the origins and content of each of his compositions. We feel heavily indebted to both these scholars.

For the English edition, Miss Emily Anderson's translation of Mozart's letters (see below) has been used wherever these are quoted, and the authors express their thanks to Miss Emily Anderson and Macmillan & Co, London, for permission to do so.

We are also indebted to the editors of all the editions of Mozart's works mentioned: their forewords and editors' reports have drawn our attention to many points. This applies particularly to the editions published by Messrs. Eulenburg, Breitkopf & Härtel, Peters and Henle.

Out of a very extensive literature which we consulted, we here list only those books and essays to which we are indebted for ideas (with which we may or may not have agreed); we also list the most important contemporary sources.

ABERT, H.: *W. A. Mozart*, two volumes, Leipzig 1919–21.

—— 'Über Stand und Aufgaben der Mozartforschung', in *Mozart-Jahrbuch*, I, 1923, pp. 7 et seq.

ALBRECHT, E.: *A Census of Autograph Music Manuscripts of European Composers in American Libraries*, Philadelphia, 1953.

ALBRECHTSBERGER, J. G.: 'Anfangsgründe der Klavierkunst', MS., library of the Gesellschaft der Musikfreunde, Vienna.

ANDERSON, EMILY: Letters of Mozart and his Family, Complete Edition, 3 volumes, Macmillan (London), 1938.

BACH, C. P. E.: *Versuch über die wahre Art das Clavier zu spielen*, published privately, 1753 (first part), second printing, Berlin, 1759: second part published, 1762. Quotations in the English edition of this book are from the translation by William J. Mitchell, published in 1949 (Cassell, London), as *Essay on the True Art of Playing Keyboard Instruments*.

BADURA-SKODA, EVA: 'Über die Anbringung von Auszierungen in den Klavierwerken Mozarts', *Mozart-Jahrbuch*, 1957, Salzburg, 1958.

BADURA-SKODA, PAUL and EVA: 'Zur Echtheit von Mozarts Variationen K.460', *Mozart-Jahrbuch*, 1959, Salzburg, 1960.

BECKING, G.: *Der musikalische Rhythmus als Erkenntnisquelle*, Augsburg, 1928.

BENINGER, F.: 'Pianistische Herausgebertechnik', in *Zeitschrift für Musikwissenschaft*, 12, 1929–30, pp. 280 et seq.

BERNET-KEMPERS, K. PH.: 'Hemiolenbildungen bei Mozart', MS.

BEYSCHLAG, A.: *Die Ornamentik der Musik*, Leipzig, 1953.

BLUME, FRIEDRICH: 'Mozart und die Überlieferung', in *Deutsche Musikkultur*, 6 (1941–2), Vols. 2–3.
—— *W. A. Mozart*, Wolfenbüttel, 1948.
BÖHM, K.: 'Mozart-Probleme', in *Österreichische Musikzeitschrift*, second year, 1947, Vols. 7–8.
BUSONI, F.: *Entwurf einer neuen Ästhetik der Tonkunst*, Trieste 1907. Reprinted Wiesbaden, 1954. An English translation, *Sketch of a New Aesthetic of Music*, was published in New York by Schirmer in 1911.
CZERNY, C.: *Vollständige theoretisch-praktische Pianoforte-Schule . . . Op. 500*, 3 vols. Diabelli, Vienna (not dated).
DENNERLEIN, H.: *Der unbekannte Mozart. Die Welt seiner Klavierwerke*, Leipzig, 1951.
DEUTSCH, O. E.: 'Erstausgaben von Mozart, Haydn, Beethoven und Schubert', in *Musikalische Seltenheiten*, Vienna, 1921 ff.
DEUTSCH, O. E. and OLDMAN, C. B.: 'Mozart-Drucke', in *Zeitschrift für Musikwissenschaft*, 13, 1931–2.
DITTERS VON DITTERSDORF, K.: *Autobiography*, trans. A. D. Coleridge (Bentley, London), 1896.
EINSTEIN, A.: *Greatness in Music*, O.U.P., London, 1945.
—— *Mozart, His Character and Work*, trans. Arthur Mendel and Nathan Broder, Cassell, London and New York, 1946.
—— 'Mozart's Handwriting and the Creative Process', in *Papers read at the International Congress of Musicology, New York, 1939*.
—— *The 10 Celebrated String Quartets by Mozart, First Authentic Edition in Score*, Novello, London, 1945.
ENGEL, H.: *Die Entwicklung des Deutschen Klavierkonzerts von Mozart bis Liszt*, Leipzig, 1927.
—— 'Probleme der Aufführungspraxis', in *Mozart Jahrbuch*, 1955.
FELLERER, K. G.: 'Mozarts Bearbeitung eigener Werke', in *Mozart-Jahrbuch, 1952*, Salzburg, 1953.
FISCHER, E.: *Reflections on Music*, Williams and Norgate, London, 1949. (Originally published in German, *Musikalische Betrachtungen*, Leipzig, 1949.)
FISCHER, W.: 'Das "Lacrimosa dies illa" in Mozarts Requiem', in *Mozart-Jahrbuch, 1951*, Salzburg, 1953.
—— 'Der, welcher wandelt diese Strasse voll Beschwerden', in *Mozart-Jahrbuch, 1950*, Salzburg, 1951.
—— 'Zur Entwicklungsgeschichte des Wiener klassischen Stils', in *Studien zur Musikwissenschaft* (volumes accompanying the *Denkmäler der Tonkunst in Österreich*), III.
—— 'Zu W. A. Mozarts Tonartenwahl und Harmonik', in *Mozart-Jahrbuch, 1952*, Salzburg, 1953.
FLOTHUIS, M.: *Mozart*, S' Gravenhage (not dated).
FRANZ, G. VON: 'Mozarts Klavierbauer Anton Walter', in *Neues Mozart-Jahrbuch*, I, Regensburg, 1941.
FURTWÄNGLER, W.: *Concerning Music*, trans. L. J. Lawrence, Boosey & Hawkes, London, 1953. (Originally published in German, *Gespräche über Musik*, Vienna, 1948.)
—— *Ton und Wort*, Brockhaus, Wiesbaden, 1955. (No English edition to date.)
GERHARTZ, K.: 'Die Violin-Schule von Leopold Mozart (1756)', in *Mozart-Jahrbuch*, III, Augsburg, 1929.
GERSTENBERG, W.: 'Zum Autograph des Klavierkonzerts KV 503 (C–Dur)', in *Mozart Jahrbuch, 1953*, Salzburg, 1954.
GIESEKING, W.: 'Mozart mit oder ohne Pedal?' in *Melos*, Schott, Mainz, 1949.
—— 'Mozarts Klavier-Werk', in the periodical *Phono*, Vol. 4, 1955.
GOTTRON, ADAM: *Mozart und Mainz*, Mainz, 1951.
—— 'Wie spielte Mozart die Adagios seiner Klavierkonzerte?', *Die Musikforschung*, thirteenth year, 1960, p. 334.
HAAS, R.: 'Aufführungspraxis der Musik', in *Handbuch der Musikwissenschaft*, edited by Ernst Bücken, Wildpark-Potsdam, 1931.

HAHN, K.: *Über die Zusammenhänge von Klavierbau und Klavierstil*, dissertation, Berlin, 1952.

HARICH-SCHNEIDER, E.: *Die Kunst des Cembalospiels*, Kassel, 1939.

HINDEMITH, P.: *A Composer's World*, Cambridge, 1952.

HOESLI, I.: *Wolfgang Amadeus Mozart, Briefstil eines Musikgenies*, Zürich, 1948.

HUMMEL, J. N.: *Ausführliche theoretisch-praktische Anweisung zum Pianoforte-Spiel*, Vienna, 1828.

HUNEKER, J.: *Franz Liszt*, Munich, 1922.

KAMIENSKI, L.: 'Zum "tempo rubato",' in *Archiv für Musikwissenschaft*, I, 1919, pp. 108 et seq.

KELLER, HERMANN: *Die musikalische Artikulation, insbesondere bei J. S. Bach*, Stuttgart, 1925.
—— *Phrasierung und Artikulation*, Kassel, 1955.

KING, A. HYATT: 'A Census of Mozart Musical Autographs in England', in *Musical Quarterly*, October 1952.
—— *Mozart in Retrospect*, London, 1955.
—— 'Musik in England zu Lebzeiten Mozarts mit einigen Bemerkungen über Mozarts Handschriften in England', in *Mozart-Jahrbuch, 1953*, Salzburg, 1954.
—— 'The Mozart Manuscripts in Cambridge', in *The Music Review*, Vol. 2, No. 1.

KNÖDT, H.: 'Zur Entwicklung der Kadenzen im Instrumentalkonzert', in *Sammelbände der Internationalen Musikgesellschaft*, 1913–14, p. 375.

KÖCHEL, L. RITTER VON: *Chronologisch-thematisches Verzeichnis sämtlicher Tonwerke Wolfgang Amadeus Mozarts*, third edition, edited by Alfred Einstein, with a supplement. *Berichtigungen und Zusätze* (Addenda and Corrigenda), by Alfred Einstein, Ann Arbor, Michigan, 1947.

LANDON, H. C. ROBBINS: *The Symphonies of Joseph Haydn*, Universal Edition and Rockliff, London and Vienna, 1955.
—— and MITCHELL, D.: *The Mozart Companion*, Rockliff, London and New York, 1956.

LUITHLEN, V.: 'Der Eisenstädter Walterflügel', in *Mozart-Jahrbuch, 1953*, Salzburg, 1955.

MANDYCZEWSKY, E.: *Vorwort zur Faksimile-Ausgabe neuaufgefundener Kadenzen*, issued by the Mozarteum, Salzburg, 1921.

MARPURG, W. FR.: *Anleitung zum Klavierspielen*, Berlin, 1755.

MATZKE, W.: *Unser technisches Wissen von der Musik*, Vienna, 1949.

MEDICI, MERINA and HUGHES, ROSEMARY: *A Mozart Pilgrimage*, London, 1955.

MIES, P.: 'Die Artikulationszeichen Strich und Punkt bei Mozart', in *Die Musikforschung*, XI, 1958, pp. 428ff.

MILCHMEYER, J. P.: *Die wahre Art das Pianoforte zu spielen*, Vienna, 1797.

MITCHELL, D.: *see* Landon, H. C. Robbins.

MOLDENHAUER, H.; 'Ein neu entdecktes Mozart-Autograph', in *Mozart-Jahrbuch, 1953*, Salzburg, 1954.

MOSER, H. J.: *Lebensvolle Musikerziehung*, Vienna, 1952.
—— 'Monumentale und intime Musik', in *Musica*, Year VIII, 1954.
—— 'Mozart-Interpretation in den jüngsten 4 Jahrzehnten', in *Wiener Figaro*, twenty-first year, Vol. 2, March 1953, pp. 5ff.

MOZART, L.: *Versuch einer gründlichen Violinschule*, Augsburg, 1756. English translation by Editha Knocker, O.U.P., London and New York, 1948.

MUELLER VON ASOW, E. H.: *Briefe W. A. Mozarts*, 2 vols., 1942.
—— 'Mozartiana', in *Musikforschung*, VIII, 1955, Vol. 1.

NIEMETSCHEK, F.: *Leben des k.k. Kapellmeisters W. G. Mozart, nach Originalquellen beschrieben*, Prague, 1798. English translation by H. Mouther, London, Hyman, 1956.

NOWAK, L.: 'Die Wiener Mozart-Autographen', in *Österreichische Musikzeitschrift*, eleventh year, 1956.

OREL, A.: *Mozarts deutscher Weg*, 1941.
—— 'Mozarts Stellung in der Geistesgeschichte', in *Österreichische Rundschau*, I, 6, Vienna, 1934.

PAUMGARTNER, B.: 'Von der sogenannten Appoggiatur in der älteren Gesangsmusik', in *Musikerziehung*, fourth year, 1953, pp. 229ff.

QUANTZ, J. J.: *Versuch einer Anweisung die flute traversière zu spielen*, facsimile reprint of the third edition, 1789, edited by Hans-Peter Schmitz, Bärenreiter Kassel and Basel, 1953.

REDLICH, H. F. : 'Mozart's C minor Concerto (K.491)', in *The Music Review*, Vol. IX, 12, 1948.

REINECKE, C.: *Zur Wiederbelebung der Mozart'schen Clavier-Concerte*, Leipzig, 1891.

RELLSTAB, J. C. F.: *Anleitung für Clavierspieler*, Berlin, 1790.

RÜCK, U.: 'Mozarts Hammerflügel erbaute Anton Walter', *Mozart-Jahrbuch, 1952*.

SCHENK, E.: 'Zur Tonsymbolik in Mozarts *Figaro*', in *Neues Mozart-Jahrbuch*, Regensburg, 1941.

SCHENKER, H.: *Ein Beitrag zur Ornamentik*, Vienna, 1908.

SCHERING, A.: 'Vom musikalischen Vortrage', *Peters Jahrbuch* for 1930, Leipzig, 1931.

SCHIEDERMAIR, L.: *Mozart, Sein Leben und seine Werke*, Munich, 1922.

SCHMID, E. F.: 'Ein neues Autograph zu KV 265', in *Mozart-Jahrbuch, 1950*, Salzburg, 1951.

SCHUBART, CHR. D.: *Ideen zu einer Ästhetik der Tonkunst*, Vienna, 1806.

SCHÜNEMANN, G.: *Musikerhandschriften von J. S. Bach bis Schumann*, Berlin and Zürich, 1936.

SENN, W.: 'Forschungsaufgaben zur Geschichte des Geigenbaues', in *Bamberger Kongressbericht*, 1953.

STEGLICH, R.: 'Das Auszierungswesen in der Musik W. A. Mozarts', *Mozart-Jahrbuch, 1955*, Salzburg, 1955.

—— *Das Tempo als Problem der Mozart-Interpretation* (reports on a musicological seminar of the Internationale Stiftung Mozarteum at Leipzig in 1932).

—— *Der Dualismus der Taktqualität im Sonatensatz* (International Musicological Congress, Beethoven Centenary, 1927).

—— 'Der Mozart-Klang und die Gegenwart', in *Acta Mozartiana 3*, pp. 9–21.

—— *Die elementare Dynamik des musikalischen Rhythmus*, Leipzig, 1930.

—— 'Expression und Gusto im Mozart-Musizieren', in *Zeitschrift für Musik*, Year 112, 1951.

—— 'Interpretationsprobleme der Jupitersinfonie', in *Mozart-Jahrbuch, 1954*, Salzburg, 1955.

—— *Mozarts Flügel klingt wieder*, Nuremberg and Salzburg, 1937.

—— 'Takt und Tempo', in *Deutsche Musikkultur*, 4, 1939–40, Vols. 5–6.

—— 'Über das melodische Motiv in der Musik Mozarts', in *Mozart-Jahrbuch, 1953*, Salzburg, 1954.

—— 'Über den Mozart-Klang', in *Mozart-Jahrbuch, 1950*, pp. 62ff, Salzburg, 1951.

—— 'Über Mozarts Adagio-Takt', in *Mozart-Jahrbuch, 1951*, Salzburg, 1953.

—— 'Über Mozarts Melodik', in *Mozart-Jahrbuch, 1952*, Salzburg, 1953.

STRAUSS, R.: *Recollections and Reflections* (trans. L. J. Lawrence), Boosey & Hawkes, London, 1953 (*Betrachtungen und Erinnerungen*, Zürich/Freiburg im Breisgau, 1949).

STRAVINSKY, I.: *Poetics of Music*, trans. Arthur Knodel and Ingolf Dahl, Harvard University Press, 1947.

TENSCHERT, R.: 'Richard Strauss und Mozart', *Mozart-Jahrbuch, 1954*, Salzburg, 1955.

TOSI, P. F.: *Opinioni di cantori antichi e moderni o sieno Osservazioni sopro il canto figurato*, Bologna, 1723.

TÜRK, G. D. FR.: *Klavierschule*, second edition, Halle, 1802.

VIRNEISEL, W.: 'Mozartiana (Berichtigung)', *Musikforschung*, VIII, 1955.

WEINMANN, A.: 'Verzeichnis der Verlagswerke des Musikalischen Magazins in Wien, 1784–1802', Vienna, 1950.

—— *Vollständiges Verlagsverzeichnis Artaria & Co.*, Vienna, 1952.

WOLF, G. F.: *Gründliche Clavierschule*, Vienna, 1801.

WORCH, H.: *Piano-makers of the Evolutionary Period*, New York, 1907.

ZOFF, O.: *Die grossen Komponisten, gesehen von ihren Zeitgenossen*, Berne, 1952.

INDEX TO WORKS DISCUSSED